The Spiritual Wisdom of the Gospels for Christian Preachers and Teachers

Year B

Eating with the Bridegroom

John Shea

LITURGICAL PRESS
Collegeville, Minnesota

www.litpress.org

Cover design by Joachim Rhoades, O.S.B.

See the acknowledgments which begin on p. vii.

ISBN: 978-0-8146-2913-0   (Year A)
ISBN: 978-0-8146-2914-7   (Year B)
ISBN: 978-0-8146-2915-4   (Year C)
ISBN: 978-0-8146-2916-1   (Feasts, Funerals, & Weddings)
ISBN: 978-0-8146-2917-8   (set)

1	2	3	4	5	6	7	8

Library of Congress Cataloging-in-Publication Data

Shea, John, 1941–
    The spiritual wisdom of the Gospels for Christian preachers and teachers
/ John Shea.
        p. cm.
    Includes bibliographical references and index.
    ISBN 0-8146-2913-X (Year A : pbk. : alk. paper)
    1. Bible. N.T. Gospels––Criticism, interpretation, etc.   2. Bible.
N.T. Gospels—Homiletical use. 3. Lectionary preaching. I. Title.

BS2555.52.S54 2004
251'.6—dc22   2003025635

Contents

Acknowledgments

This four-volume set, *The Spiritual Wisdom of the Gospels for Christian Preachers and Teachers*, has been a long time in the making. Along the way, there have been many collaborators, people whose critical comments and ongoing support have kept me thinking, meditating, and writing about Gospel texts. Although it is impossible to mention every student or workshop participant who asked a question or volunteered a comment that improved my understanding and articulation, I am thankful to all of them.

In particular, there have been some key organizations, congregations, and people who have told me, "This is useful," "Keep doing it," "Stay here," "Talk to us," "What do you need," and "When are you ever going to put this stuff in print." This is what writers yearn to hear, so I am grateful:

To Lilly Endowment, Inc., especially to Fred Hofheinz, who saw the contribution a spiritual-literary interpretation of Gospel texts would make to Christian preachers and teachers and graciously and generously funded this project.

To Rev. Jack Wall, Roger Hughes, Al Hellwig, Janette Nunez, Bob Kolatorwicz, and the staff and community of Old St. Patrick's Church who pioneered Awakenings, an early morning group of Gospel lovers, and became the home base for this project.

To the ecumenical advisory group: Rev. Wayne Priest of Queen of All Saints Basilica, Rev. Dean Francis of First United Methodist Church of Evanston, Rev. Paul Koch of Ebenezer Lutheran Church, Canon Linda Bartholomew of Christ Church Cathedral, and Rev. Carol Allen of Fourth Presbyterian Church. These creative Christian preachers and teachers provided valuable assistance to the first volume of this series and helped to set the general direction for this project.

To Rev. Andrew Greeley, John Cusick, Edward Beck and many others who offered insights I eagerly received.

To Robert Demke, who gave much-needed computer advice and administrative assistance.

To Grace Lutheran Congregation and School, for their gracious hospitality.

To Peter Dwyer, director, Mark Twomey, Rev. Cyril Gorman, O.S.B., Rev. Linda Maloney, Colleen Stiller, and all the staff at the Liturgical Press for their interest in this project and their expertise in helping to implement it.

Finally, to Anne, companion, lover, wife, friend of the Spirit.

Page 51: Excerpt from Robert Frost, "Mending Wall" in *The Poetry of Robert Frost* (New York: Holt, Rinehart, and Winston, 1969) 33–34, reprinted with permission of the copyright holder. All rights reserved.

Page 55: John Updike, "Fever" in *Collected Poems, 1953–1993* (New York: Knopf, 1993) reprinted with permission of the copyright holder. All rights reserved.

Page 60: John Shea, "A Prayer to the Pain of Jesus" in *The Hour of the Unexpected* (Allen, Tex.: Thomas More, 1992) reprinted with permission of the copyright holder. All rights reserved.

Page 88: Sufi tale from Sharafuddin Maneri in James P. Carse, *Breakfast at the Victory: The Mysticism of Ordinary Experience* (San Francisco: HarperSanFrancisco, 1994) 187, reprinted with permission of the copyright holder. All rights reserved.

Page 96: Excerpt from *Paradiso* of Dante Alighieri, *The Divine Comedy,* trans. Henry Wadsworth Longfellow. Originally published Boston and New York: Houghton Mifflin Company, 1900.

Pages 101, 256: Excerpts from the Gospel of Thomas, trans. Stephen Patterson and Marvin Meyer in *The Complete Gospels: Annotated Scholars Version,* ed. Robert J. Miller, rev. ed., Sonoma, Calif.: Polebridge Press, 1994.

Page 103: Goethe, "The Holy Longing," trans. Robert Bly in *The Soul Is Here for Its Own Joy: Poems from Many Cultures,* ed. Robert Bly (Hopewell, N.J.: Ecco Press, 1995) reprinted with permission of the copyright holder. All rights reserved.

Pages 103–04: Kabir, "The Time before Death," in *The Soul Is Here for Its Own Joy: Poems from Many Cultures,* ed. Robert Bly (Hopewell, N.J.: Ecco Press, 1995) 81, reprinted with permission of the copyright holder. All rights reserved.

Page 125: Excerpt from the English translation of *Rite of Marriage* © 1969, International Committee on English in the Liturgy, Inc. (ICEL). All rights reserved.

Page 147: Poem of Hildegard of Bingen in *The Enlightened Heart: An Anthology of Sacred Poetry,* ed. Stephen Mitchell (New York: Harper & Row, 1989) 41, reprinted with permission of the copyright holder. All rights reserved.

Pages 152–53: Paul Murray's "Know Yourself" in *The Absent Fountain* (Dublin: Dedalus Press, 1991) 12, reprinted with permission of the copyright holder. All rights reserved.

Pages 153–54: From *Five Stages of the Soul* by Harry R. Moody and David Carroll, copyright © 1997 by Harry R. Moody and David Carroll. Used by permission of Doubleday, a division of Random House, Inc.

Page 158: Story from *Living Presence: A Sufi Way to Mindfulness and the Essential Self* (New York: Jeremy P. Tarcher/Perigee, 1992) 23–24, reprinted with permission of the copyright holder. All rights reserved.

Pages 166–67, 233: Excerpts from Rachel Naomi Remen, *Kitchen Table Wisdom* (New York: Riverhead Books, 1996) 59–60, 218–19, 240, reprinted with permission of the copyright holder. All rights reserved.

Pages 176–77: From *The Illuminated Rumi* by Coleman Barks, Michael Green, copyright © 1997 by Coleman Barks and Michael Green. Used by permission of Broadway Books, a division of Random House, Inc.

Pages 176, 198: From *After the Ecstasy, the Laundry* by Jack Kornfield, copyright © 2000 by Jack Kornfield. Used by permission of Bantam Books, a division of Random House, Inc.

Pages 186–87: From *Meetings at the Edge* by Stephen Levine, copyright © 1984 by Stephen Levine. Used with permission of Doubleday, a division of Random House, Inc.

Pages 199–200, 254: Excerpts from Ram Dass and Paul Gorman, *How Can I Help?: Stories and Reflections on Service* (New York: Knopf/Random House, Inc., 1985) 33–34, 191–92, reprinted with permission of the copyright holder. All rights reserved.

Page 238: From *What Really Matters* by Tony Schwartz, copyright © 1995 by Tony Schwartz. Used by permission of Bantam Books, a division of Random House, Inc.

Page 258: Excerpts from *A Passion for Truth* by Abraham Joshua Heschel. Copyright © 1973 by Sylvia Heschel. Reprinted by permission of Farrar, Strauss and Giroux, LLC.

Page 263: Story from Frederic C. Craigie, Jr., "The Spirit and Work: Observations about Spirituality and Organizational Life," *Journal of Psychology and Christianity* 18 (1999) 43–53, reprinted with permission of the copyright holder. All rights reserved.

Page 271: From T. S. Eliot, "East Coker," 2.3, in *Four Quartets* (New York: Harcourt, Brace and Co., 1943) reprinted with permission of the copyright holder. All rights reserved.

If there are any remaining claims, Liturgical Press would like to be contacted so that proper settlement can be made.

Introduction

Working with the Mind: ⁑
The Art of Jesus the Teacher

The major section of the introductory essay, "Preaching and Teaching
the Gospels as Spiritual Wisdom," in *On Earth As It Is In Heaven*, the
first volume (Year A) of *The Spiritual Wisdom of the Gospels for Christian
Preachers and Teachers*, explored the vision of spiritual transformation
in the Gospels. This transformation entails a change of consciousness
and action from a condition characterized as blind, deaf, asleep, lost,
and dead to a condition characterized as seeing, hearing, awake,
found, and risen. The catalyst of this change is the Word. Once this
Word is heard, it can be dismissed, received in a shallow way, overcome by competing interests, or fully realized and integrated. Therefore, spiritual transformation is always an invitation offered by the
Word to which people respond in varying degrees.

A key insight into this transformative process was that the Word
functions as spiritual wisdom. Spiritual wisdom is a form of artful
language that tries to open the person to receive Spirit from God and
to release that Spirit into the world. In order to do this, spiritual wisdom targets the mind. The mind is the gatekeeper of both the soul's
access to God and the soul's capacity for creative action in the world.
Spiritual wisdom acts on the mind to increase attention to the spiritual,
to develop an understanding of the spiritual, and to integrate the spiritual with physical, social, and mental life. This is its agenda.

In some circles spiritual wisdom is presented as a series of ideas that
detail how the divine and human interact. But in the stories of the
Gospels spiritual wisdom is never abstract. Jesus is not a spiritual phi-
losopher who thinks to himself and talks out loud to the stars. He is
primarily an interpersonal event, dialoguing with people whose mental openness ranges from recalcitrant to receptive. But no matter where
their minds are at, he works with them in the service of Spirit. So he
shapes his words as skillful means—confronting one moment and
consoling the next moment, carefully constructing an argument one
moment and spinning a tale the next moment, asking a question one
moment and answering a question the next moment. Jesus lives in a

1

person-to-person, eyeball-to-eyeball, spoken-word-to-heard-word world. His spiritual wisdom unfolds in the context of concrete conversations, however stylized those conversations may be.

This introductory essay of the second volume (Year B) of *The Spiritual Wisdom of the Gospels for Christian Preachers and Teachers* focuses on the conversational patterns that communicate spiritual wisdom. It presupposes the transformative process from blindness to sight, from deafness to hearing, from asleep to awake, from lost to found, and from dead to risen. But it watches that process unfold on a one-to-one basis, in the interaction of the character of Jesus with other characters. In particular, it pays attention to the art of Jesus' teaching style, how he gears what he says to the mindsets of people and how he marshals his rhetoric in the service of breakthroughs in consciousness.

In order to explore how Jesus the teacher works with the mind in the service of Spirit, I will first consult the teaching style of a contemporary spiritual teacher. Then I will examine in detail the conversational exchanges between Jesus and an insincere lawyer (Luke 10:25-37), Jesus and a sincere seeker (Matt 19:16-22), and Jesus and his favorite foil, Peter (John 13:3-11). Finally, I will conclude by connecting Jesus the teacher with Jesus the lover.

How a Spiritual Teacher Works

Reuven Gold was a sacred storyteller and, more covertly, a spiritual teacher. The second time I met him he told me a story I didn't understand. My "flat response" to the story began a series of events I still remember. It also became a springboard into a reflective process that has influenced how I see Jesus the Teacher, how I meditate on his teaching art, and how I use Gospel stories in my own teaching.

However, the first time I meet Reuven Gold he did not tell me a story. It was at a conference on Faith and the Imagination. I was giving the opening lecture, a presentation filled with what at the time I considered exciting ideas. On looking back, it was a talk on the imagination without using the imagination, a rational appreciation on the indispensability of imaginative forms for the expression and communication of faith.

Reuven sat in the first row, right beneath the lectern. As soon as I started, his head nodded, and his three chins rested gently in his salt and pepper beard. Throughout the talk his body rose and fell noiselessly in the gentle rhythms of sleep. When the talk was over, he searched me out, embraced me, and told me it was one of the finest talks he had ever heard. I was skeptical.

Reuven was at the conference to tell stories. He was billed as a sacred storyteller, and his main fare was teaching stories from the Jewish Hasidic and the Islamic Sufi traditions. But his real interest was in the spiritual consciousness these stories could evoke. Reuven believed that if spiritual consciousness was ever to be evoked in the listeners, it first had to be present in the teller. So when Reuven told his stories, he tried to tell them from a clear and luminous interior space. In a sense, he was both teller and listener, discovering with delight and inquisitiveness one inner state after another. If no one else followed the stories into higher states of consciousness, Reuven did. If others wanted to listen in, fine. If they responded, the game was afoot.

The second time I met Reuven was on a plane, a late night flight out of Pittsburgh to Chicago. In a nearly empty 737, he waved me into the seat next to him.

"I have a story," he said. Rarely have I seen so much pleasure in a man. He did not wait for my response. He launched in:

> A very advanced disciple was very distraught and pounded insistently on the door of his teacher's house at midnight. The teacher opened the door. The house was darkened, but the teacher held a candle in his hand. The disciple blurted out that he was filled with anxiety and had to see the teacher at once. The teacher opened wide the door. The disciple entered and the teacher closed the door. Then the teacher blew out the candle.

At the sentence, "The teacher blew out the candle," Reuven's eyes widened and a grin of revelation spread across his face.

I sat there, blank. Finally, I shrugged, making it clear I was in the dark. Reuven offered help. "A very advanced disciple, John. A very advanced disciple." It was help that didn't help. I didn't get it.

We went on to other things. One of which was work for Reuven. There is not a great call for sacred storytellers, and Reuven was hurting for cash. At the time, I was directing a Doctor of Ministry program. So I hired Reuven to come and tell his stories. He was delighted.

A month later, twenty-four Doctor of Ministry students sat in two semicircles. Reuven sat on a chair in front. I introduced him, and he immediately told a story. It was the story of the very advanced disciple. Silence followed. This was my second run at the story, and I was still floundering. I looked around at the students. Many were studying their shoes. All the faces I could see were puzzled.

Then suddenly a young priest began to talk. He told us about his recent decision to change ministries. He had accepted an assignment in Hispanic ministry, and he was scheduled to go to Mexico and learn Spanish. But now he was vacillating. Had he done the right thing? He told us he was "no great shakes" in school and was not a natural linguist. Certainly, he would learn Spanish well enough to say Mass and do sacraments. But would he ever be fluent? Would he get jokes and be comfortable around kitchen tables and street corners? The more he talked, the more anxious he became.

Reuven stopped him, saying, "I understand that in Madrid even the children of the poor speak Spanish."

The group laughed uneasily. We were all "nice" people. We were not comfortable with mocking someone's anxiety. At first, the young priest seemed not to hear what Reuven said. He continued down his negative track. Then he stopped. Reuven's remark had finally sunk in. It slowed him down. He managed a smile. "Thanks," he said, "I feel better."

Then in a very loud voice that had no anger in it but tremendous force, Reuven shouted, "DON'T WORSHIP YOUR EMOTIONS!" Reuven's eyes widened, and a grin of revelation spread across his face.

Reuven looked over at me, his eyebrows went up, and his body shook with laughter. He knew I got the story. I knew what the problem was with the very advanced disciple. But I got it the way a door opens and closes, the way a light flashes against the darkness. I saw something very valuable. But it was gone as quickly as it arrived. It was a momentary shining but not a steady seeing. I am not sure what immediate and/ or long-lasting effects this encounter had on the young priest.

As this episode reveals, Reuven was more a spiritual teacher than a storyteller. He used stories in combination with injunctions and other language forms to guide people toward spiritual consciousness and action. It would omit something essential to characterize Reuven as communicating knowledge, even spiritual knowledge. He was more an interpersonal event in which spiritual wisdom was involved. He engaged you: with his eyes, body, laugh, etc. You could feel him wanting access to the interior ways you thought and felt. Instinctively, I, and I think most people, would pull up the drawbridge and casually mention that there were crocodiles in the mote. Reuven never forced entry. But he would wait around for the drawbridge to go down.

Reuven's teaching style was a mix of very direct and very indirect ways of relating. It was direct because Reuven inhabited the role of teacher. The students assumed he knew more, and they allowed him, within limits, to control the conversation. This "teaching role" did not mean Reuven would not learn from the students or that he would impose his own position on them. But, by tacit agreement, he could stop and start the action, and he had every intention of doing so. Reuven himself was on a spiritual path; and he presupposed that if anyone sat and listened to his stories, they were also spiritually interested and were open to whatever wisdom might arise. When the wisdom arose, so did Reuven.

Reuven's teaching style was also indirect, for it included participation from the students. He had to find out where they were at so he could bring them the next step. They had to volunteer the working of their minds. The stories were tools to uncover those workings. Then Reuven would either develop or confront what emerged. Of course, when the teaching started Reuven did not know the exact shape of the workings of the mind that would be evoked. So he had to be attentive and quick. He was just that. What I watched in that long ago class was high art.

This teaching episode planted a seed. I remember it, not the way a video recorder would have captured and stored it. But the way an impression is made that is powerful enough to be memorable. I host that memory every so often and consult it. When I do, the seed grows or, less imaginatively, I simply understand more. In this way it has become an informal spiritual exercise that opens my mind to Spirit.

In the years since it happened, I have become more familiar with Eastern forms of spirituality. One of their insights is that the mind tends to cling to negative experiences. This clinging can be so powerful that it pulls the person into the emotion until they identify with it. So the negative emotion owns the person. Something must be done to reestablish the transcendence of the person over their emotional life. The *very advanced* disciple of the story should be able to "disidentify" from his anxiety. Yet he runs at midnight to his teacher who both accepts his situation and refuses to solve it for him. He accompanies him in the darkness. At least that is some of the meaning I have derived from the story and Reuven's interaction with the student. I know there is more.

But what I return to again and again is the loud shout, the booming injunction not to worship emotions. It was geared to stop the runaway mind, a mind that was dragging its owner down a remorseful and overly self-critical road. The loud injunction was not showing the young priest how he is always more than thoughts and emotions in a rational way. It was an intervention into his mental processes, not to try to alter their course but to change his relationship to them. The emotions could go up and down, but he did not necessarily have to soar and crash with them. This was an attempt to teach with authority, to bring this person to a level of freedom where a new possibility awaited his decision.

I do not think there is any direct correlation between Reuven Gold and the diverse portraits of Jesus the Teacher in the Gospels. But when I ponder the Gospel portraits of Jesus the teacher, Reuven often comes to mind. I find myself replaying my limited but important interactions with him. He helped me see something that is useful in appreciating Jesus as a teacher.

Jesus the Teacher is not a straightforward conveyer of information. He is an encounter with a higher consciousness that is bent on opening whomever he meets to the indwelling Spirit. Everything he says and does is geared to the spiritual transformation of disciples, crowds, religious authorities, and individual seekers. "I came that they may have life and have it abundantly" (John 10:10). This means he knows the workings of their minds, either by careful attention to what they say and do or by direct intuition into their interiors. Then it is "whatever it takes"—confrontation or compassion, story or discourse, image or injunction, commendation or critique—to bring their awareness and action under the influence of Spirit. To watch him at work is to grasp the power of the Word Made Flesh (see John 1:14, especially the KJV Bible). He is embodied spiritual wisdom, bursting with "grace upon grace," and seeking to share its blessings (see John 1:16).

I would like to watch Jesus the Teacher at work with three people. The first is an exchange with a learned lawyer. This interaction will be a success. The man will learn how to *do* love of God and neighbor. The second encounter is with a man seeking eternal life. This conversation will be a failure. The man will not get what he wants. The third is intimate conversation with Peter. This conversation will be unresolved. The art of Jesus the teacher is displayed in these encounters. Yet, despite the art, the outcomes are uneven. There is a "Yes," a "No," and a "Not now." But, deeper than the art, is person of the Teacher sensitively working with how the mind opens and closes and offering to all a fullness he knows in himself (John 1:16).

Learning to Do Love of God and Neighbor

Luke 10:25-37

Just then a lawyer stood up to test Jesus.

"Teacher," he said, "what must I do to inherit eternal life?"

He said to him, "What is written in the law? What do you read there?"

He answered, "You shall love the Lord your God with all your heart, and with all your soul, and with all your strength, and with all your mind; and your neighbor as yourself."

And he said to him, "You have given the right answer; do this, and you will live."

The conflicted consciousness of the lawyer is captured succinctly. Although his speech acknowledges Jesus as teacher, interiorly he sees himself as the teacher. He will be the one who will test, and Jesus will be the one who either passes or fails the test. The words of the lawyer's mouth (Jesus is teacher) and the thoughts of his heart (I am teacher) are not integrated.

Although the lawyer is eager to dispute, Jesus is not interested in *"mano a mano"* ego games. Instead, he asks the lawyer about what he knows; the teacher inquires after the consciousness of the one seeking everlasting life. The lawyer cannot refuse this chance to shine. He deftly combines Deuteronomy 6:4-9 with Leviticus 19:18 to produce the double commandment to love. Jesus compliments his correctness. But also he indicates something more is needed. Knowing the law is one thing; doing the law is another. When you do the law, everlasting life is not a future reward; it is a present experience: "do this, and you will live" (v. 28).

However, the lawyer's knowledge is not deep enough to overflow into a doing. He has mechanically memorized a text, but he lacks the realization of what both commandments mean and how they are intimately linked. Mere knowledge of what the law says cannot unfold into doing. This lawyer's mental condition reflects a type often found in religious traditions. They can read the sacred books, even make insightful connections. They are excellent at recital. But they lack an in-depth appreciation of what the texts are meant to express and communicate. "[Love the Lord your God with all your heart, and with all your soul, and with all your strength, and with all your mind; and your neighbor as yourself" (v. 27) is a call to spiritual consciousness and transformation. But, at this moment, for the lawyer it is retrieved information.

But wanting to justify himself, he asked Jesus, "And who is my neighbor?"

In the lawyer's mind, the first exchange with Jesus, initiated by the question about inheriting everlasting life, has gone poorly. Jesus was not subjected to his scrutiny; he was guided by Jesus' skilled teaching. The second exchange, initiated by the question of, "[W]ho is my neighbor?" is driven by the lawyer's attempt to gain the upper hand and claim the role of teacher. However, this exchange will go the way of the first one. The one who wishes to test will be tested, and once again he will answer correctly. However, this exchange is on a deeper level.

Although the lawyer flails about seeking superiority, Jesus is steady in his resolve to bring the lawyer into the true consciousness of the intimate and dynamic relationship between love of God and love of neighbor. Jesus will be successful, and for a second time he will tell the lawyer to "do." However, this time the "knowing" of the lawyer will be sufficiently deep so that the "doing" is a possibility.

Jesus replied, "A man was going down from Jerusalem to Jericho, and fell into the hands of robbers, who stripped him, beat him, and went away, leaving him half dead. Now by chance a priest was going down that road; and when he saw him, he passed by on the other side. So likewise a Levite, when he came to the place and saw him, passed by on the other side.

The priest and Levite who pass by the hurting man presumably know the Law. They are able to recite it, just as the lawyer did. But they are not able to do this double commandment. Since the story does not want to dwell on these non-responses, it does not tell us their reasons for not stopping. But scholars have made suggestions. Perhaps there is a conflict of commandments in their minds. Laws about becoming impure by contacting bleeding and/or dead bodies may stop them from helping. Or perhaps this man does not qualify as a neighbor for they cannot identify him without his clothing. But the more we speculate about the possible justifications for their failure to help, the more we stay in the territory of the lawyer. This is what he would love to debate. Are they breaking the commandment to love their neighbor or do they have a legitimate excuse? This fine print is the air the lawyer breathes, and it is the air that suffocates Jesus.

But a Samaritan while traveling came near him; and when he saw him, he was moved with pity. He went to him and bandaged his wounds, having poured oil and wine on them. Then he put him on his own animal, brought him to an inn, and took care of him. The next day he took out two denarii, gave them to the innkeeper, and said, 'Take care of him; and when I come back, I will repay you whatever more you spend.'

The appearance of the Samaritan changes the flow of the story and the flow of consciousness in the lawyer listening to the story. The Samaritan is outside the Law, so no external entanglements or prescribed obligations constrain him. He does not travel in the maze of Jewish motivations. Instead, he is interiorly driven by compassion. In other words, he loves his neighbor as himself.

But the path to loving the neighbor as yourself is to "love the Lord your God with all your heart, and with all your soul, and with all your strength, and with all your mind" (v. 27). When you are interiorly centered on God, the ultimate Source, Sustainer, and Transformer of all Creation, you become aware that all Creation arises from the same source as you do. The differences that the surface of life displays are rooted in more foundational sameness. In traditional spirituality, the many arise out of the One. In this sense, all creation shares your identity as related to the One and, in this sense, becomes yourself. Compassion for others is the natural interior state of someone centered in the love of God.

Also, if you are interiorly in communion with God, you also share God's ecstatic and abundant nature. The Divine goes out from itself in overwhelming care. This overwhelming care is reflected in the detailed and extravagant actions of the Samaritan. What he does is over and above any social expectation. It is the abundance of God manifesting itself through the Samaritan, the one who is helping with an energy that goes well beyond a legally refined obligation. This is how to do both love of God and love of neighbor.

But does the story work? Does the lawyer understand the double commandment deeply enough to have a chance at doing it?

Which of these three, do you think, was a neighbor to the man who fell into the hands of the robbers?"

He said, "The one who showed him mercy."

Jesus said to him, "Go and do likewise."

It worked. The lawyer gets it.

In the first exchange, Jesus changed "do something now and inherit everlasting life later" to "do something now and live in everlasting life now." In this second exchange, he changes the legalistic "Who is my neighbor?" to the existential "Who was neighbor?" Anyone who loves God is universally proactive in responding to the needs of all people. The outer discernment of neighbor, enemy, neutral other, etc. is not what determines action. Earlier in the Gospel Jesus teaches:

> "But I say to you that listen, Love your enemies, do good to those who hate you, bless those who curse you, pray for those who abuse you. If anyone strikes you on the cheek, offer the other also; and from anyone who takes away your coat do not withhold even your shirt. Give to everyone who begs from you; and if anyone takes away your goods, do not ask for them again. Do to others as you would have them do to you. If you love those who love you, what credit is that to you? For even sinners love those who love them. If you do good to those who do good to you, what credit is that to you? For even sinners do the same. If you lend to those from whom you hope to receive, what credit is that to you? Even sinners lend to sinners, to receive as much again. But love your enemies, do good, and lend, expecting nothing in return. Your reward will be great, and you will be children of the Most High; for he is kind to the ungrateful and the wicked. *Be merciful, just as your Father is merciful.*" (Luke 6:27-36)

The Samaritan loves his enemy. He has no social obligation to the robbed and beaten man. Therefore, where does his motivation come from? It can only be from his interior love of the merciful God and his doing of that love by becoming a neighbor. That is what the lawyer grasps because he designates the Samaritan as "The one who showed him mercy" (v. 37). Under the loving guidance of Jesus the Teacher, the lawyer now knows how to *do* love of God and neighbor. The only thing left is to go and do it. "Go and do likewise" (v. 37).

Luke has put the high art of Jesus the Teacher on display, showing how spiritual wisdom works in an interpersonal encounter. Jesus discerns the lawyer as wanting a battle of egos. He refuses. He also discerns him as someone who can read the Law but cannot do it. Further, the lawyer does not know the intrinsic coincidence of action and reward. He sees them as separate and only extrinsically connected: actions done now receive rewards later. Jesus does not directly confront these shortcomings. Rather he works with them.

Jesus tells a story of how an enemy (the Samaritan), who from a legal point of view cannot possibly be considered a neighbor, becomes a neighbor. Therefore, his consciousness must be on a level deeper than social obligations. Also, the abundant nature of his help, his going beyond all expectations, reveals an interior centering of heart, soul, strength, and mind in the overflowing God. Jesus' wagered that a story would increase the lawyer's understanding of love of God and neighbor to such an extent that he would know how to do it. The wager was successful.

Failing to Possess Eternal Life

Matthew 19:16-22

Then someone came to him and said, "Teacher, what good deed must I do to have eternal life?"

And he said to him, "Why do you ask me about what is good? There is only one who is good. If you wish to enter into life, keep the commandments."

Since Jesus' agenda is to open people to eternal life, this man has come to the right teacher. But Jesus immediately confronts the way he has phrased his quest. He can never have what he wants if he thinks it is a matter of good deeds getting rewards. Jesus has to work with his mind so that his desire can be fulfilled.

The man attributes goodness to himself. But earlier Jesus has taught, "let your light shine before others, so that they may see your good works and give glory to your Father in heaven" (Matt 5:16). There is only one who is good, the Father in heaven. When people do good works, it is because God is working through them. Spiritually illumined people can discern the Divine as the source of their actions. So the idea of doing good to gain eternal life is the wrong way around. It is when people are participating in eternal life that good works flow from them.

Jesus instructs the man to purify his desire, to understand his drive for eternal life in a more appropriate way. His desire should not be to "have"; it should be to "enter into." One does not possess eternal life; one enters into it. The way to do this is to keep the commandments. Jesus is pointing to the commandments as a path. If the man tries to keep the commandments, something will happen that will show him how to enter into eternal life.

> He said to him, "Which ones?"
>
> And Jesus said, "You shall not murder; You shall not commit adultery; You shall not steal; You shall not bear false witness; Honor your father and mother; also, You shall love your neighbor as yourself."
>
> The young man said to him, "I have kept all these; what do I still lack?"

The man has not heard Jesus' correction of his mindset. In his eagerness, he thinks Jesus has told him the good works he must do. He must do the commandments. He is still in the framework of doing in order to possess and not in the framework of doing in order to discover how to enter. So naturally his concern is to get more information. There are many commandments. He is an earnest seeker, and so he wants to make sure he has the right ones. "Which ones?" is the misguided question of a man who thinks he is getting closer to his goal.

Jesus tells him the second part of the Decalogue and finishes it with the universal and mystifying command to "love your neighbor as yourself" (v. 19). The strategy of the Teacher is in place. The only way love of neighbor can be enacted is if it is empowered by love of God. The second part of the Decalogue is dependent on the first part, the commandments that embody the relationship to God. If the man did not register Jesus' first correction about how his goodness and God are related, certainly he will acknowledge the essential link between the relationship to God and the ability to do good by the neighbor as it is enshrined in the tradition. The link between the first and second parts of the Decalogue is essential.

However, the man's response shows he did not take Jesus' lure. For the first time, the storyteller confesses he was a *young* man; and he must have been a very young man indeed to have kept all those commandments. More to the point, he had to be spiritually immature to *think* he had kept all those commandments. He asks Jesus what he lacks, and to Jesus' consciousness what he lacks is obvious. He lacks a sense of dependency on God as the Source and energy of whatever goodness he is able to do. The teacher will now give him instructions of how to fill this lack:

> Jesus said to him, "If you wish to be perfect, go, sell your possessions, and give the money to the poor, and you will have treasure in heaven; then come follow me."

When the young man heard this word, he went away grieving, for he had many possessions.

The young man does not lack desire; he lacks understanding. So Jesus the teacher reinforces his desire as, at the same time, he reconstructs his understanding. The "wish to be perfect" corresponds to Jesus' teaching in the Sermon on the Mount, "Be perfect, therefore, as your heavenly Father is perfect." (Matt 5:48). Although this perfection consists in embodying a love as universal and impartial as the sun and the rain, the point here is to insist that perfection as well as goodness belong to God. So if one is to be perfect, one will have to be united to God and allow God's perfection to manifest itself in your life.

The path to this communion with God is to give up the possessive spirit. The young man's first, and fiercely retained, desire was to possess eternal life. Acquisition is what he is about. This acquisitive spirit is basically ego centered, caring about itself first and foremost. But the spiritual is not like physical or social goods. It cannot be possessed. In fact, the way to participate in the Spirit is through dispossession. He must sell what he has and give it to the poor. In this way, he will give up the drive for possessions and, at the same time, consider the well-being of others. This will do for him what his conversation with Jesus has not been able to do. It will break him out of his individual, wrong-headed quest and set him on the right path. "Blessed are the poor in spirit, for theirs is the kingdom of heaven" (Matt 5:3).

It will also give him treasure in heaven. But treasure in heaven is not eternal life and is not the goal of his quest. Treasure in heaven is the beginning of a transformative process that Jesus sets out in the Sermon on the Mount (Matt 6:19-21). People are encouraged to store up treasure in heaven rather than treasure on earth. Earthly treasures are prey to moths, rust, and thieves. Heavenly treasures are immune from temporal decay because they participate in eternal life. The teaching concludes: "For where your treasure is, there your heart will be also" (Matt 6:21). If the young man begins to value the spiritual, his relationship with God, this value will become more and more integrated into his life. It will become his heart, the radiating center of his being. In other words, he will cooperate with the transformative process of his own growth. That is why he must come back and follow Jesus. His quest is not over. It is just beginning. He will finally be on the right path.

But it is not to be. The story emphasizes that the young man hears this final word of Jesus. The implication is he has not grasped what

Jesus has previously said to him. Although now he understands the very different path of spiritual participation, he does not walk it. Instead, he walks away. His spiritual immaturity holds; it has him in its grip. It so completely owns him that it causes him to grieve. His is the way of possessions, and he has to have it his way. If he cannot acquire eternal life, he will live in sadness and forsake the quest. Jesus the Teacher has done what he could. He tried to bring the young man to wisdom, but the one who persisted in acquisition also persisted in ignorance.

Awaiting Another Time

In the Gospel of St. John, Jesus is both Lord and Teacher. "You call me Teacher and Lord—and you are right for that is what I am" (John 13:13). As Lord, Jesus is one with the Father and reveals Divine Love to the alienated world. As Teacher, he helps people understand and receive that Love and work out its implications for all areas of human life. In a passage that begins the "Last Supper," Jesus first reveals the full purpose of Divine Love and then works with the mind of Peter to help him receive it.

John 13:3-11

Jesus, knowing that the Father had given all things into his hands, and that he had come from God and was going to God, got up from the table, took off his outer robe, and tied a towel around himself. Then he poured water into a basin and began to wash the disciples' feet and to wipe them with the towel that was tied around him.

This is an intimate look into the interior of Jesus, a sketch of his God consciousness. He knows his wither and his whence, his origin and his destiny— he has come from God and is going to God. He is also aware that God is love (the Father) and that all things are in his hands. This echoes his identity as the Word who "was God" and "through" whom "[a]ll things came into being" (John 1:1, 3). He is the mediator between God and Creation, and the next thing he does will reveal the mystery of God and the love of the Father. In order for this revelation to be seen, he rises from table and takes off his outer robe. The deep secret of Jesus' relationship with God is out in the open.

Divine Love is interested in washing and drying people's feet, in revitalizing them for their journey on earth. This love flows like water pouring into a basin. The God consciousness of Jesus (the highest) drives him all the way down to feet (the lowest). Spirit is not an escape from the earth; it is a commitment to its transformation. This is a picture of the Word Becoming Flesh (see John 1:14), of God embracing the struggling life of people. If this washing and drying can be received, it will save the weary world.

> **He came to Simon Peter, who said to him, "Lord, are you going to wash my feet?"**
>
> **Jesus answered, "You do not know now what I am doing, but later you will understand."**
>
> **Peter said to him, "You will never wash my feet."**
>
> **Jesus answered, "Unless I wash you, you have no share with me."**
>
> **Simon Peter said to him, "Lord, not my feet only but also my hands and my head!"**
>
> **Jesus said to him, "One who has bathed does not need to wash, except for the feet, but is entirely clean. And you are clean, though not all of you"**
>
> **For he knew who was to betray him; for this reason he said, "Not all of you are clean."**

Jesus the Lord now becomes Jesus the Teacher, working with the mind of Peter. Peter recognizes a revelation has occurred because he calls Jesus "Lord." His problem seems to be a reversal in his expectations. He is Peter and on a lesser level than Jesus. He should be washing Jesus' feet. There is a hierarchical order, and it should not be violated. In Peter's mind God relates to the world as a ruler relates to a realm. God issues orders, and everyone obeys or is punished. Subjects grovel at God's feet. God does not attend to the bruised and battered feet of people. Peter is the servant and soldier of this transcendent King. What Jesus is doing bewilders his mind.

Jesus sees that bewilderment and realizes that Peter does not understand. At the present moment Peter does not comprehend fully this new revelation, and so he cannot receive it. But Jesus foresees a time when understanding will arrive. That time will be "the dark night" of Peter's ego. Later, Peter tells Jesus, "I will lay down my life for you."

Jesus responds, "Will you lay down your life for me? Very truly, I tell you, before the cock crows, you will have denied me three times" (John 13:37-38). Peter will come to illumination (the cock crowing; see Mark 14:72 and parallels) after he has denied Jesus three times (a sacred number). When his strength fails him, he will grasp the need to receive grace and strength from God. The denials of Peter will bring him to the illumination of morning, the time when the cock crows.

But for now Peter is adamant. He fiercely holds to what he knows and refuses the new revelation. Jesus tells him there is no other way. Jesus cannot conform to the fantasies of Peter's mind. Jesus only does what he hears from his Father (see John 14:31); he can only do what reveals the love of God. Jesus washes feet; and if Peter will not open to that activity, he cannot share in Jesus' life.

Although Peter does not understand Jesus, he loves him. So he moves from refusing to have his feet washed to suggesting a whole bath. Unfortunately, this poignant openness is wrongheaded. It focuses on physical bathing, and, as Jesus points out, it is not about cleanliness. If people have bathed, they are clean. Jesus' foot washing and drying is about spiritual receptivity. But Peter's lack of understanding and consequent resistance is acceptable and will continue to be worked with. This exchange with Jesus has not been a failure. It is one piece in the ongoing conversion of Peter. Its exact role will only be clear when the conversion is complete.

However, the last line suggests that Judas cannot be worked with. Satan has closed him in an irrevocable way. Even when Jesus gives himself to Judas in the dipped morsel, it is Satan that enters him, and not Jesus (John 13:27).

Conclusion

Thomas Aquinas defined love as the affective willing of the good of the other. From a spiritual perspective, the good of others is that they know themselves as living in intimate communion with God and in service of the neighbor. However, there are many mental tapes and holdings that block this consciousness. These holdings come from negative personal experiences, conventional thinking, and, as the rabbis insisted, evil imaginings. For the most part, these blocks cannot be overcome by individual effort. Someone who lovingly wills this good for others must work with the blocks until they are no longer obstacles.

Therefore, loving others is more than just willing they awaken to the love of God and neighbor. It is actually working to bring it about.

In the Gospels, Jesus is the one who wills this good for others and engages them in such a way that it can happen. He is highly qualified for this teaching task. At his baptism Jesus realizes he is the Beloved Son who is on a Spirit guided mission (see Mark 1:9-11 and parallels). This identity is not his special preserve. It is extended to others. All who hear and respond to his proclamation and teaching enter into his identity and discover the same structure of selfhood within themselves. So Jesus sees in others what he knows in himself. And he works with these others until they see and love in themselves what he sees and loves in them. It is this patient and perseverant working with the minds of others that manifests his love.

When Jesus interacts with others, what does he know about the working of the mind that helps him? If the encounters with the lawyer, the young man, and Peter are any indication:

• He knows that the mind must open to love of God for love of neighbor to happen because love of God provides the vision to compassionately see the neighbor as yourself and the energy to complete the arduous task of caring.

• He knows that when the mind is attached to ego games of testing, it is not possible to seek true wisdom.

• He knows that the mind that retrieves information has to take another step into realized knowing.

• He knows a story has the power to sneak past mental defenses and touch the heart so directly that a new consciousness emerges.

• He knows that the illumined mind can trace what it sees and hears on the outside to the source on the inside.

• He knows the illumined mind manifests itself as a new freedom to do compassionate acts.

• He knows that when the mind claims moral actions as self-promotional trophies, it is mistaken.

• He knows that the minds of immature seekers are centered on themselves and overestimate their ability to do good.

• He knows that moving the mind to centeredness in God entails relinquishing the mind's drive to acquire worth on its own terms.

• He knows that the mind's drive to possess is so entrenched that it is easier to walk away without what you want than to change and receive what you want.

• He knows that the conventional mind would rather serve a God of transcendent demands than open to a God of imminent revitalization.

• He knows the minds of disciples do not have to get it all at once.

• He knows that love can help disciples persevere when mental understanding is lacking.

• He knows that when he talks about the spiritual, people's addicted minds will hear it as remarks about the physical.

• He knows that even when he gives himself totally, some minds are so closed that he will not be received.

The spiritual wisdom of the Gospel is more than a message, more than a revelation of theological truths. It happens in the encounter with Jesus, and this encounter is always with particular people with particular mindsets. Jesus addresses those mindsets and works with them in the service of Spirit. The secret energy of Jesus' commitment and creativity to work with the mind is the love of God that wills and brings about the good of the other. Therefore, Jesus the Teacher who works with the mind and Jesus the Lover who embodies divine care are one and the same.

For a fuller introduction to the origin and direction of *The Spiritual Wisdom of the Gospels for Christian Preachers and Teachers* project, see the preface in the first volume (Year A).

First Sunday of Advent
Mark 13:24-37

Working and Watching

A Spiritual Commentary

[Jesus said to his disciples:] "In those days, after that suffering, the sun will be darkened, and the moon will not give its light, and the stars will be falling from heaven, and the powers in the heavens will be shaken. Then they will see 'the Son of Man coming in clouds' with great power and glory. Then he will send out the angels, and gather his elect from the four winds, from the ends of the earth to the ends of heaven.

"From the fig tree learn its lesson: as soon as its branch becomes tender and puts forth its leaves, you know that summer is near. So also, when you see these things taking place, you know that he is near, at the very gates. Truly I tell you, this generation will not pass away until all these things have taken place. Heaven and earth will pass away, but my words will not pass away.

"But about that day or hour no one knows, neither the angels in heaven, nor the Son, but only the Father. Beware, keep alert; for you do not know when the time will come. It is like a man going on a journey, when he leaves home and puts his slaves in charge, each with his work, and commands the doorkeeper to be on the watch. Therefore, keep awake—for you do not know when the master of the house will come, in the evening, or at midnight, or at cockcrow, or at dawn, or else he may find you asleep when he comes suddenly. And what I say to you I say to all: Keep awake."

This cosmic imagery expresses and conveys the impact and importance of the revelation of Jesus. When a way of thinking, feeling, and acting has held sway for a long period of time, it can be imagined as heaven and earth, an unshakeable cosmic backdrop. Human affairs may be tumultuous; history may be on the loose. But the implacable sky and the solid earth stand firm. They are the stable stage, the orderly succession of time and seasons. "A generation goes, and a generation comes, but the earth remains forever" (Eccl 1:4).

However, when a new way of thinking, feeling, and acting arrives and threatens the established order of things, the best way to express it is cosmic collapse. The sun and moon are snuffed out; stars fall. Angels search heaven and earth, collecting the ones who will survive into the new world. The old arrangements are over. Heaven and earth are passing away, and it is the words of Jesus, words that are creating an alternative way to be human, that is bringing them down. These words are the new reality, and they will not pass away.

This radical transition has a cost. Many will go down with the world they promoted and within which they prospered. But from the point of view of those who followed Jesus, this destruction is favorable. It makes way for the advent of summer, not the full-blown summer of high heat, but the first bud, difficult to detect but bursting with promise. The new way is in its infancy. Its understandings are piecemeal and progressive. Its actions are experimental and tentative. Therefore, it is necessary to both work and watch, to be both a servant ("each with his or her own work") and a doorkeeper ("on the watch").

In this context working is really co-working. The Lord is active and at work in the world bringing about a new humanity. God lures people into the same activity, making them servants of divine activity. But in order for them to join the Lord's activity, they must be awake to what God is doing. They must notice the Spirit's arrival, the sudden presence and voice whose time cannot be predicted. The old ways, the ways of the heaven and earth that are passing away, are always predictable. There is no need to be awake to follow them. They are ingrained habits, mindless and oppressive business as usual. The Word of God that was embodied in Jesus is novel in each situation. Only those who both work and watch can hear this Word.

This injunction to work and watch, especially to watch, is strident. The text shouts it; the repeated imperatives assault the ear. And the final line, "What I say to you, I say to all," suggests a universal application. Therefore, this advice is not a temporary strategy. Hang in there for awhile, and then you will be able to get some sleep. It is an adaptive challenge, a permanent way of being in the world. Can Christians live engaged in God's work and ever open to the arrival of the new? This strange combination, immersed in the present and on the edge of the future, is the way of discipleship.

Teaching

When I was thirteen years old, I was introduced to meditation. The seminary high school I attended required all students to purchase a copy of *Meditation Mechanics*. As well as I can remember, this book had an introduction on the dynamics of attention and distraction. The body of the book was a series of Gospel texts with instructions on how to slowly ponder them and benefit from their inspiration. My spiritual director told me the best place to meditate was in church before morning Mass.

So there I was at 6:30 in the morning in a back pew of a large, Gothic, urban church. However, I was not alone. Even at this early hour, the church was flooded with regulars. Pious men and women were clanging coins down the steel chutes of the votive stand and lighting candles with brightening hopes. Widows, dressed in black, were whispering to one another about who was ill and where to go for breakfast. An occasional girl, my own age, would wander down the main aisle. Christian courtesy demanded my eyes see her safely to her seat. There was a lot going on. Meditation was not one of them.

I told my spiritual director that the early morning church was too noisy. He said, "Go at night when there is no one there." So there I was at 7:30 at night, kneeling in the pew with my meditation book, more often than not a basketball on the bench behind me. Only a few other people were in the church. No outer distractions.

On my first night, just as I had begun to meditate, a voice said, "Kneel up straight." It was the voice of my grandmother. She wasn't in the church; she was in my head. And she was not alone. The whole neighborhood had taken up residency between my ears. The lack of noise on the outside made me aware of the considerable noise inside. Meditation was in jeopardy from both outer and inner distractions.

Over the years and with practice, I have learned how to steady my mind, to gently resist every distraction that wants to steal my attention—except the really good distractions. Sustaining attention is a great learning. This human possibility is symbolized by the Latin spiritual advice, *Age quod agis* (Do what you are doing.) However, it has also made me something of a Neanderthal. I cannot watch television and read at the same time, or seriously listen and talk to a friend with the radio on. I walk without earphones and when I eat alone, I often eat in silence—only eating. In this way I learned some of the tricks that hover around the dynamic of distraction and attention.

This was part of my early adventures following the injunction, "Watch!" But there was more to come. When spiritual traditions praise attention and say it is the key to spiritual development, they mean more than the ability to stay focused for a period of time on one particular task. They propose a deeper watching, an inner vigilance that notices not only the comings and goings of the outer world but the rising and perishing of inner thoughts and emotions. In the first moment this sustained watching is a witness, acknowledging but not investing in the contents of consciousness. The depth of the person is always on reserve, waiting, watching, staying awake.

Paradoxically, this deep watching does not preclude activity. It coexists with work, with doing what has to be done. What the watching brings to the working is an added dimension. Some have called this dual consciousness, and Meister Eckhart has imagined it as a hinge and a door. (See Robert K. C. Forman, *Meister Eckhart: The Mystic as Theologian: An Experiment in Methodology* [Rockport, Mass.: Element, 1991] 134.) The door swings back and forth engaging what is happening, but the hinge stays steady, anchoring the door and allowing it to move freely. The unmoved watcher and moving worker live side by side. The Christian tradition has called it recollection in action. We remember our ultimate identity as we engage our proximate tasks. So the watcher and worker combine to actualize the full human potential.

However, there comes a time when the watcher and worker join forces. This is the second moment, the true fulfillment of the life of the watcher. When consciousness cultivates the watcher, it waits beyond the mind, and peers through the screen of conventional and customary thoughts. When it does, it begins to discern a component of every arising and perishing situation that is often missed. In every experience there is a lure to redemption, to maximizing value, to making something the best it can be. When "watcher consciousness" sees this lure, it pours everything it has into the work of responding to and engaging this possibility. In symbolic code, the Lord has arrived and the watcher and worker unite to greet him.

This is a difficult possibility to envision. Here is one person who witnesses to how it works: Eckhart Tolle, a contemporary spiritual teacher, is talking about a "dimension of consciousness that is unconditioned." When consciousness rests in this dimension, "You'd be surprised at the alertness that is there when you allow what is. It is the alertness out of which action arises, should it be necessary." Andrea Kulin, who has interviewed Tolle, supplies a piece of her own experience, a time when action was necessary. "I've had the experience, while teaching, of sitting with a distressed child and being uncertain how to help. Sometimes, rather than going into my own reaction of distress, I was able to be there quietly, openly, just 'taking in' the child, and from somewhere, something came that was the right thing, the thing the child needed. I don't know where that came from but it felt like a different form of intelligence."

In Andrea Kulin the watcher and worker joined to greet the arrival of the Lord, "the right thing, the thing the child needed."

Of course, this is the surprise that the injunctions "beware, be alert, be on the watch, stay awake" hold. The Lord is arriving in every moment, and when the watchers see him, they become workers in the kingdom.

Second Sunday of Advent
Mark 1:1-8

Beginning before It Begins

Spiritual Commentary

The beginning of the good news of Jesus Christ, the Son of God.

This summary opening line seems like a trumpet blast to start a story of glory. But once the last page of Mark's Gospel is turned and the stunned and confused readers return to this first line, they understand it in a startling and bold way. Every word—"beginning," "good news," "Jesus," "Christ," and "Son of God"—vibrates differently because of the story that has unfolded.

What does "beginning" mean when there is no ending?

Mark's Gospel is notorious for not having a tidy conclusion. The last line has the women disciples, although charged with a mission to tell Peter and the disciples that the crucified Jesus goes before them into Galilee, running away from the empty tomb in silence and fear (see Mark 16). This is not an ending that ties a neat ribbon on the narrative. Rather it is an indication that the story of Jesus continues and that fear is an essential feature of discipleship. Therefore, "the beginning" of the first verse of this Gospel is still the operative word for the last verse. Readers may roll up the parchment of the Gospel and return it to a shelf, but the reality of the "good news" continues to unfold. This is a story of a beginning that has no ending.

Mark's story also will not respect the normal understandings of "good news," "Christ," and "Son of God." The "good news" will not be the standard fare of political ascension, triumph over enemies, and glorious recognition, and the conventional meanings of "Christ" and "Son of God" that convey privilege and prestige will be reversed. The destiny of Jesus will be to encounter deadly resistance from political and religious authorities; incomprehension and abandonment from his disciples; and eventually to suffer, die, and rise. Strangely, in the mind of the author, all this will be considered good news and will supply revolutionary insight into the standard religious titles of "Christ" and "Son of God."

So, in the light of the story to follow, the opening line is a stunning expression of transformed Christian consciousness. None of these words: "beginning," "good news," "Christ," and "Son of God"—survive in tact. They are all stripped of conventional understanding because of their relationship to the unyielding reality of one word: Jesus

> **As it is written in the prophet Isaiah, "See, I am sending my messenger ahead of you, who will prepare your way; the voice of one crying out in the wilderness: 'Prepare the way of the Lord, make his paths straight,'"**
>
> **John the baptizer appeared in the wilderness, proclaiming a baptism of repentance for the forgiveness of sins. And people from the whole Judean countryside and all the people of Jerusalem were going out to him, and were baptized by him in the river Jordan, confessing their sins.**
>
> **Now John was clothed with camel's hair, with a leather belt around his waist, and he ate locusts and wild honey.**
>
> **He proclaimed, "The one who is more powerful than I is coming after me; I am not worthy to stoop down and untie the thong of his sandals. I have baptized you with water; but he will baptize you with the Holy Spirit."**

The good new of Jesus Christ "begins" *before* "it begins." John the Baptist comes out of the past prophetic tradition. The prophet Isaiah (Malachi and Exodus) wrote about him. He lives in the wilderness, a locale prophets haunt. John's camel hair garment is reminiscent of Elijah; and his diet is the ascetic fare of prophets, paradoxically hinting at more nourishing spiritual food. Most telling is his message. He preaches repentance, echoing God's eternal plea, "Come back to me." So John lives where prophets live, dresses like a prophet, eats like a prophet, and talks like a prophet.

As a prophet, John's primary work is freeing people from their identification with sin. He does this through a call to change their minds (interiors) and behaviors (exteriors) and to experience and symbolize this change in the act of baptism, going under the water to die to sin and emerging above the water open to the sky. This is a strenuous undertaking. It entails courageous self-examination, and it can be a rigorous and exhausting affair. To authentically undergo the baptism is to experience a dizzying sense of freedom. To shake off the shackles of the past, to walk away from destructive habits and alliances, to say "no" to what has mastered a person for so long could seem like the finish line, a successful conclusion to a long process.

This is precisely the impression John does not want to give. Therefore, he witnesses to the incompleteness of himself and his work. He does not want his newly baptized people thinking they are a "completed conversion." The mission is not accomplished. All that has happened is: now people are ready.

The "path" image clarifies John's work. Often path images are developed from the point of view of the traveler. In order to arrive at a desired destination, the one journeying has to deal with fallen branches, stones, landslides, etc. But in the "path" image of the prophesy, the obstacles are not in the way of the one journeying but in the way of the one arriving. Someone wants to come toward people, but he or she is blocked by the "fallen branches, stones, landslides, etc." In particular, the path is twisted. The point of making straight the path is for someone to smoothly and straightforwardly arrive.

This way of working with the image of path reflects a theological perception. God and the ones who manifest God's love are very proactive. They come after people. People do not have to search them out. In Mark's Gospel, although Jesus hides from the celebrity that accompanies his teaching, exorcisms, and healings, he is, at the same time, driven to reach out to all people. What people must do is learn to wait and welcome. If people empty themselves of sin, they will wait and welcome the Holy Spirit whom Jesus brings. In this way John's work is essential preparation for the reception of the more powerful one, the thong of whose sandals John is not worthy to untie.

Teaching

Once I was teaching seminarians a course in spirituality. Two priests who were visiting the seminary asked if they could sit in on the class. I agreed, and afterwards we talked about changes in seminary life and priesthood. One of the priests said, "I never knew what spirituality was until I went through AA."

"You know remarks like that make those of us in seminary formation and teaching wonder if we are getting anything across," I said.

"Oh, there was nothing wrong with the programs I had in my seminary years. The problem was not there. The problem was me. I wasn't ready."

When he was a seminarian, the priest had been exposed to many opportunities for spiritual formation. But he seized none of them. He wasn't ready.

Some facilitators of group process have a saying: "It begins before it begins." On a first level, this means that if the group starts at nine, it really starts as people gather in the room at 8:30. On a second level, it means that people bring their history of group interaction into the room with them and, to the degree it is possible, it must be taken into account as the process and conversation unfold. What is the readiness level of people? Are they willing and open? Can they engage the people and the tasks?

This question of readiness may be a partial answer to why the teachings of Jesus fell on many deaf ears. People had not let go of sin, so they could not embrace grace. They had not undergone John's baptism, so they were not open to Jesus' banquet. It is not just a matter of exposure to Christ. It is a matter of what we are able to let in, of what we can truly hear and integrate. Some theologians call this the question of pre-evangelization. What has to happen to the person so they are ready for the revelation, so they absorb what they hear? Encountering Jesus the Word may be a beginning, but, after all, it begins before it begins.

Any list of experiences and qualities that make for readiness would be as extensive and complicated as the human race itself. However, this gospel text focuses on the desire for the forgiveness of sins. Although Mark is certainly exaggerating, he portrays this desire as widespread. "People from the whole Judean countryside and all the people of Jerusalem" went out to John, seeking baptism and "confessing their sins." Historians may tell us that these people thought the end of the world was about to happen, and they were playing the odds that John's baptism would protect them from eternal destruction. Their desire for shedding sins was merely an insincere, last ditch effort to save themselves.

But, in my mind's eye, I imagine a readiness that is real but not pretty, a readiness that flows from frustration and dissatisfaction. If sin is understood as any thought, deed, or disposition that breaks the flow of life between God and the self, as well as between the self, other people and the earth, then a different picture of the desire for forgiveness presents itself. Perhaps people wake up one day and find that there is no "life" in their lives. The passion, pleasure, and purpose of what they do and who they are with is no longer there. They go through the paces and fulfill their duties, but there is something wrong. Beneath the surface they are out of sync. Although they still fight for money and position, they know the payoff will not be all that it promises. Also, vast social inequalities are not as easy to tolerate as they once were, and their accumulated possessions are more burden than pleasure. Although they may not be able to list their sins, this is a sinful condition. The flow of life has dried up, and they want out. It is often said that the longing for liberation begins when you notice you are in prison.

It is these people, the dissatisfied and desperate, who venture from the cities and the villages into the desert. They come to John with a "God, I hope this works" look in their eye. They may not have the full picture, but they know a first step when they see it. Desperate women and men risk the future because the past has become intolerable. They are feeling dead, and they sense they are dying at their own hands. The first step is stripping, purification, letting go. The current of the Jordan will carry away whatever they can manage to release. "Do that," they say to themselves, "and then see if there is a next step. I can no longer go on as I am."

The Baptist watches them emerge from the waters. He deflects their gratitude and praise. He tells them about the "more powerful" one who will provide the Spirit of their new life. This life will start when they realize and integrate his wisdom. They are on the edge of a beginning, ready, eager, open. Then the Baptist reveals himself, tells them who he is, "I am the beginning before it begins."

Third Sunday of Advent

John 1:6-8; 19-28

Looking for One You Do Not Know

A Spiritual Commentary

There was a man sent from God, whose name was John. He came as a witness to testify to the light, so that all might believe through him. He himself was not the light, but he came to testify to the light.

The storyteller sums up what John will say directly in the following series of exchanges. He is a witness to someone else; he is someone people go "through" rather than "arrive at." What people are looking for is "the light," a full awareness of what is real, an illumination of the ultimate structures of human existence, a consciousness of God, self, neighbor, and creation. The One who can do this is "the true light, which enlightens everyone" (John 1:9). John cannot muster that much wattage. Jesus may have called him "a burning and shining lamp" (John 5:34), but he knew this from the vantage point of his own full illumination. The larger light renders the lamp a reflection, a testimony, a preparation.

This is the testimony given by John when the Jews sent priests and Levites from Jerusalem to ask him, "Who are you?"

He confessed and did not deny it, but confessed, "I am not the Messiah."

And they asked him, "What then? Are you Elijah?"

He said, "I am not."

"Are you the prophet?"

He answered, "No."

Then they said to him, "Who are you? Let us have an answer for those who sent us. What do you say about yourself?"

He said, "I am the voice of one crying out in the wilderness, 'Make straight the way of the Lord,'" as the prophet Isaiah said.

John is sent from God; the priests and Levites are sent from the higher-ups of Jerusalem. The rest of the text is told from their point of view, and my sympathy is with these minions. They start with a direct question about who John is, and he tells them who he is not. If they are looking for the big fish, the "Messiah," they are in the wrong place.

But they need more than this confession of denial. So they supply identities. But John refuses to let them name him either Elijah or the prophet. In their messianic schemes these figures would be precursors of the Messiah. The toadies have tried, but they have not bettered their situation. They cannot return to Jerusalem with a list of what John is not. Telling the "Jews" (the top religious authorities) that John is not the Messiah, Elijah, or the Prophet will not be seen as mission accomplished.

When they say, "Let us have an answer for those who sent us," are they pleading with John? Is there frustration in their request? Is the real communication, "Give us a break. We have a job to do." But what John tells them positively is not much better than his strings of denials. In fact, it is another way of saying they are in the wrong place. He is someone who is preparing for someone else.

> **Now they had been sent from the Pharisees.**
>
> **They asked him, "Why then are you baptizing if you are neither the Messiah, nor Elijah, nor the prophet?"**
>
> **John answered them, "I baptize with water. Among you stands one whom you do not know, the one who is coming after me; I am not worthy to untie the thong of his sandal."**
>
> **This took place in Bethany across the Jordan where John was baptizing.**

As a prelude to further questioning, the storyteller reminds us these inquisitors had been sent from the Pharisees. Does this mean they do not give up easily? Does it mean they dare not return without incriminating evidence? Does it mean their questioning is hostile and not genuine inquiry? Whatever it means, their next ploy is to try to arrive at John's identity through his activity. Supposedly, his baptizing would be appropriate if he was "the Messiah," "Elijah," or "the prophet." Since he is none of the above, why does he baptize? The path is open for an identity avowal with John finally naming himself, or an identity slip-up with John inadvertently revealing what he wants to hide.

Instead, John sidesteps them. If they want to know who he is and why he is baptizing, they have to know the one who is coming after him. Although there is a qualitative difference between John and the one coming after him, John's water baptism prepares for this one. The baptism only makes sense in light of the future one. However, the future one is already standing among them and they do not know him. Their knowledge about the Messiah is not accurate and cannot help them discern his presence. They came to solve the mystery of John; they have been directed to the mystery beyond John and among them.

The interview is over. The bottom line is: those who have been sent to ascertain John's identity only find out he does not fit their identity categories. The identity category John himself supplies is not helpful because it includes as an essential feature an unnamed "one" who is already among them but whom they do not know. It will not go well with these minions when they return to their suspicious, unforgiving leaders in Jerusalem.

Teaching

The first sacred storyteller I ever met was Reuven Gold. Reuven told Sufi and Hasidic stories, smiling and laughing as the stories came out of his own mouth and entered his own ears. He valued the stories as torches that pushed back the darkness and revealed the play of Spirit. His pleasure was contagious.

Shortly after we had met for the first time, we unexpectedly found ourselves on a plane together. He quickly pulled from his bag a copy of Thomas Merton's rendering of Chuang Tzu's stories, poetry, and reflections. He gave it to me with the inscription, "To my new friend, John." I opened it for a quick look, but he reached over and closed the book.

Instead, he slid into my hand two folded pieces of paper. They were wrinkled from use and slightly torn along the creases. "Just so you know people are still writing sacred stories." I opened the papers and read a story that was typed out in double space. There were a number of spelling errors. Since that time I have both heard the story told and seen it in print. It is never quite told the same way or written down the same way. In print I have seen the story attributed to "unknown origin" (Elisa Davy Pearman, *Doorways to the Soul: 52 Wisdom Tales from Around the World* [Cleveland, Ohio: Pilgrim Press, 1998]) and classified as "Chassid" (*Stories of the Spirit, Stories of the Heart*, ed. by Christina Feldman and Jack Kornfield, [San Francisco: HarperSan Francisco, 1991]).

It is a story about a monastery that had fallen on hard times. The monks did not talk with one another; they were no new, young monks; and people had stopped coming for spiritual solace and direction.

> In the woods that surrounded the monastery a rabbi lived in a small hut. Occasionally, the monks would see the rabbi walking in the woods and, almost hypnotically, they would say to one another, "The rabbi walks in the woods."
>
> The abbot was greatly distraught at the decline of the monastery. He had prayed and pondered over the situation and admonished the mood and behavior of the monks. All to no avail. One day he saw the rabbi walking in the woods and decided to ask his advice. He walked up behind the rabbi. The rabbi turned, and when the abbot and the rabbi faced one another, both began to weep. The sorrow of the situation affected them deeply. The abbot knew he did not have to explain the decline of the monastery. He merely asked, "Can you give me some direction so the monastery will thrive again?"
>
> The rabbi said, "One of you is the Messiah." Then he turned and continued to walk in the woods.
>
> The abbot returned to the monastery. The monks had seen him talking to the rabbi who walks in the woods. They asked, "What did the rabbi say?"
>
> "One of us is the Messiah," the abbot said the words slowly, almost incredulously.
>
> The monks began talking to one another. "One of us? Which one? Is it Brother John? Or perhaps it is Brother Andrew? Could it even be the abbot?"
>
> Slowly, things began to change at the monastery. The monks began to look for the Messiah in each other and listen to each other's words for the Messiah's voice.
>
> Soon new, younger monks joined, and people returned to the monastery for spiritual solace and direction.

I folded the papers and gave them back to Reuven. Awaiting the Messiah is not part of the theology I carry or the spirituality out of which I try to live. Yet as I looked at this round, middle-aged man, with a Jewish skull cap, African dashiki, salt and pepper beard, and more beads than a hippie on Mulberry Street, who was smiling at me because he could see the gift he gave me, I could not help but ask, deep inside myself where lives the transformative energy of the heart, "Is Reuven the Messiah?" And when I did, I felt such a quickness in my being, such an awakened alertness, that everything became vivid and intensely interesting. I realized the truth of the story was not in the objective fact of whether one of the monks was the Messiah or not. It was in what it had done to my consciousness, at the new level of attention it had created in me. I listened to his every word.

So years later when I stumbled upon this poem by Hafiz, "How Do I Listen?" I knew exactly what it meant.

How
Do I
Listen to others?
As if everyone were my Master
Speaking to me
His
Cherished
Last
Words.

(*The Gift: Poems by the Great Sufi Master,*
trans. Daniel Ladinsky [New York: Arkana/Penguin, 1999])

Fourth Sunday of Advent

Luke 1:26-38

Conceiving through Courage

A Spiritual Commentary

In the sixth month the angel Gabriel was sent by God to a town in Galilee called Nazareth, to a virgin engaged to a man whose name was Joseph, of the house of David. The virgin's name was Mary.

It has been six months since God last dispatched Gabriel. At that time he appeared to the aged Zachary at the right hand of the altar of incense in the Holy of Holies. He promised the birth of a son from the old and barren womb of Elizabeth, Zachary's wife. The message was clear: God is at work in this birth because it could not come about from merely natural causes. The spiritual is seeding physical and social life with new possibilities, possibilities that physical and social life do not have on their own.

Now Gabriel is at it again. His activity is not restricted to the Temple precincts. He is in Nazareth, a town so small that the larger territory of Galilee must be named first so the reader will have some idea where it is. This time his assignment is not an old man who cannot grasp the possibility of conception but a virgin who thinks it is impossible.

The virgin is someone whose physical (no sexual contact) and social (unmarried) identity is not established. Therefore, the angel will address her spiritual identity. This spiritual identity is closely tied to the heritage of the man to whom she is engaged. The "house of David" is the reality God has pledged to build. "I will establish his throne forever. I will be a father to him, and he shall be a son to me. I will not take my steadfast love from him . . . [B]ut I will confirm him in my house and in my kingdom forever, and his throne shall be established forever" (1 Chr 17:12-14). The scene is set: Gabriel will visit the spiritual center of Mary and recruit her to build God's house, a house that cannot be built by human hands.

And he came to her and said, "Greetings, favored one! The Lord is with you."

But she was much perplexed by his words and pondered what sort of greeting this might be.

Gabriel knows something about Mary she does not know about herself. She is full of grace (the traditional and, by far, the better translation). Her center is an abundant, overflowing spirit. This spirit is in service of a divine mission. "The Lord is with you" means God is working out divine purposes through her life. This is how an angel greets "a virgin" for a virgin is someone who belongs to God and is dedicated to what God is doing.

However, this revelation of Mary to herself is troubling. The angel sees her ultimate identity more clearly than she does. Although his words are perplexing, she does not dismiss them. She ponders them. She will not symbolize rocky ground that hears the Word but does not develop it in any depth (Luke 8:6, 13). The first step in becoming pregnant by the Spirit is to seriously heed the transcendent Word that reveals a dimension with which we may not be completely comfortable. Pondering is the response to angel-speak.

The angel said to her, "Do not be afraid, Mary, for you have found favor with God. And now, you will conceive in your womb and bear a son, and you will name him Jesus. He will be great, and will be called the Son of the Most High, and the Lord God will give to him the throne of his ancestor David. He will reign over the house of Jacob forever, and of his kingdom there will be no end."

The angel senses Mary's discombobulation. His words counter her fear with the assurance of favor. The presence of divine grace in the center of her being may at first cause fear, but at last it will be recognized as a gift of love. Also, further understanding will mitigate her fear. So Gabriel spells out the mission in more detail and in increasingly mind-blowing proportions. It demands that she become pregnant and bring forth God's son who will bring about God's kingdom on earth, a kingdom that fulfills Israel and reaches beyond it. However, this explanation of her mission encounters an obvious obstacle.

Mary said to the angel, "How can this be, since I am a virgin?"

The angel said to her, "The Holy Spirit will come upon you, and the power of the Most High will overshadow you; therefore the child to be born will be holy; he will be called Son of

God. And now, your relative Elizabeth in her old age has also conceived a son; and this is the sixth month for her who was said to be barren. For nothing will be impossible with God."

Mary's physical virginity is not an obstacle to conceiving and bearing God's Son. Conceiving the Son of God does not happen in the same way as conceiving a physical body. This type of conception entails openness to the Holy Spirit. Beyond openness, it entails cooperation with that Spirit. Essential to this cooperation is the insight that opening and cooperating with God enables people to accomplish things they previously thought were impossible. What is considered impossible from a strictly human standpoint becomes possible when God is working through the human.

This conversation with Gabriel has increased Mary's understanding. Her center is a spiritual reality, open to God's loving presence and invited to share in God's work. This means her identity and mission cannot be imprisoned by physical and social laws. She has to think in terms of Spirit becoming flesh, not flesh restricting Spirit. This angelic instruction develops Mary's realization of what she is called to be and do. However, it also brings her to a moment of decision.

Then Mary said, "Here am I, the servant of the Lord; let it be with me according to your word."

Then the angel departed from her.

The understanding part of the angelic dialogue is over. It has led her, as it always does, to the terror of decision. She stands on the ledge of courage and leaps. Her tenacious will engages her illumined mind in a total act of commitment. She echoes Isaiah's offer, "Here am I; send me!" (Isa 6:8). The result is conception. The transcendent Word has initiated a process of understanding and willing that has made her pregnant. The angel has accomplished his task. He departs.

Teaching

St. Augustine said that Mary conceived Christ through the ear. This jarring remark makes it clear we are talking about spiritual rather than physical dynamics. It also points to the importance of the Word. Hearing a transcendent Word through the ear initiates the process of conception.

St. Augustine also said Mary conceived in her heart before she conceived in her womb. This jarring remark points to the process of understanding and willing that is necessary to become pregnant by the Spirit. The path of spiritual conception is marked out—hearing a transcendent Word, struggling to understand it, and finally uniting our will to it.

The transcendent Word is meant to awaken in us the identity called "full of grace, the Lord is with you." Kallistos Ware, the Eastern Christian Bishop of Diokleia, reflects on the tradition of the "virgin point."

> By "virgin point" Massignon, interpreting al-Hallaj, means "the last, irreducible, secret center of the heart," "the latent personality, the deep subconscious, the secret cell walled up [and hidden] to every creature, the 'inviolate virgin," which "remains unformed" until visited by God; to discover this virgin point is to return to our origin. Thus *le point vierge* or the innermost heart is, in the words of Dorothy C. Buck, the place "where God alone has access and human and Divine meet"; it embodies "the sacredness hidden in the depth of every human soul." (Kallistos Ware, "How Do We Enter the Heart?" In *Paths to the Heart: Sufism and the Christian East,* ed. James S. Cutsinger [Bloomington, Ind.: World Wisdom, 2002] 3)

This description explains both Mary's perplexity and our own. We are not accustomed to thinking about ourselves in this way. We need to ponder any greeting that names us in this way.

Of course, there will be a need for greater understanding. Since at this level we belong entirely to God, our mission will be to join in God's work, to help construct the house the divine is building. Grasping this profound personal truth will mean conceptual transformation. We will no longer be just physical and social beings struggling to promote and protect ourselves. We will be sons and daughters of God struggling to change physical and social reality to reflect our common, innate dignity. Our smaller plans and self-centered ambitions will have to be integrated into a more comprehensive vision. This is not a fast process, and even angelic explanations are questioned. But eventually the mind does move from darkness to light, and the light beckons to the will to follow. This is the moment when many of us are paralyzed. Fear is more powerful than favor. Playing it safe is the entrenched habit; risking it all is dangerous territory.

Denise Levertov's poem, *Annunciation*, ends with what the Christian tradition calls "Mary's *Fiat* " (Latin, "Let it be!").

> She did not cry, "I cannot, I am not worthy."
> nor, "I have not the strength."
> She did not submit with gritted teeth,
>   raging, coerced.

> Bravest of all humans,
>> consent illumined her.
>
> . . . .
> Consent,
>> courage unparalleled,
> opened her utterly.

> (*A Door in the Hive* [New York: New Directions, 1989])

This is the difficult truth. Understanding is intimately coupled with willing. Knowing is deepened and increased through engagement. The mind is important, but we cannot completely open through mental understanding. It is only with the courage of consent that we open utterly. It is only when we say, "Yes," that we become pregnant with the Spirit.

Earlier in the poem, Levertov reflects on the annunciations in all of our lives.

> Aren't there annunciations
> of one sort or another
> in most lives?
>> Some unwillingly
> undertake great destinies,
> enact them in sullen pride,
> uncomprehending.
>> More often
> those moments
>> when roads of light and storm
>> open from darkness in a man or woman
> are turned away from
> in dread, in a wave of weakness, in despair
> and with relief.
> Ordinary lives continue.
>> God does not smite them.
> But the gates close, the pathway vanishes.

This is an even more difficult truth. Many would point to the exceptional privilege of Mary and in the process take themselves off the hook. Angelic visitations are for special people, yet Denise Levertov thinks every life is visited by revelations and calls to commitment. But we either begrudgingly agree and become joyless people, cursed by our own call, or we turn away in weakness and relief. Levertov thinks when this happens, the gates close, the offer is rescinded.

I think God sends another angel.

Second Sunday in Ordinary Time
Second Sunday after Epiphany

John 1:35-42 *LM* • John 1:42-51 *RCL*

The Gospel text for users of the *Lectionary for Mass* for the Second Sunday in Ordinary Time is John 1:35-42. A spiritual commentary and teaching for that text is given in the first volume of this set, *The Spiritual Wisdom of the Gospels for Christian Preachers and Teachers,* Year A, *On Earth as It Is in Heaven,* p. 55.

Finding the Thin Place

A Spiritual Commentary

For users of the *Revised Common Lectionary:*

> **The next day Jesus decided to go to Galilee. He found Philip and said to him, "Follow me."**
>
> **Now Philip was from Bethsaida, the city of Andrew and Peter. Philip found Nathanael and said to him, "We have found him whom Moses in the law and also the prophets wrote, Jesus son of Joseph from Nazareth."**
>
> **Nathanael said to him, "Can anything good come out of Nazareth?"**
>
> **Philip said to him, "Come and see."**

Jesus sought out Philip; he went looking for him. When he found him, he called him, invited him, perhaps even commanded him, "Follow me." Their meeting is not portrayed as a fortuitous happenstance. Jesus has a game plan. "I know whom I have chosen" (John 13:18). To call someone presupposes knowledge of them. Is Jesus' knowledge of Philip a particular application of his insight into people in general? "[H]e knew all people and needed no one to testify about anyone; for he himself knew what was in everyone" (John 2:24-25). Or does Jesus see so deeply into the particular person of Philip that, even without conversation, he knows he is ready for discipleship? Whatever the case, Philip follows.

Philip talks to Nathanael and tells him about his find. Although Jesus found him, signifying God's mysterious knowledge and initiative, Philip sees himself as discovering the promised one. There is mutuality involved. The one called simultaneously finds the caller. What Philip found was the Scriptures being fulfilled. He hooks the writings of the Law and the Prophets to a concrete person, "Jesus, son of Joseph, from Nazareth."

Nathanael is not impressed. In a cultural milieu where origin is destiny, Nazareth is hardly the home of messiahs. It is too insignificant a place to grow such a significant figure. But Philip does not argue about the adequacy of his witness. He invites Nathanael to experience for himself the one "whom Moses in the law and also the prophets wrote." Nathanael accepts the invitation.

> **When Jesus saw Nathanael coming toward him, he said of him, "Here is truly an Israelite in whom there is no deceit!"**
>
> **Nathanael asked him, "Where did you get to know me?"**
>
> **Jesus answered, "I saw you under the fig tree before Philip called you."**
>
> **Nathanael replied, "Rabbi, you are the Son of God! You are the King of Israel!"**

The mysterious knowledge of Jesus is once again on display; and it is having the same stunning impact. It is presupposed that Jesus knew something essential about Philip to pursue him in such a direct and unequivocal way. Now Jesus sees into Nathanael and discerns someone who has integrated the faith of Israel and is open to the truth. Where there is no deceit, the one who brings "grace and truth" (John 1:17) will be welcomed. But where did this knowledge come from? How could Jesus come to this intimate assessment of Nathanael whom he had just met?

Jesus knew Nathanael before Philip called him. Just this fact alone suggests an extraordinary type of knowing, one not confined to the normal ways of introduction and the slow processes of interpersonal exchange. The social path of knowing is: Jesus knows Philip, Philip knows Nathanael, Philip brings Nathanael to Jesus, Jesus gets to know Nathanael. However, this is not how Jesus knows Nathanael. His knowing arises from outside this chain of interactions.

How Jesus knows Nathanael is symbolized in the phrase "I saw you under the fig tree." However this symbol is interpreted and scholars have mentioned many options, it further reinforces a mysterious way of perception (see Francis J. Maloney, *The Gospel of John* [Collegeville:

Liturgical Press, 1998] 56; Bruno Barnhart, *The Good Wine: Reading John from the Center* [New York: Paulist, 1993] 241–75). In fact, the type of knowledge Jesus has of Nathanael is heart knowledge, a grasp of his core being, his foundational goodness. It is the type of knowing that the psalmist attributes to God:

> O LORD, you have searched me and known me.
> You know when I sit down and when I rise up;
>   you discern my thoughts from far away.
>   . . . .
> Such knowledge is too wonderful for me;
>   it is so high that I cannot attain it.
>   (Ps 139:1-2, 6)

This is what overwhelms Nathanael. To be known at this intimate depth is to be seriously searched. What Jesus knows is too wonderful for human attainment. So Nathanael instantly revises his skepticism. The earthly origins of Jesus do not determine his identity. The son of Joseph from Nazareth is indeed the Son of God and the King of Israel.

Jesus answered, "Do you believe because I told you that I saw you under the fig tree? You will see greater things than these."

And he said to him, "Very Truly, I tell you, you will see heaven opened and the angels of God ascending and descending upon the Son of Man."

No matter how wonderful is Jesus' ability to know the interior depth of people, there is still another level. Coming to believe that Jesus is the inheritor of titles like "Son of God" and "King of Israel" may be a first step. But it is a step that has to lead to another.

In Genesis, Jacob is journeying to find a wife from among the daughters of Laban (Gen 28:10-17). One night he falls asleep and dreams of a ladder connecting heaven and earth and the angels of God ascending and descending on it. The Lord stands beside the ladder and tells Jacob that he will be fruitful and "all the families of the earth shall be blessed in you and in your offspring" (v. 14). When Jacob wakes, he says, "Surely the LORD is in this place—and I did not know it! . . . How awesome is this place! This is none other than the house of God, and this is the gate of heaven" (vv. 16-17). He calls the place *Bethel* (House of God).

This is the greater sight Nathanael must see. Jesus, the Son of Man, is the connection between heaven and earth. If people receive him, they will enter into the flow of angels, be fruitful, and bless the earth.

Teaching

A woman returned from a trip to the isle of Iona. When her gardener heard where she was, he quietly said, "Iona is a thin place."

"A thin place?" she asked.

"There is very little between it and God," the gardener explained.

Are there thin places, places where the usual thickness between the sacred and the profane is only a fine membrane?

A friend of mine, whose house of faith is built on the strong timbers of reason sunk into a bedrock of unassailable convictions and lashed together with crossbeams of irrefutable logic, recently visited the Holy Land.

When he returned, I asked, "How was it?"

"I saw where they whipped him," he said. His eyes filled. "The real place, historically certain. I saw where they whipped him."

My friend's trip to the Praetorium evoked deep religious feelings. Of course, these feelings were tied into a whole christological gestalt that he carried in his mind. But probably these affections would never have surfaced if his mind had not been in the "real place, historically certain" where Jesus suffered. For Christians the Holy Land, with its many sites of the events of Jesus' life, is just that: holy.

Pilgrims, even those for whom it is more a social occasion than a religious event, think there are thin places. When we journey to sacred sites, it is with the express purpose of having a heightened possibility of experiencing God. There are certain natural and historical sites that facilitate our consciousness of the sacred. If we can put ourselves in that atmosphere, God is more accessible and we are more open. From a cosmological point of view, there may or may not be thin places. But from a psychological point of view, there are definitely thin places.

However, in the Gospel of John Jesus redirects the Samaritan woman's quest for a thin place. "Our ancestors worshiped on this mountain, but you say that the place where people must worship is in Jerusalem" (John 4:20). Which mountain is the thin place, Mount Gerazim or Mount Zion? Jesus responds, "Woman, believe me, the hour is coming when you will worship the Father neither on this mountain nor in Jerusalem . . . God is spirit and those who worship him must worship in spirit and truth" (John 4:21, 24). This seems to say the quest for the right place is not the right quest. The real quest is to understand spirit and truth, and spirit and truth is universally available.

Eknath Easwaren, a teacher of meditation, expresses a similar point of view in regard to the Hindu classic, the Bhagavad Gita.

> Once I was on a train going from Delhi to Simla, high on the Himalayas, and on the way we passed through Kuruksherra, the historical battle-field of the Bhagavad Gita. My fellow passengers were talking about the tremendous battle which took place there, and when we arrived at the scene, they eagerly climbed out to have a look. To me there was no need to disembark, because I already had an inkling that the real battlefield of the Gita was right inside each passenger on the train. (*The End of Sorrow*, The Bhagavad Gita for Daily Living, vol. 1, [Tomales, Calif.: Niligiri Press, 1975] 24)

What if the thin place, the gate of heaven, the house of God, the ascending and descending angels is "right inside" each person?

Thomas Merton is both sure of it and eloquent about it.

> At the center of our being is a point of nothingness which is untouched by sin and by illusion, a point of pure truth, a point or spark which belongs entirely to God, which is never at our disposal, from which God disposes of our lives, which is inaccessible to the fantasies of our own mind or the brutalities of our own will. This little point of nothingness and of absolute poverty is the pure glory of God in us. It is so to speak his name written in us, as our poverty, as our indigence, as our dependence, as [sons and daughters of God]. It is like a pure diamond, blazing with the invisible light of heaven. It is in everybody, and if we could see it we would see these billions of points of light coming together in the face and blaze of a sun that would make all the darkness and cruelty of life vanish completely . . . I have no program for this seeing. It is only given. But the gate of heaven is everywhere. (*Conjectures of a Guilty Bystander* [Garden City, N.Y.: Doubleday, 1966] 142).

In another passage Merton calls this gate of heaven the "secret beauty" of the human heart, personal "core of reality," and "the person that each one is in God's eyes" (pp. 156–58).

Finding the thin place is an interior journey.

Third Sunday in Ordinary Time
Third Sunday after Epiphany

Mark 1:14-20

Calling, Leaving, Following

A Spiritual Commentary

Now after John was arrested, Jesus came to Galilee, proclaiming the good news of God, and saying, "The time is fulfilled, and the kingdom of God has come near [alternative trans., *is at hand*]; repent, and believe in the good news."

John is confined; Jesus is free. The torch is passed. The time of waiting is over. God is actively at work in human history bringing about a better world. In order to join this activity, there is a need to change our minds and give ourselves to this "good news." But this revelatory activity is not Jesus' alone. He will need companions to teach, preach, heal, and exorcise along side of him, and, eventually, to carry on in his name and in the power of his Spirit. Where will he find them?

As Jesus passed along the Sea of Galilee, he saw Simon and his brother Andrew casting a net into the sea—for they were fishermen.

And Jesus said to them, "Follow me and I will make you fish for people."

And immediately they left their nets and followed him. As he went a little farther, he saw James son of Zebedee and his brother John, who were in their boat mending the nets. Immediately he called them; and they left their father Zebedee in the boat with the hired men, and followed him.

This episode begs for expansion. A playful storyteller might insert a rejoinder to Jesus' metaphoric call. If the woman at the well can tease Jesus about not having a bucket for his living water (John 4:11) Andrew and Simon might laugh and reply, "Fish for people? Where's your net?" It would be Jesus' first frustration with his followers, a harbinger of the many misunderstandings to come.

Or James and John's father might shout after them, "What do you think you're doing? This boat will be yours someday. All you have to do is put in the time. Don't leave me with these unreliable hirelings. Besides, you owe me." This would foreshadow the family-disciple tension that haunts Jesus' fledgling community.

Or Simon, Andrew, James, and John might be far behind Jesus, struggling to keep up and discussing among themselves, "Did he mention benefits?" This would be the beginning of the suspicion that the disciples might not be ready for the road to Jerusalem.

Obviously, these two terse encounters are not an actual reporting of events. Real life accounts would demand conversation, argument, hand wringing, and that greatest of human pastimes—the weighing of options. But the Gospel rendition bypasses the dynamics of decision making in favor of a symbolic statement of essentials.

Jesus recruited disciples to join him in the mission of bringing people to the spiritual consciousness and action he called the "near-at-hand kingdom of God." This recruitment entailed hearing a call, leaving family and occupation, and following Jesus. These dynamics are similar to the sequence found in the parables of the treasure buried in a field (Matt 13:44) and the pearl of great price (Matt 13:45-46). In those stories a person finds (call), sells (leaves), and buys (follows). This model seems so right on, so woven into the fabric of human experience, so core to human adventure, it can claim to be universal.

Perhaps that is one way to interpret the fast-paced action. There is no time between call and leaving. "Immediately" upon hearing the call, the four men leave nets, boat, father, and hired hands. "Call" and "leaving" are paired experiences. One inevitably leads to the other. Calling unfolds into leaving; and leaving unfolds into following.

I said, "Why not?" and before you know it, I was arguing with a learned Pharisee in a synagogue in Capernaum."

Human actions do not take place in vacuums. They unfold in rapid, intrinsically connected sequences. Calling, leaving, and following are a natural continuum.

Teaching

The Dogmatic Constitution on the Church *(Lumen Gentium)* from the Roman Catholic Council, Vatican II, talks about a universal call to holiness and mission: "Accordingly, all Christians, in the conditions, duties and circumstances of their lives and through all these, will grow constantly in holiness if they receive all things with faith from the hand of the heavenly Father and cooperate with the divine will, making manifest in their ordinary work the love with which God has loved the world" (§41; *Vatican Council II: Constitutions, Decrees Declarations: The Basic Sixteen Documents*, ed. Austin Flannery [Northport, N.Y.: Costello, 1996]).

This seems direct and simple enough. But in the mid 1960s it represented a shift to a more inclusive way of thinking. The popular approach was that men and women who heard the call of Jesus became priests, sisters, and brothers. As Simon, Andrew, James, and John did, they left family and worldly occupations and followed Jesus to preach, teach, heal, and exorcise. Lay people did not hear the same call and so were not under the same obligations to holiness and mission. If the question was asked, "Do you have a vocation?" it meant do you want to be a priest, sister, or brother. Vatican II thought everybody, in their own way, hears the call of Jesus to holiness and mission.

In this context, the universal call to holiness and mission could not mean a literal leaving of family and occupation. In fact, near the same place just cited, the document encourages workers "to imitate, by their active charity, Christ who worked as a carpenter" (§41). Instead of leaving boats and nets, they are encouraged to pick up hammers and saws. This is how it has to be. Most people live in families and are committed to one another. They are also not about to leave their occupations—unless there is a good early retirement package. So how does calling, leaving, and following work in this setting?

In different ways and under different circumstances, people sense life is not what Macbeth called it, ". . . a tale / Told by an idiot, full of sound and fury, / Signifying nothing" (5.5.26-28; *The Plays and Sonnets of William Shakespeare*, vol. 2, ed. William George Clarke and William Aldis Wright, Great Books of the Western World, ed. Robert Maynard Hutchins, vol. 27 [Chicago: Encyclopædia Britannica, 1952]). There is something afoot in the universe, and each person is called to cooperate with it. Rumi, the Sufi mystic and poet, puts this sentiment in the mouth of a master:

> The Master said, "There is one thing in this world that must never be forgotten. If you were to forget everything else, but did not forget that, then there would be no cause to worry; whereas if you performed and remembered and did not forget every single thing, but forgot that one thing, then you would have done nothing whatsoever. It is just as if a king had sent you into a country to carry out a specified task. You go and per-

form a hundred other tasks; but if you have not performed that particular task on account of which you had gone to the country, it is as though you have performed nothing at all. So [each human being] has come into this world for a particular task, and that is [each one's] purpose; if [one] does not perform it, then [that one] will have done nothing." (*Discourses of Rumi*, trans. A. J. Arberry [London: J. Murray, 1961] 26).

The "one thing" to which everyone is called is to participate in and mediate the creative energy of God in bringing about a better world or, in biblical terms, in restoring creation. This is the core of Jesus' proclamation of the kingdom of God, and people will have to repent or, as the literal Greek has it, "change their mind" to enter it.

This change of mind means leaving family, occupation, and wealth (if you had hired hands, you were wealthy)—but not literally. Repentance means reestablishing priorities. What can never be lost sight of is the divine invitation to build a better world through whatever path you choose. But it is fairly commonplace for people to totally identify with family and work and lose sight of the one purpose for which they were made. If we symbolically leave that identification and follow Jesus, we will dwell in our families and engage in our work in such a way that "God's creation will be restored" or "the kingdom of God will come." This way of being is captured in the phrase, "In the world, but not of it" (see John 15:18–16:33).

When we hear the call and leave all things, we embark on the following of God's kingdom that Jesus revealed. For the disciples in the Gospel this is a long adventure and one that they did not expect. It is a following filled with misunderstandings, failures, suffering, and finally hope. My guess is that it will not be any different for us. If we persevere in the call and steadily try to bring God's mission into human machinations, it will not be the glorious life we fantasize. In stories of spiritual transformation from every culture, conventional expectations that seekers bring with them never materialize. We might be able to remember the past, but we cannot foresee the future, no matter how furiously we squint. We never know all that we are getting into. Although that may appear to be a regretful limitation, it often proves to be the way to find a hope larger than our individual lives.

Fourth Sunday in Ordinary Time
Fourth Sunday after Epiphany

Mark 1:21-28

Creating and Crossing Boundaries

A Spiritual Commentary

[The disciples] went to Capernaum; and when the Sabbath came, [Jesus] entered the synagogue and taught. They were astounded at his teaching, for he taught them as one having authority, and not as the scribes.

Jesus enters into the sacred space (synagogue) and sacred time (Sabbath) of Jewish religion. In that space and time he teaches. This simple fact involves a claim. He is asserting the right to interpret the covenant tradition, to articulate its most profound meanings. However, this is not teaching as usual. It is not a poor parody of the predictable scribal material. It has a quality called "authority" or "power." But at this stage in the episode, it is not clear what the teaching is or how it is authoritative or how it contrasts with what the scribes teach.

Just then there was in their synagogue a man with an unclean spirit, and he cried out, "What have you to do with us, Jesus of Nazareth? Have you come to destroy us? I know who you are, the Holy One of God."

But Jesus rebuked him, saying, "Be silent, and come out of him!"

And the unclean spirit, convulsing him and crying with a loud voice, came out of him.

This encounter of Jesus with the man possessed of an unclean spirit is what the teaching is about and how it is a teaching with authority. The teaching has to do with purity codes, a favorite topic of scribal discussion. People could become defiled by contact with an unclean spirit. In fact, the simple presence of the unclean spirit in the synagogue contaminates the entire synagogue. The scribal advice was avoidance. The people and individuals were holy to the degree they kept their distance from what was unholy. So maintaining purity meant excluding certain actions, certain foods, and certain people. A man possessed of an unclean spirit qualifies as contagious. To be in his presence is to become impure. Therefore, the scribal teaching without authority was: "Steer clear!"

The unclean spirit knows this and counts on it. But it senses something different in Jesus. So it asks a first question, "What have you to do with us, Jesus of Nazareth?" (v. 24). This means, "It is customary to leave us alone and to let us torment those we have inhabited. To do anything else is to become impure yourself. You are not thinking of anything else, are you?" The second question intuits the answer to the first question. "Have you come to destroy us?" means "Are you seriously considering polluting yourself? Do you think you can destroy us without being drawn into our uncleanliness?" Finally, the unclean spirit clinches the argument. It knows that Jesus is the Holy One of God and God, by essence, is not impure. So it is unthinkable that God's Holy One would risk defilement. The unclean spirit has made the case. It owns the man, and anyone who prizes holiness, as certainly God's holy one does, will have the theological good sense to stay away.

But Jesus of Nazareth, the Holy One of God, has another theology. He does not respect purity boundaries. He trespasses them. The false theology of the unclean spirit, its only hope to continue its vicious domination of God's good creation, is silenced. Jesus responds, "Shut up!" That whole way of thinking, rooted in ineffectual fear, is over. A new teaching is being articulated and it comes into existence with power and authority, "Get out!" Convulsing and screaming, the unclean spirit leaves the man. It does not go willingly. It has not been argued into submission. It has not met its match. A higher authority has appeared, and it will be obeyed.

They were all amazed, and they kept on asking one another, "What is this? A new teaching—with authority! He commands even the unclean spirits, and they obey him."

At once his fame began to spread throughout the surrounding region of Galilee.

They are amazed because they have seen another way to deal with the fear of impurity. Do not avoid it; bring your own stronger purity to it and cleanse it. However, this teaching is new and its full implications are not known. Although it is attractive, it cannot be immediately grasped. But the people in the synagogue know authority when they see it—as the centurion in St. Matthew's Gospel: "For I also am a man under authority, with soldiers under me; and I say to one, 'Go,' and he goes, and to another 'Come,' and he comes, and to my slave, 'Do this,' and the slave does it" (Matt 8:9). The higher Spirit of God who descended upon Jesus at his baptism (Mark 1:10 and par.) and leads his mission does not allow lesser beings to harm those whom God loves. It commands them, "Get out!" And they get out, taking with them all the pain they have caused.

Teaching

Legend tells of a training session between Merlin, the master magician, and young Arthur, a boy destined to be King. Merlin takes Arthur into the forest, turns him into a hawk (they could do that in those days) and send him sailing into the sky:

> From the earth Merlin shouts to Arthur, "What do you see?"
> Arthur shouts back, "I see rivers and trees."
> "No," an irritated Merlin responds and repeats his question, "What do you see?"
> "I see cattle and sheep and . . ."
> "No," Merlin interrupts and asks a third time, "What do you see?"
> "I see villages and . . ."
> "Come down," orders Merlin. Arthur, the hawk, returns to earth and becomes Arthur, the young boy. Merlin tells him, "Some day you will know what you saw."

The day Arthur knew what he saw was the day after his dream of Camelot died. He saw no boundaries. When he was in the sky and looking at the earth, everything was distinct yet also part of a unity. In the universe there may be many lines, but the lines can be viewed as either divisions or meeting places. Both divisions and meeting places are created by the mind.

People create boundaries for many reasons. One of these reasons is that it is the loving thing to do. It respects rights and diversities. Psychologists tell us people who do not know limits—where they leave off and others begin—do damage to themselves and others. To demarcate is a way of clarifying responsibilities and focusing consciousness. Without boundaries things become a formless mass, and we do not know how to proceed. We often emphasize the need for community.

We insist on connecting lines, both straight and dotted, in our relational and work lives. But we also need to draw circles, to close off others to avoid being swamped.

People cross boundaries for many reasons. One reason is that it is the loving thing to do. St. Paul said, "There is no longer Jew or Greek, there is no longer slave or free, there is no longer male and female; for all of you are one in Christ Jesus" (Gal 3:28). The revelation of Jesus crossed these well-established boundaries. In the Gospel, Jesus crosses the boundary of clean and unclean. This boundary had become a division, and the division had lead to exclusion. Jesus represents God's loving outreach to those whom society, in the name of holiness, had pushed away and whom Jesus, in the name of holiness, draws in. The path of love in a deeply divided society is to cross boundaries.

This combination of creating and crossing boundaries is captured in the famous poem of Robert Frost, "Mending Wall." Frost is the narrator and his position is clear. "Something there is that doesn't love a wall" (line 1). But it is spring, and hunters and winter have damaged the wall between his neighbor's property and his own. So he and his neighbor meet to mend the wall. His neighbor can only say, "Good fences make good neighbors" (line 27). Frost picks a fight in his mind:

> *Why* do they make good neighbors? Isn't it
> Where there are cows? But here there are no cows.
> Before I built a wall I'd ask to know
> What I am walling in or walling out,
> And to whom I was like to give offense.

> (*The Poetry of Robert Frost,* ed. Edward Connery Lathem [New York: Holt, Rinehart, and Winston, 1969] 33–34).

Frost pictures his neighbor as "an old-stone savage" (line 41) who will not go beyond his saying. In fact "He likes having the thought of it so well / He says again, "Good fences make good neighbors" (line 46).

Is Frost right? If there is no reason for a wall, or the reason for a wall is long gone, it should be taken down. Or is his neighbor right? Even if there is no reason, boundaries in and of themselves make for good relations between people. The traditional adage, "Good fences make good neighbors," has wisdom far beyond what the rational mind can surmise. It must be respected and the wall must be mended, even when the reason for the wall has vanished.

In my life I have created boundaries and crossed boundaries. Sometimes I have created boundaries instinctively out of fear and crossed boundaries recklessly out of desire or anger. At other times I have created and crossed boundaries thoughtfully, with much pondering within and conversing without. It has been a judgment call, and love has always been a major player in whatever I decided. Therefore, I am convinced that loving can embrace both activities.

But, if truth be told, I respect boundaries more than I defy them. I play it safe more than I risk. I think that is why when I encounter this boundary crossing Jesus who leaps off the pages of St. Mark's Gospel, I know he will not respect the wall around myself that I mend every spring.

Fifth Sunday in Ordinary Time
Fifth Sunday after Epiphany

Mark 1:29-39

Curing, Healing, and Serving

A Spiritual Commentary

As soon as [Jesus and his disciples] left the synagogue, they entered the house of Simon and Andrew, with James and John. Now Simon's mother-in-law was in bed with a fever, and they told him about her at once. He came and took her by the hand and lifted her up. Then the fever left her, and she began to serve them.

That evening, at sunset, they brought to him all who were sick or possessed with demons. And the whole city was gathered around the door. And he cured many who were sick with various diseases, and cast out many demons; and he would not permit the demons to speak, because they knew him.

The word is out. Jesus has the power to restore human life to wholeness, to banish what torments it. The sick and demon-possessed may be too debilitated to come to him on their own. But others can bring Jesus to them or bring them to Jesus.

It is not hard to understand that "they" told Jesus immediately about Simon's fevered and bedridden mother-in-law. Nor is it difficult to grasp that the moment the sun set and the Sabbath's regulations about movement no longer applied, "they" brought the whole city of the sick to his door. Curing sickness and driving out demons restores individuals to better functioning. But it also restores the person to family and community, to the circles of love that grieve at loss and rejoice at reunion. We know who these "they" are. "They" are us. Is there someone alive who has not brought a sick loved one to a person reputed as a healer with both more hope and more fear than their heart could hold?

These cures and exorcisms are quickly recorded. Their wonder can be appreciated, but their wonder is not the point. There is no razzle-dazzle in their description. The demons may know something of the point and may have a glimpse of the deeper meaning because they know who Jesus is. But their knowledge is incomplete. If they speak, they will spew titles. These titles, "Holy One of God" (Mark 1:24), "Messiah," etc., will be misconstrued (Mark 1:28). They will be equated with miracle working; and when miracle working does not happen or cannot happen (Mark 6:5), the popularity of Jesus will fade as quickly as it appeared. Silencing the demons is not because they know the truth but because they know half the truth, and half the truth is the most seductive falsehood.

> **In the morning, while it was still very dark, he got up and went out to a deserted place, and there he prayed. And Simon and his companions hunted for him.**
>
> **When they found him, they said to him, "Everyone is searching for you."**
>
> **He answered, "Let us go on to the neighboring towns, so that I may proclaim the message there also; for that is what I came out to do."**
>
> **And he went throughout Galilee, proclaiming the message in their synagogues and casting out demons.**

As the mission of Jesus unfolds, he stays in touch with the ultimate driving force of his words and actions. He seeks out the desert and his prayerful communion with God. Prayer provides the clarity and direction that will be necessary. There will be subtle distractions and downright wrong paths to his mission. Jesus will have to choose. Prayer will center him for decision.

One subtle distraction is Jesus' popularity. His cures and exorcisms attract crowds. They are magnets that draw people to Jesus and spread his fame. To the disciples the crowds mean success. Fame and reputation are the heady energy that drives Simon and his companions to hunt down Jesus. But Jesus does not bask in notoriety. He may call followers, but he does not court fans. His concern is to get the message out. The cures and the exorcisms are signs of a new revelation of God, visible manifestations of a spiritual revolution. This message must be made known. This is why he came. His foundational identity, reclaimed in prayer, moves him away from the crowds that seek him. He must move on. The message must be preached and taught in word and deed.

Teaching

Contemporary spiritual teaching often maps a different path of curing, healing, and service than is portrayed in this episode from St. Mark's Gospel. But a similar challenge emerges in both renditions.

Ram Dass, an American spiritual teacher in the Hindu tradition who suffered a debilitating stroke in 1997, makes this distinction between healing and curing. "While cures aim at returning our bodies to what they were in the past, healing uses what is present to move us more deeply to Soul Awareness, and in some cases, physical "improvement." . . . [A]lthough I have not been cured of the effects of my stroke, I have certainly undergone profound healings of mind and heart" (*Still Here: Embracing Aging, Changing, and Dying,* ed. Mark Matousek and Marlene Roeder [New York: Riverhead Books, 2000] 67). Therefore, healing can happen without cure.

In fact, it is in the sickness that the healing begins. Michael Lerner, who works with people diagnosed with cancer, offered this description of what he would do if faced with a cancer diagnosis. "I would pay a great deal of attention to the inner healing process that I hoped a cancer diagnosis would trigger in me. I would give careful thought to the meaning of my life, what I had to let go of and what I wanted to keep" (Dass, 74). In his poem, "Fever," John Updike, in an almost playful way, tells about one facet of the inner healing that may accompany sickness:

> I have brought back a good
> message from the land of 102 degrees:
> God exists.
> I had seriously doubted it before;
> but the bedposts spoke of it with utmost
> confidence,
> the threads in my blanket took it for granted,
> the tree outside the window dismissed all
>   complaints,
> and I have not slept so justly for years.
> It is hard, now, to convey
> how emblematically appearances sat
> upon the membranes of my consciousness;
> but it is truth long known,
> that some secrets are hidden from health.

(*Collected Poems, 1953–1993* [New York: Knopf, 1993] 28)

Healing is initiated in the sickness. It does not wait for cure to arrive.

In fact, in some illness literature patients report a greater sense of being alive and in communion with others when they were sick. When they were cured, they returned to normal life, a life often characterized by numbness and rote obligation. Cure actually threatened healing. This was the case with a man by the name of Fred. He was diagnosed with terminal cancer. After an initial period of distress, "something amazing happened. I simply stopped doing everything that wasn't essential, that didn't matter." His terminally ill life became vital and peaceful. But the doctors changed their mind. He was not terminally ill. He had a rare but curable disease. "When I heard this over the telephone, I cried like a baby—because I was afraid my life would go back to the way it used to be" (Peter Senge and others, *Presence: Human Purpose and the Field of the Future* [Cambridge, Mass.: SoL, 2004] 25–26). Holding together cure and healing is the challenge.

This is the same challenge the Gospel presents, only in a quite different context. Jesus' cures and exorcisms are signs of the kingdom of God. They both complement and embody Jesus' more explicit teachings. People are supposed to interpret these signs as God's loving response to human need. This interpretation, in turn, is meant to change minds and initiate new ways of being with one another. The proper response to cures and exorcisms, like the proper response to proclamation and teaching, is repentance, a change of mind and behavior. Just remaining dazzled by the miraculous activity is insufficient.

Although the consciousness of Simon's mother-in-law is not presented in the text, the indication is that both cure and healing occurred. Fever lays her low. Jesus takes her hand (v. 31). His touch becomes a transfusion, his life flowing into hers. In loving the person at the hidden center of the sickness, he lifts her up. The fever leaves and service begins. God's service to her becomes her service to others.

The cure provides physical relief, but it is also accompanied by profound healing. Healing reconnects us to the deepest center of ourselves and through that center to God and neighbor. The flow of life and love through the intimate communion of God, self, and neighbor results in the dignity of service. As the whole Gospel will attest, service is not menial work. It is the hallmark of the new humanity that Jesus came to establish (see John 13:1-17). "The Son of Man came not to be served but to serve" (Mark 10:45).

The contemporary path suggests that suffering is an invitation to healing our alienation from God and neighbor. This healing may or may not result in a cure. If cure happens, the struggle is to persevere in the healing that was begun in sickness. The Gospel path begins with cures and exorcisms, restorations to physical and mental health. But these cures must affect the minds and hearts of those cured and those witnessing the cures. They are meant to be catalysts of personal transformation, relating people in a new way to the love of God and the well-being of their neighbor (see Mark 12:29-31).

Sixth Sunday in Ordinary Time
Sixth Sunday after Epiphany

Mark 1:40-45

Cultivating Compassion

A Spiritual Commentary

A leper came to [Jesus] begging him, and kneeling he said to him, "If you choose, you can make me clean."

Moved with pity, Jesus stretched out his hand and touched him, and said to him, "I do choose. Be made clean!"

Immediately the leprosy left him, and he was made clean.

Leviticus clearly states the fate of the leper. "The person who has the leprous disease shall wear torn clothes and let the hair of his head be disheveled; and he shall cover his upper lip and cry out, 'Unclean, unclean.' He shall remain unclean as long as he has the disease; he is unclean. He shall live alone; his dwelling shall be outside the camp" (Lev 13:45-46). These instructions make lepers the ultimate outsiders. They are symbols of those whom no one can help, of those without hope. A leper who was left alone to face his deteriorating future must have experienced excruciating isolation. The deep pain of leprosy is the growing realization that no one cares.

This inner world of leper is revealed in his request. He has heard of Jesus' power to heal. More importantly, he has heard that Jesus cares about those whom no one else cares about. He includes the excluded. This reputation of Jesus emboldens the leper to come forward. He does not keep his distance. His faith is that Jesus has the power to make him clean. His hesitancy is that Jesus might not be disposed to do it. The leper's self-image is that he is beyond human and divine concern. His uncleanness means that God and people remove themselves from him. However, Jesus' inner compassion for this isolated human being moves him to reach out and touch him, symbolically welcoming him back into the circle of the human. The cleansing reveals God's outreach to the outcasts more than it celebrates divine power to cure a physical malady.

After sternly warning him he sent him away at once, saying to him, "See that you say nothing to anyone; but go, show yourself to the priest, and offer for your cleansing what Moses commanded, as a testimony to them."

But he went out and began to proclaim it freely, and to spread the word, so that Jesus could no longer go into a town openly, but stayed out in the country; and people came to him from every quarter.

Jesus gave the leper what he requested. The leper does not return the favor. Jesus' compassionate outreach was intended, at least in part, to restore the leper to community. So Jesus commands him to show himself to the priests and make ritual offerings (see Lev 14). This is the way back into the community. The story does not tell us whether he obeys this command. But it does tell us he disobeys the command to say nothing to anyone.

He tells everyone everything. The ironic result is that Jesus could no longer go into a town openly. Is the reason that Jesus is now unclean? Having touched the leper he falls under the Leviticus sentence of exclusion. The cleansed leper can now enter the town, but the one who cleansed him must keep his distance. This is the social consequence of the cleansed leper's "freely proclaiming it." But whether Jesus is in the town or country, people find him. What he is saying and doing are what people want to hear and see.

There may also be a mystical hint in Jesus' sudden leper status, in the holy one becoming unholy. It is captured in a poem, "A Prayer to the Pain of Jesus":

> When crutches were thrown away
> did Jesus limp
> after the running cripples?
>
> Did his eyes dim
> when Bartimaeus saw?
>
> Did life ebb in him
> when it flowed in Lazarus?
>
> When lepers leapt in new flesh,
> did scales appear
> on the back of his hand?
>
> The gospels say
> Jesus felt power go out from him

but neglect to say
whether at that moment
pain came in.

Did the Son of God
take on ungrown legs and dead eyes
in the terrifying knowledge
that pain does not go away
only moves on?

(John Shea, *The Hour of the Unexpected*
[Allen, Tex.: Thomas More, 1992])

Jesus' compassion may have included experiencing within himself the total situation of the leper. The touching constitutes an intimate sharing. God's love in Jesus does not heal by exterior contact but by a mutual indwelling whereby two lives become one.

Teaching

We all have bodies, yet at any given moment some bodies are healthy and some are ill. We all have minds, yet some minds are first in the class and the corporation, and some minds are forever catching up or permanently left behind. We all have relationships and social position, yet some relationships are loving, and some are indifferent, and some social positions are important, and some are menial. We are all souls, yet some souls are conscious of their communion with the Divine Source and living in peaceful action, and other souls are unconscious of their connection to the Divine Source and struggling painfully with life. We are both separate and the same, isolated and connected to one another.

This realization of sameness and connection is the first step to cultivating compassion. When the pope gets off an airplane in any country, he kisses the earth. He does this in every land for all the earth is sacred. There is a sameness to the different terrains of every country. Although many may think the earth of their country is sacred in a way the earth of other countries is not, this gesture tries to awaken another perception. When the Dalai Lama arrives in a country, he announces to all who are there, "Everyone wants happiness and doesn't want suffering." This is true of all, so all are bound together.

Both the pope's gesture and the Dalai Lama's sentence could be turned into profound spiritual practices. Although one may seem to be politically inspired and the other to be a throwaway line of a banal philosophy, they are both strenuous efforts to reverse separatist thinking. If you kiss with mindfulness the floor of every house you enter and say internally to every person you meet, "Everyone wants happiness and doesn't want suffering," you will be on a path of realizing your neighbor is yourself.

This consciousness of sameness and connection is often a gradual process. In the Middle Ages, Christians were encouraged to meditate on the mystical rose. The meditation began at the top of the rose where the tips of the petals do not touch. At this point they would realize the truth of separateness. Then their eyes would glide down the rose and rest on the overlapping sections of the petals. This sight would encourage consciousness to realize similarities and commonalities among what appeared as separate. When the eyes reached the base of the rose, all the petals came from the same stem. This was the deepest realization of the one source of all things and, therefore, a fundamental communion among all things.

However, getting to the base of the rose is not an easy trip. We are used to identifying with our competitive edges, with the physical, psychological, and social benefits that separate us from others. I am in better health, have a higher I.Q., and have more money than you. But, alas, I am in poorer health, have a lower I.Q., and have less money than someone else. Within this way of thinking we alternate between being better or worse off; we swing back and forth between pitying those who have less and envying those who have more. In the presence of suffering this mental framework generates inner fear that makes us recoil. The leper is someone worse off who could bring us down to his condition. Avoidance is the strategy and, of course, prayers are made to the protective God to keep us from this fate.

When the consciousness of sameness and connection replaces the consciousness of separation, compassion arises. Compassion is a felt perception of sharing a common world that drives us toward action. We do not recoil, we reach out. Jesus' compassion is the engine of his touching and making clean the leper. It is also the unwavering firmness in the response which I've seen translated as, "Of course, I want to."

Therefore, to cultivate compassion you can kiss the floor of all houses, interiorly size up each person met with "this person desires to be happy and doesn't want to suffer," and spend a longer time with the roses in gardens and flower shops. You can also meditate on this wild poem of Hafiz, "Why Aren't We Screaming Drunks?":

The sun once glimpsed God's true nature
And has never been the same.

Thus that radiant sphere
Constantly pours its energy
Upon this earth
As does He from behind
The veil.

With a wonderful God like that
Why isn't everyone a screaming drunk?

Hafiz's guess is this:

Any thought that you are better or less
Than another man

Quickly
Breaks the wine
Glass.

(*The Gift: Poems by the Great Sufi Master,*
trans. Daniel Ladinsky [New York: Arkana/Penguin, 1999])

Seventh Sunday in Ordinary Time
Seventh Sunday after Epiphany

Mark 2:1-12

Carrying Our Mats

A Spiritual Commentary

When [Jesus] returned to Capernaum after some days, it was reported that he was at home. So many gathered around that there was no longer room for them, not even in front of the door; and he was speaking the word to them.

Jesus may be at home, but he is not alone. In escalating phrases the storyteller paints the crowded house—many, so many no room, not even at the door. Earlier Peter had said, "Everyone is searching for you" (Mark 1:37). They seem to have found him. In Peter's mind this is obviously a sign of success. And surely this tendency to see crowds as a sign of success is part of the apostolic succession. Every pastor since Peter has been pleased with high attendance. The first question of every worship service is, how many? Answer: packed. Jammed to the rafters. Spilling into the street. Breaking the fire codes. They couldn't get in the door.

Jesus is speaking to them the word (v. 2). But we do not get to hear what Jesus is saying. There will be an interruption. Jesus the Speaker of Words will be replaced by Jesus the Engager of People. What we will see is what Jesus was speaking about. The story will show the teaching-preaching in action. The Word will become flesh once again (see John 1).

Then some people came, bringing to him a paralyzed man, carried by four of them. And when they could not bring him to Jesus because of the crowd, they removed the roof above him; and after having dug through it, they let down the mat on which the paralytic lay.

When scholars talk about narrative, they often mention that it reflects the unpredictability of life. The mind creates "logical sequences." It plots how things should happen, arranging events like flowers in a vase. Often "things" are compliant. They go along. Then the unforeseen happens. We scramble for a response and everything flows in a different direction. The arrival of the four bearers and the paralytic is not prepared for in the story. It is the unforeseen that changes everything.

However, their top-down entry has been anticipated. The crowded house that signaled the success of Jesus' ministry is now seen from another perspective. The people anxious to hear Jesus are blocking the entrance. They have come close, but now no one else can get close.

Is this a critique of the Church? Is the predicament of the Church that while it has gathered to listen to Jesus, it is simultaneously blocking access to him? It should be clearing a path à la John the Baptist. But it has created a huddle, rear ends to outsiders. In particular, the paralyzed are being blocked. This is especially unfortunate for Jesus has peculiar understanding of paralysis and a peculiar way of dealing with it.

It is hard to restrain the imagination from picturing the descent. Suddenly dust and debris fall from the ceiling. (I once asked a group what was the first question they thought of after hearing the story. A man answered, "Who is going to pay for the roof?" He was in insurance.) People scatter. Jesus looks up. Where there was only roof, the sky appears. Then coming down from the sky through the roof is a pallet. Four men are lowering it. When it comes down far enough, the paralyzed man can be seen. Are his eyes the only part of him still capable of movement? And then there are Jesus' eyes. The story will tell us what they see.

When Jesus saw their faith, he said to the paralytic, "Son, your sins are forgiven."

When Jesus sees the bearers, he sees people of faith. Could it be that what comes down from above signifies the divine will? It is God's will that the paralyzed find Jesus. Even when people block the way, the divine will is not thwarted. It finds creative contributors who ingeniously gain access to the source of healing. These bearers are people of faith because they carry the paralyzed to a place of possibility, a place that God desires.

Jesus connects the bearers and paralytic by his sequence of actions. He *sees* their faith but he *talks* to the paralytic, tying them together through his sight and sound. What Jesus says to the paralytic is abrupt and unexpected. If the arrival of the paralyzed one was unforeseen, so is this sudden introduction of sin. All the story has provided is "paralyzed one on a pallet." Jesus' remark focuses on the forgiveness of sin. The symbol is established: sin paralyzes.

Jesus addresses the paralyzed one as "Son." This does not mean he (or any other man or woman similarly addressed) is a youngster. It is an acknowledgement of the "child of God" dimension. What sin does is cripple the child of God in us. What is unable to walk is the human person who is made in the image and likeness of God. This understanding of sin as restraint is reflected in Neil Douglas-Klotz's translation from the Aramaic of the "trespass" verse of the Lord's prayer: "Loose the cords of mistakes binding us, as we release the strands we hold of others' guilt" (*Prayers of the Cosmos: Meditations on the Aramaic Words of Jesus* [San Francisco: HarperSanFrancisco, 1990] 30).

> **Now some of the scribes were sitting there, questioning in their hearts, "Why does this fellow speak in this way? It is blasphemy! Who can forgive sins but God alone?"**

The scribes are seated, the official position of teachers, and their objection to what Jesus has said is theological. Their theological frowning might be strung together in this way. "Sin is an offense against God. Therefore, only God can forgive sins. If someone who is not God attempts to forgive sins, that person is arrogating to oneself the power of God. This usurping of God's right by someone who is not God constitutes blasphemy." The scribes are guarding the divine prerogative. They think God is constantly concerned about people infringing on divine turf.

> **At once Jesus perceived in his spirit that they were discussing these questions among themselves; and he said to them, "Why do you raise such questions in your hearts?**

It is dangerous to hang around Jesus. Even though you do not talk, he knows what you are thinking. The question of why they are thinking these things is important. It is not rhetorical, but probative, exposing the constructive and reconstructive powers of the mind. They are "putting things together" in one way. It is possible to put them together in another way. Knowing the role of the mind in framing "reality" is an important step in spiritual development. We do not mistake our current categories for the "way things are." We are open to alternate approaches. For the scribes this openness will be helpful for Jesus is about to propose another way of seeing what is happening.

> **Which is easier, to say to the paralytic, 'Your sins are forgiven,' or to say, 'Stand up and take your mat and walk'?**

This question focuses Jesus' way of seeing the situation. He is not concerned with divine honor and privilege. His obsession is not authority but human liberation. If sin alienates people from their child of God identity, then forgiveness restores it. Forgiveness of sins and "rising, carrying, and walking" are two sides of the same coin. The word "rise" (NRSV: "stand up") indicates resurrected life, life back in touch with the Divine Source. The path back to this relationship is by cutting the knot we have tied to the wrongs done to us and wrongs we have done to others. Forgiveness of sins is the power to walk. The answer to "Which is easier . . . ?" (v. 9) is that they are the same thing. Forgiveness of sins is the power to walk.

> **But so that you may know that the Son of Man has authority on earth to forgive sins"—he said to the paralytic—"I say to you, stand up, take your mat and go to your home."**

> **And he stood up, and immediately took the mat and went out before all of them; so that they were all amazed and glorified God, saying, "We have never seen anything like this!"**

Earlier Jesus connected the four bearers to the paralytic by looking at one and talking to the other. Now he connects the scribes to the paralytic by first talking to one and then to the other. In this way the exiting paralytic becomes the walking witness to real authority. The Son of Man is the Son of God engaging the renewal of the earth. The type of authority the Son of Man exercises is not concerned about "who has the right." It is concerned about authoring new life, about freeing people from paralysis. And it is effective. It brings about real change. It is not words. It is Word Made Flesh (John 1).

Three times in this short story a phrase is repeated with some variation. It is obviously significant: "Stand up and take your mat and walk (v. 9); "stand up, take your mat and go to your home" (v. 11); "he stood up, and immediately took the mat and went out before all of them" (v. 12).

The command to rise ("stand up") is appropriate. It corrects the death dealing effects of sin. Although death usually refers to bodily demise, we lose life in many ways. Relationships die, creativity declines, productivity fades, finances are lost, zest for life disappears, a way of thinking is discarded, a habit is killed. We are continually in the processes of dying and rising. In the story, sin has destroyed this man's ability to walk in the light, to do good deeds. His reemergence is a coming back from the dead.

This once paralyzed person does not stay in the religious gathering. Nor is he enjoined to leave all things and follow Jesus. He is told to go home. The purpose of the healing is for him to reengage his life. His relationships and work that have suffered from his paralysis can now be revitalized. Obediently he goes out before them all.

The most intriguing symbol is the mat. It is prominently featured in the story. The storyteller could have had the man rise and go home singing psalms. But in place of the expected jubilation is the injunction to drag along the mat.

Why?

Is it a sign of his healing? He has overcome that which paralyzed him. What he was carried in on he now carries with him, walking out.

Or is it meant to be a reminder? The pallet is the sign of his paralysis. His continuing memory of what once was will keep him in the world and mercy and gratitude. He will not harden into self-righteousness because there, in his home, is the pallet of his paralysis.

Or is he meant to use it to carry others to the source of healing as he was carried? Personal healing is not personal privilege. His new life is a mission to bring new life to others. He must find others paralyzed by sin, put them on the pallet that was once his, and carry them as he once was carried to the Source of Healing. Do not forget that the door will be blocked, but the roof will open.

The episode ends with astounded people. But we are not told exactly what "they had never seen before." Did they always think that physical disability was a punishment from God, and now they are being told that God is the release of suffering not the cause of it? Does their astonishment mean they are exhilarated by the miracle they have witnessed but befuddled by what it means? Are they better at amazement than understanding? Or does the authority and assertiveness of Jesus simply overwhelm them?

A Teaching

The man crept into the back of the church. Early Sunday mass, 8:00 a.m., last row, aisle seat. Barely in, quickly out if need be.

It was his habit since the divorce. He was afraid not to go to Mass—and he was afraid to go to Mass. So he snuck in and out. It was not that he was well known in this parish. When people looked at him, they would not be thinking, "Poor Don, what a messy divorce!" But *he* was thinking it. It was how he saw himself. In his head he was guilty, a major failure at matrimony—and at a young age! It was hard to handle. No matter how much they talked about forgiveness, there was very little room for matrimonial failure in the Catholic Church. The last row, aisle seat was a perfect place. It was where he belonged.

An old priest was saying Mass. He was soft spoken, but if you paid attention, he made you think. He preached that people could rise out of their sins, that the child of God is never completely paralyzed. "If you hear this truth," he almost whispered, "you can walk."

As usual, Don did not go to communion.

After communion a woman soloist sang a haunting rendition of Amazing Grace. Every "wretch that was saved" was moved.

Except one. Suddenly the old priest was on his feet and walking toward the congregation.

"I hate that song. I am not a wretch. You are not a wretch. The Gospel is right. You are a child of God. Perhaps momentarily paralyzed, but called to rise."

Then the old priest began moving down the center aisle. "This is my recessional song," he shouted.

He began to point to people in pew after pew. "You are a child of God. You are a child of God. And you."

"Oh no!" thought Don, as the priest approached with his jabbing finger. "Oh no!"

"And you are a child of God" said the old priest in voice that was now quiet, not from exhaustion, but from the intuition the truth he was saying had nothing to do with loudness.

Last man, last row, aisle seat: "You are a child of God."

Don tried but he could not stop the tears. After a while he even stopped trying. Everyone walked by him. Finally, he stood up, walked out, and went back home.

We tie knots to our failures so tight we can barely breathe. We know we have to untie those knots, but we do not know how. Sometimes we untie them slowly, patient as a sailor, knowing the sea waits once we loose the rope.

Other times it is a swift blow that frees us. An unlikely Jesus comes out of nowhere and wields the words of freedom. An old priest finds us hiding with our guilt in the last row and breaks through our self-hatred. We are "unparalyzed" and on our feet, striding out of the place we crept into, knowing that forgiveness and walking are the same thing.

Eighth Sunday in Ordinary Time
Eighth Sunday after Epiphany

Mark 2:18-22 *LM* • Mark 2:13-22 *RCL*

Eating with the Bridegroom

A Spiritual Commentary

For users of the *Revised Common Lectionary:*

> Jesus went out again beside the sea; the whole crowd gathered around him, and he taught them.
>
> As he was walking along, he saw Levi son of Alphaeus sitting at the tax booth, and he said to him, "Follow me."
>
> And he got up and followed him.
>
> And as he sat at dinner in Levi's house, many tax collectors and sinners were also sitting with Jesus and his disciples—for there were many who followed him.
>
> When the scribes of the Pharisees saw that he was eating with sinners and tax collectors, they said to his disciples, "Why does he eat with tax collectors and sinners?"
>
> When Jesus heard this, he said to them, "Those who are well have no need of a physician, but those who are sick; I have come to call not the righteous but sinners."

For users of the *Lectionary for Mass* and the *Revised Common Lectionary:*

> Now John's disciples and the Pharisees were fasting; and people came and said to [Jesus], "Why do John's disciples and the disciples of the Pharisees fast, but your disciples do not fast?"

Fasting, the act of refraining from eating, gains its meaning from the consciousness of those fasting. People fast for physical reasons. They may want to lose weight, or recover after a binge of food and drink, or calm a volcanic stomach. People fast for psychological reasons. They may sense an unhealthy attachment to food, and they refrain to find greater freedom and more control. People fast for social reasons. It is a way of compassionate identification with hungry brothers and sisters, or a way of protesting an unjust situation, or a way of remembering a tragedy, or a way of calling attention to a cause. Deliberately not taking food when hunger goes against the biological rhythms of the body. Therefore, the consciousness of the ones fasting must be explored to find the reason for resisting what is instinctive and natural.

People may also fast for spiritual reasons. In fact, religious traditions unanimously praise fasting. It is a universal practice and ardently recommended by spiritual teachers. Along with prayer and almsgiving, it is seen as indispensable. Even two groups as diverse as the disciples of the Baptist and the Pharisees share this common practice. They may have deep disagreements and even be outright hostile toward one another. But both groups fast.

The text does not spell out what their fasting might mean. It does not mention motives of commitment to God, atonement for sin, a companion activity for prayer, obedience to the prescriptions of the law, subduing the flesh in the name of the spirit, seeking an interior (or mystical) illumination, or refusing consolation until final justice is accomplished. Rather it assumes that fasting is so common a religious practice that it does not need explanation. What requires an explanation is the behavior of Jesus' disciples. They do not fast.

> **Jesus said to them, "The wedding guests cannot fast while the bridegroom is with them, can they? As long as they have the bridegroom with them, they cannot fast. The days will come when the bridegroom is taken away, and then they will fast on that day.**
>
> **No one sews a piece of unshrunk cloth on an old cloak; otherwise, the patch pulls away from it, the new from the old, and a worse tear is made. And no one puts new wine into old wineskins; otherwise, the wine will burst the skins, and the wine is lost, and so are the skins; but one puts new wine into fresh wineskins."**

Jesus recommends both feasting and fasting, and he ties them to different situations and the corresponding states of consciousness these situations evoke. The wedding imagery refers to the communion of the divine and the human. The Spirit of God enters into and lifts up physical, mental, and social life. This situation of intimacy between God and humankind is the consciousness that Jesus, the bridegroom, embodies in his own being and makes possible for others. The physical expression of this consciousness of Spirit permeating flesh is eating and drinking, a sign of joy and celebration. If we are full spiritually, we express this inner awareness by feasting into physical fullness. Fasting would be inappropriate, a sign that God's presence in Jesus was not perceived and appreciated.

But situations change and consciousness shifts. The bridegroom is ripped from the guests. The sense of divine presence permeating and elevating all things is lost. In this situation eating and drinking would be physical substitution for spiritual loss, a way of dulling the pain, a pretense that we are no more than our stomachs. The physical expression of this spiritual absence is fasting. If we are empty spiritually, we manifest it by being empty physically. Eating and drinking would be a cover-up, a sign we are camouflaging the actual state of our consciousness.

But these two spiritual situations and their physical embodiments are not on an equal level. It is not just a matter of fluctuating fate and its corresponding inner states: one day high and the next day low. The presence of the bridegroom is primary and foundational. The wedding guests have experienced the Spirit enlivening flesh—sacred clothes, sacred music, sacred dance, sacred food, sacred wine, and sacred sex. This experience makes them sensitive to times when flesh is not enlivened by Spirit—clothes, music, dance, food, wine, and sex are just that and nothing more. It is now time to fast, not just because physical emptiness expresses spiritual emptiness but because physical emptiness awaits the reappearance of spiritual fullness. Fasting is an act of hope that recognizes loss but will not absolutize it.

This is the Christian consciousness of fasting. Feast is the context of fast. This way of thinking about and practicing fasting is new. Sometimes when a new consciousness for a traditional religious practice appears, it can be grafted onto the old. There is no need for a radical break. The tattered coat can be mended; the old wine skins can welcome and safely embrace the new wine. This is not the case with the Christian combination of feasting and fasting. The old cannot accommodate the new. The tattered coat must be discarded; the old wineskins must be thrown away. When Christians refuse to put food and drink in their mouths, it is to put a different type of food and drink in their mind. All other reasons must be subordinated to this consciousness.

Teaching

Fasting enhances the experience of eating.

Philip Zaleski tells about a time he contracted a mysterious illness that made everything he put in his mouth taste like liquid fire. For over three weeks he had barely eaten; and when the mysterious illness suddenly abated, he had eaten nothing for two days. He decided to celebrate his return to eating with a blood orange. "The taste of the blood orange flooded my mouth, and with it came a wave of gratefulness for all that had helped to produce this food and deliver it into my hands. Sun, soil, and rain; planters, harvesters, and retailers; apiculture and horticulture; evolution, whose slow-motion magic wand had transformed an inedible Jurassic fruit into the ambrosia of the gods; God, fount of all fruitfulness—I gave thanks to one and all" (P. Zaleski and Paul Kaufman, *Gifts of the Spirit: Living the Wisdom of the Great Religious Traditions* [San Francisco: HarperSanFrancisco, 1997] 43–44). His fast was not intentional. Nevertheless, as a result of fasting, eating had become a spiritual experience of gratitude.

What was it like to eat with Jesus?

Scholars tell us that table fellowship was a hallmark of his ministry. But few venture beyond this bland remark to speculate on what went on inside people as they received cup and bread from his hands, and from the hands of one another. How did the mind process the tastes and the slow move from hunger to satisfaction, from emptiness to fullness? Was it possible that eating with Jesus was an experience that changed the consciousness of those eating? Did people become aware, as Philip Zaleski did, of the interconnectedness of all things and feel unfeigned gratitude fill their entire being with such completeness that the food, no matter what it was and how much there was, was a feast? Did they realize they were all sustained by the same Source and thus brothers and sisters to one another? Did this realization bring into minds their countless violations against one another at the same time as their deeper sense of unity allowed them to forgive these violations from their hearts, freely and gratuitously?

No matter what they ate, was it always one loaf they shared?

Was this—or something like this—what it was like to eat with the bridegroom?

We eat three times a day. And, as a friend says, "more when we're lucky." It can become a mindless act, stoking the furnace. Even worse, stoking the furnace in front of the television. Anything we do often can become repetitious, monotonous, routine. The symbolic potential of eating and drinking lost.

The way to recover this symbolic potential is to fast. Not eating out of habit wakes us up to the change of consciousness eating and drinking can effect in us. As Christians we fast in the memory of feast. The fast jolts us out of mindlessly responding to biological needs and encourages us to trace our hungers and thirsts into love of God and love of neighbor. We are united to God and in communion with one another. When we remember to eat and drink like this, the fasting has found its true meaning. The bridegroom has returned.

Ninth Sunday of Ordinary Time
Ninth Sunday after Epiphany

Proper 4

Mark 2:23–3:6

Critiquing Traditions

A Spiritual Commentary

One Sabbath [Jesus] was going through the grainfields; and as they made their way his disciples began to pluck heads of grain.

The Pharisees said to him, "Look, why are they doing what is not lawful on the sabbath?"

And he said to them. "Have you never read what David did when he and his companions were hungry and in need of food? He entered the house of God, when Abiathar was high priest, and ate the bread of the Presence, which it is not lawful for any but the priests to eat, and he gave some to his companions."

Then he said to them, "The sabbath was made for humankind, and not humankind for the sabbath; so the Son of Man is lord even of the sabbath."

In the book of Genesis, life, fresh from the hands of God, is pictured as good and harmonious. Humankind is at peace with God, nature, and themselves. Innocent hungers, hungers flowing from natural appetite, are innocently fed. "Out of the ground the LORD God made to grow every tree that was pleasant to the sight and good for food" (Gen 2:9). But when humankind ate from the tree of the knowledge of good and evil, everything changed. Strife replaced peace; separateness replaced harmony. The man and the woman hid from one another and from God (see Gen 3). The earth became recalcitrant, yielding food only when humans toiled over it.

In reflective theology these two contrasting states became known as the Creation and the Fall. Creation was often explained as prehistory, a time before the disastrous consequences of Adam and Eve's decision. This original state of blessedness is gone forever, a tale of paradise lost.

We now live east of Eden, struggling in broken and violent relationships. What we know and feel in our bones is alienation.

However, Creation and Fall can also be understood as two different states of consciousness. Life, in this present moment, can be appreciated as a gift from God and lived in peace and harmony, or it can be appreciated as alienated from God and lived in discord and strife. Although "Fall consciousness" has dominated the human race, "Creation consciousness" has been preserved by mystics and prophets. It also enters sporadically into the life of those who live largely in Fall consciousness. In fact, on the Sabbath, one day a week, all people are called to creation consciousness, to live life together as God's gift without discord and strife.

Jesus and his disciples are strolling through flowering fields of grain, and the disciples are plucking and nibbling. What a glorious way to celebrate the Sabbath! "[O]n the seventh day God finished the work that he had done, and he rested on the seventh day from all the work that he had done. So God blessed the seventh day and hallowed it, because on it God rested from all the work he had done in creation" (Gen 2:2-3).

Jesus and the disciples are doing what God does. They are blessing and hallowing creation. This activity is characterized as rest, not in the sense that they are not doing anything, but in the deeper meaning of delighting in the very being of themselves and the earth. As they walk in harmony with the earth, the earth gives them its bounty as food. They do not have to force the earth to provide. They do not have to sow and reap, or grind the grain at the mill and bake it in the oven. It comes to them of its own accord. They are living at ease with creation, gathering food without "the sweat of their brow" (Gen 3:19; NIV). This creation consciousness of life as a gift is what Sabbath is meant to celebrate.

However, the Sabbath consciousness of creation has been translated into laws. The laws try to safeguard the consciousness of creation as gift by forbidding any and every form of human effort. Both walking through the fields and picking grain is human effort. But these Sabbath regulations have lost contact with the underlying spirit of Sabbath rest. They exist as laws, but the larger purpose they were meant to serve is not remembered. Therefore, the law has become its own reality. As its own reality, it no longer leads to the sacred. It usurps the sacred. Therefore, the sacred law has been violated, and these Pharisees want to know why.

Jesus is only too willing to tell them. However, the parallel between David taking the sacred bread to feed himself and his starving men and Jesus and his disciples strolling through grainfields and plucking kernels is difficult to discern. It may be the simple fact that Jesus compares himself to David. If David could make an exception to Sabbath laws, then Jesus can also. As Jesus will declare, "The Son of Man is lord even of the Sabbath" (2:28). But this is not an appeal to authority, as if "Son of Man" was a credential that put Jesus above the law. Rather it means the Son of Man, the one living in essential communion with God and creation, understands what regulations are appropriate and what regulations are not.

The parallel with the David episode is in "the bread of the Presence" (2:26). Creation consciousness knows that God gives food out of the fullness of the earth for all to eat, not just priests. Bread offered to God implicitly acknowledges all sustenance comes from God. When people eat this bread, bread they know is sacred, they open to a fuller understanding of creation. When David and his men eat the sacred "bread of the Presence of God," it is appropriate Sabbath behavior because it facilitates Sabbath consciousness. It is in the same category as Jesus and his disciples eating the sacred grain that flows out of the flowering earth. In this activity they receive life as God's gift.

Creation consciousness is primary. The celebration of the Sabbath is meant to facilitate this awareness. If Sabbath regulations have lost sight of this goal or keep people from this goal, they are not to be followed. The Son of Man is also the second Adam (see 1 Cor 15), the one who embodies original creation consciousness, the one who can discern how the Sabbath should be kept.

> Again he entered the synagogue, and a man was there who had a withered hand. They watched him to see whether he would cure him on the sabbath, so that they might accuse him.
>
> And he said to the man who had the withered hand, "Come forward."
>
> Then he said to them, "Is it lawful to do good or do harm on the sabbath, to save life or to kill?"
>
> But they were silent.
>
> He looked around at them with anger; he was grieved at their hardness of heart and said to the man, "Stretch out your hand."
>
> He stretched it out and his hand was restored.
>
> The Pharisees went out and immediately conspired with the Herodians against him, how to destroy him.

There were two trees in the Garden of Eden, "the tree of the knowledge of good and evil," and "the tree of life" (Gen 2:9). When Adam and Eve were being expelled from the garden, the Lord God said, "[The man] might reach out his hand and take also from the tree of life, and eat, and live forever" (Gen 3:22). Sabbath consciousness of creation means that people reach out for life.

However, this human desire and ability is stunted. In its place, the laws have set up a consciousness that fears infraction more than it desires life. This consciousness constrains and imprisons people. It does harm and kills the spirit. It lies in wait for mistake. It conspires to destroy. It does not opt for goodness and life. In fact, it refuses to answer the most basic of choices between a Creation consciousness that rejoices in goodness and life and Fall consciousness that focuses on harm and death. The Sabbath regulations keep hands withered.

Jesus is the Son of Man, a person living in the consciousness of God's good Creation and celebrating life. Earlier, he had called himself a bridegroom in whose presence no one could fast (Mark 2:19). Now in the sacred space of the synagogue and at the sacred time of the Sabbath, he is setting out the feast and encouraging people to eat and live. There is no more fitting Sabbath behavior than restoring this withered desire in people.

But those addicted to Fall consciousness watch for sin and wait for accusation. Their allegiance to laws that block life has killed their spirit. They have already died. Their hearts are hard; they no longer pump life through their bodies. This inner deadness is offended by life and conspires to destroy it.

Teaching

Christian faith is carried by a historical community, and so it is thicketed with traditions. To name just some of the variety, there are liturgical, moral, doctrinal, ascetical, and ecclesiological traditions. Some go all the way back to Gospel times, and some stem from the intervening centuries. Some have fallen by the wayside; some have been modified more than once; some claim to have weathered the years in tact. When people contact a historical faith, what they initially meet is a baffling array of traditions.

Traditions are always under scrutiny. The contemporary scene boasts tradition "undertakers," "miracle workers," and "birthers." Tradition undertakers are quick to bury the traditions that no longer seem relevant. They point out how a particular tradition comes from another time, place, and culture. It no longer makes any sense. It is time to bury it. Bury it with honor, but bury it.

Tradition miracle workers take the opposite point of view. Every tradition, no matter how peripheral—and no matter how little used—is capable of being revived and honored. These people continually talk of something "coming back." Resurrecting the dead excites them.

Tradition birthers are busy creating something new. The new cultural moment with its new understandings and behaviors has to be incorporated into the tradition. This means experimenting with new' forms, forms that fit contemporary consciousness.

I deliberately did not give any examples of Christian traditions that should be buried, resurrected, or created. This is where the fight begins. What one person thinks should be buried, another thinks should be resurrected, and a third thinks something new should be created. These arguments about how to treat and complement traditional forms can be fierce, and the criteria for sustaining, changing, and creating them are hotly debated. Words like "Neanderthal," "traitor," and "panderer" are never far from the minds of those involved, and often they are upfront in the discussion.

In the Gospel, Jesus is a fierce critic of the inherited traditions. He takes on purity-dietary laws (7:1-23), temple traditions (11:15-17), divorce traditions (10:1-12), etc. Although his critiques vary from tradition to tradition, his overall complaint is that they reflect and strengthen a hardened heart. A hardened heart has walled itself off from God and neighbor. The walls it has built are the traditions, and their builders rigorously walk the parapets to make sure God and neighbor do not breach them.

Jesus' criteria for evaluating the Sabbath traditions might be paraphrased this way: Do they serve life? To the legal and organizational mind, this is maddeningly vague. How is one to make this judgment? How is one to give evidence for it? But to the mystical mind, this criterion is essential. The heart of a faith tradition is its spiritual perception of the flow of life between God, self, and the world. This spiritual awareness transcends forms, and it is expressed and communicated through forms. These forms are always partial and historically conditioned. Therefore, they have to be continually evaluated and adjusted. Are they bringing people to the spiritual awareness at the living heart of the tradition? Or are they contributing to the hardening of the heart?

Who can answer this question?

The one who lives out of the God of life and so can discern what makes for life and what makes for death. "The Son of Man is lord even of the sabbath" (2:28).

First Sunday of Lent

Mark 1:9-15

Repenting and Believing in the Good News

A Spiritual Commentary

In those days Jesus came from Nazareth of Galilee and was baptized by John in the Jordan. And just as he was coming up out of the water, he saw the heavens torn apart and the Spirit descending like a dove on him.

And a voice came from heaven, "You are my Son, the Beloved; with you I am well pleased."

Conventional consciousness envisions heaven and earth as two different spheres, separate and distant from one another. There may be periodic contact, but this contact will most likely be explosive: an angry father reminding a disobedient son to behave. Also, the heavenly divine and the earthly human may be more intimately connected in life after death when the flesh has fallen away and only the soul remains. But now, in the realm of space and time, there is no continuous communion. This is presumed to be the divine-human condition in which all participate.

This is not Jesus' experience as it is symbolically expressed in the story. He comes out of the depths of water, leaving behind sin, what separates the divine and the human. His emergence is an act of human reaching, an ascending openness. He finds the heavens torn apart, not for a moment, but permanently. "God has ripped the heavens apart irrevocably at Jesus' baptism, never to shut them again. Through this gracious gash in the universe, he has poured forth his Spirit into the earthly realm" (J. Marcus, in Francis J. Moloney, *The Gospel of Mark: A Commentary* [Peabody, Mass.: Hendrickson Publishers, 2002] 36). This "gracious gash" allows the Spirit of love to descend. But the Spirit does not merely descend "on" him; it descends "into" him, fully inhabiting his being and preparing him for his mission. The reaching human is met by the reaching divine; the ascending human is met by the descending Divine. A loving Father embraces an obedient son. Union replaces separation; pleasure replaces anger. A new divine-human condition is revealed.

And the Spirit immediately drove him out into the wilderness. He was in the wilderness forty days, tempted by Satan; and he was with the wild beasts; and the angels waited on him.

This spiritual union between the divine and human in Jesus does not erupt into an individual celebration. The Spirit does not drive God's Son into green pastures and set a banquet before him. Instead he is immediately driven into the wilderness for forty days, an allusion to the trials of Israel as they tried and largely failed to be faithful to the God of their liberation. The baptismal gift of Spirit is not a personal privilege but the foundation for a struggle. The consciousness of being loved immediately unfolds into the consciousness of being faithful. This wilderness, like the wilderness of old, will be a place and time of testing and conflict.

The testing and conflict will be conducted by Satan, the Adversary. Satan is associated with wild beasts, symbols of the violent reprisals that will afflict Jesus if he pursues the path of uniting God and creation. Will the fear of violence keep Jesus from carrying out his mission? But Jesus is not only attacked by wild beasts, he is supported by his spiritual union with God, symbolized by angels ministering to him. He has the inner resources and ability to "stay the course." Although this quickly sketched picture reveals the basic tension of the story, it does not, in itself, disclose the outcome. Do the wild beasts devour Jesus? Or do the ministering angels sustain him?

St. Mark's Gospel is not simply good news. It is good news in a bad world. The mythological character of Satan is not just one more character. Satan should not be imagined as encountering Jesus in a definite individual form. Satan is the inner, invisible energy of people, groups, and social and political structures that inflict suffering on people. This adversary of God manifests itself through these people, groups, and social and political structures—and turns them into "wild beasts" who devour God's good creation. This inner invisible force of Satan and the demons will quickly sense Jesus' opposition and move against him. They know who Jesus is because he is their polar opposite. As their polar opposite, he threatens their possessions and seeks the territory they inhabit (see Mark 3:27). Satan and the demons actively keep people alienated from God and divided among themselves. Jesus actively seeks to unite people to God and to one another. These two are irreconcilable.

Now after John was arrested, Jesus came to Galilee, proclaiming the good news of God, and saying, "The time is fulfilled,

and the kingdom of God has come near; repent, and believe in the good news."

At the present moment in the story, Satan holds sway. Working through the wild beast Herod, he has arrested John. But Jesus is not intimidated. He preaches the good news of God in a bad world. The ministering angels are sustaining him in the midst of the wild beasts.

Jesus not only preaches the kingdom; he is the kingdom in himself. His baptismal experience structures his consciousness. He is sustained by divine love and suffused by divine pleasure. His life in time is permeated by eternity. Therefore, time is fulfilled. The promise of union that lurks in every moment has happened. But it has happened in the one human being, Jesus. It has yet to happen in others. Jesus' mission is to offer to others that potential that has become actual in himself. This offer makes the kingdom of God near.

But the mere offer of the kingdom does not make the kingdom arrive. There must be human reception. Arrival depends on repentance and belief. Repentance entails turning away from ways of thinking and acting that reinforce alienation from God and separation from people. These ways of thinking and acting are many and complex, interwoven with one another and often masquerading as true knowledge and righteous deeds. They are deeply ingrained, and their continued power is due, in no small part, to lethargy. We are often not "up" to the required change. Turning away, refusing to allow alienating thinking and acting to have influence, takes persevering and attentive activity.

As difficult as it is, turning away by itself does not make the kingdom of God arrive. Turning away must be complemented by turning toward, by believing in the "good news." But this good news is not easy to grasp; and, if grasped, not easy to integrate into all the dimensions of the human makeup. In the parable of the sower there are three soils that cannot welcome the seed of "the word" (good news) and bring it to fulfillment; only one soil successfully nurtures the seed into incredible abundance (Mark 4:3-20). In general, Mark provides more information about intransigency and the failure to believe than about resiliency and the emergence of belief.

The arrival of the near kingdom depends on the repenting and believing potential of the people who hear the proclamation and experience its actualization in the person of Jesus. Jesus is soliciting human freedom to become a new humanity, a restored creation. Although we may fantasize that human freedom has been waiting for this offer a long time and will enthusiastically embrace it, Mark's narrative keeps us from any easy optimism. Satan's holdings may be safe. It may be a standoff between the wild beasts and ministering angels.

Teaching

Question: Why is it so difficult to repent and believe the Gospel—that we are loved by God, and are called to embody that love in the time and space of earthly life?

Answer: Because we harbor so many other beliefs that do not fit into this Good News.

Beatrice Bruteau names some of these beliefs: "Health and beauty, money and power are necessary for happiness." "I am identified by my body, personality, and possessions." "My welfare is more important than yours." "No one willingly gives up power." "The world is here for us to exploit." "No one can be trusted." "There have to be winners and losers." "They hurt me, so I must get even." "I can't feel good about myself unless I'm better than somebody." "Some people are supposed to dominate other people." "If everyone were good, life would be boring" ("Following Jesus into Faith," *The Journal of Christian Healing* 10 [Fall 1988] 24).

Of course, we are not always aware we hold these beliefs or other beliefs that block us from embracing the good news. We often discover our own beliefs by tracing our actions back to their source. We shrug at injustice because "some people 'get the shaft' and some don't." We read about a tragedy befalling someone, and we respond, "Thank God, it's not me." We cheat a customer because if we don't have a certain amount of money, we won't be happy. Our instinctive and repetitive responses reveal our hidden beliefs.

Repentance entails finding and letting go of beliefs that compete with or contradict the Good News. Two observations are helpful for this "letting go" to occur. First, notice where the competing or contracting beliefs come from. Some of them come from the mindless internalization of cultural assumptions. Others come because we have universalized one of our negative experiences. Instead of allowing it to be a partial and painful piece of life, we have made it into a norm that must be obeyed.

Second, realize that we are holding the belief. The belief has not been imposed on us. It may appear to be a universal truth that we must heed. But the real truth is that we are holding it, nurturing it, sustaining it in existence by our attention and obedience. We enshrine it by allowing it to dictate our moods, decisions, and actions. Deeply realizing the origins of competing beliefs and our role in their continued power allows us to open the grasping hands of our mind. Once we cease to hold onto these beliefs, they lose their power and eventually drop away.

In spiritual teaching, it is always appropriate to ask the question a second time:

Question: Why is it so difficult to repent and believe the Gospel—that we are loved by God, and are called to embody that love in the time and space of earthly life?

Answer: Because the Gospel is about spiritual reality and how we come to believe in spiritual reality is an involved, lifelong process.

The Good News/Gospel originates with Jesus. He is the one who is conscious of divine love and human solidarity. Although his ministry and mission entails passing on this consciousness to all who follow him, initially there is a need to have faith in Jesus without having his consciousness of divine love and pleasure. The Christian community and tradition initiates all its members into this faith and supports it with strong argumentation and multiple practices. But eventually this "faith seeks understanding," as St. Anselm would say. It wants to move away from "complete" dependency on Jesus and become personally affirmed and deeply understood by each believer. This is a process of growing in faith, a gradually putting on "the mind of Christ" (1 Cor 2:16) so that our consciousness is more and more congruous with the consciousness of Christ.

There are many renditions of how this growth process takes place, but there is a passage from the Sermon on the Mount that is particularly practical: "Do not store up for yourselves treasures on earth, where moth and rust consume and where thieves break in and steal; but store up for yourselves treasures in heaven, where neither moth nor rust consumes and where thieves do not break in and steal. For where your treasure is, there your heart will be also" (Matt 6:19-21).

We can value ourselves in many ways, lay up treasure in many places. We can value our beauty, our brains, our achievements, our ability to make friends, our wit, our charms, or any number of attributes. All this may be the natural activity of our social natures, but it is treasure on earth. It is passing material, subject to the corrosions and thievery of time.

The text says we should "store up . . . treasures in heaven" (Matt 6:20), value ourselves in a way that time cannot destroy. This means identifying ourselves more and more as beloved sons and daughters of God sent into the world to bring love onto the earth. If we do this consistently, our sense of ourselves will change. Our faith *in* Jesus will gradually change to a faith *with* Jesus. We will see for ourselves what once we could only see by trusting in Jesus. According to the text, what we treasure and where our heart is will come together. Our sense of being loved by God will enter our heart, the center of our being, the source of our thinking and acting. The Good News will be central to our identity, and we may be surprised to find our decisions and behaviors flow from this treasure in our hearts (see Matt 12:34). We are doing what Jesus proclaimed, believing in the Good News.

Repenting and believing in the good news is not a project for the beginning of Lent, or even a project for the whole of Lent. It is the adventure that permeates all of life. We never finish letting go of false beliefs, and we never finish entering the kingdom of God, embracing and embodying the transcendent love at the center of our being.

Second Sunday of Lent

Mark 9:2-9

Radiating Outward

A Spiritual Commentary

Jesus took with him Peter and James and John, and led them up a high mountain apart, by themselves. And he was transfigured before them, and his clothes became dazzling white, such as no one [Greek, *no fuller*] on earth could bleach them.

The Teacher brings an inner circle of disciples into the depths of himself. He leads them "up a high mountain" (v. 2) to the place where he and God are in loving communion. This inner communion of love radiates a white light outward. It permeates the entire being of Jesus, moving through mind and body until it affects even his clothing. Clothing is the outer expression of a person's inner identity, how this identity becomes visible to others. "Dazzling white clothes" symbolize Jesus is completely integrated. The white light at the center transfigures his entire being.

The storyteller stresses the divine source of this radiant Jesus. He remarks that this whiteness goes beyond what earth can accomplish. Bleaching is blackness next to this dazzling white. The disciples are witnessing a divine manifestation mediated through Jesus. Its purpose is to renew their desire to follow Jesus. Discipleship has proved to be a difficult task. Everything that is unfolding is for their benefit.

And there appeared to them Elijah with Moses, who were talking with Jesus.

Even more is revealed to them. Elijah and Moses enter into the vision. These great past prophets are familiar with high mountains. They have communed with God and struggled to make divine plans happen on the recalcitrant earth. However, they too appear to be disciples. They are talking to Jesus; Jesus is not consulting them. The disciples do not overhear the conversation. It is enough for them to know that the whole Jewish tradition, Moses of the Law and Elijah of the Prophets, is involved.

> **Then Peter said to Jesus, "Rabbi, it is good that we are here; let us make three dwellings: one for you, one for Moses, and one for Elijah." He did not know what to say, for they were terrified.**

Peter, speaking for the three, addresses Jesus as "Rabbi" (that is, "Teacher"). His words reflect a mix of emotions. He gushes that it is good for them to witness this. Perhaps they can feel their commitment deepening. He wants it to last and suggests that he, John, and James build dwellings. All they know is that they need more of this.

But Peter's words were not a considered response. They were the stammerings of someone in over his head. What was unfolding was well beyond the comfortable boundaries of the disciples' consciousness. Their attraction to this transcendent meeting was shot through with trepidation. They exhibit the classic human response to the appearance of the holy: *mysterium tremendum et fascinans* (overwhelming and fascinating mystery). They are caught up in an overwhelming mystery that they cannot adequately articulate and to which they are simultaneously attracted and terrified.

> **Then a cloud overshadowed them, and from the cloud there came a voice, "This is my Son, the Beloved; listen to him!" Suddenly when they looked around, they saw no one with them any more, but only Jesus.**

But the revelation is not over. Jesus has brought them up the high mountain: now a cloud descends to meet them. The sense of transcendence and mystery is deepened. The presence of God overshadows them while still remaining shrouded. They are as close as humans get to the divine and still live. A voice from the cloud reveals to them what it revealed to Jesus at his baptism. "This is my Son, the Beloved" (v. 7). The revelation is meant to make them obedient. In fact, all that has happened is an encouragement for them to listen. Not argue. Not balk. Listen.

This transcendent experience, as all transcendent experiences, dissolves. Moses and Elijah are gone. The disciples know the Beloved Son is not one of these past prophets. The Beloved Son is "prophesy plus." But the transfigured Jesus is also gone. The dazzling clothes now need bleach to become white. Who remains is "Jesus alone" (v. 8; NASB). The mystical door that graciously opened has closed. What remains is the memory of the deepest truth of this Rabbi they are following.

> **As they were coming down the mountain, he ordered them to tell no one about what they had seen, until after the Son of Man**

had risen from the dead. So they kept the matter to themselves, questioning what this rising from the dead could mean.

However, the other shoe has not dropped. The mystical vision may reinforce Jesus as God's beloved, the inheritor of the law and the prophets. Its desired effect might be to sustain the disciples' commitment to Jesus. But it did not increase their comprehension. They know the divine approval of Jesus, but they have not advanced their understanding of the divine plan.

The divine plan is tied to the mysterious question of the Son of Man "rising from the dead" (v. 10). At the moment, this rising from the dead is beyond their grasp. Until they understand both the divine identity and the divine plan, they are charged to be silent. They heed the voice from the cloud: they listen and are obedient. But, instead of waiting for another revelation, they try to puzzle out "rising from the dead" among themselves. Perhaps the voice from the cloud gave the wrong advice. Instead of "[L]isten to him!" (v. 7) it should have said, "Talk to him!"

A Teaching

Paul Tillich described sin as a state of estrangement comprised of three interlocking factors (*Systematic Theology,* vol. 2, *Existence and the Christ* [Chicago: University of Chicago Press, 1957] 47–55): In unbelief people turned away from their grounding in God. This left them isolated and turned in on themselves in hubris. This hubris unfolded into a panicky concupiscence, in which people tried to pull the world into themselves to fill the hole that was created when they turned away from God. Unbelief, hubris, and concupiscence were the deep dynamics of the countless individual sins people commit.

If there is some cogency to this model of estrangement, and I believe there is, grace would be a reversal of the process. People grounded in God would not feel separate but in communion. This communion would fill them with spirit that would propel them outward. They would not try to grab and hold everything, fantasizing it could fill their inner emptiness. They would give their lives away knowing that more life from the source of life is always available. The proper flow is bringing inner strength to the troubled outer world.

In commenting on Meister Eckhart's spirituality, Cyprian Smith points out this movement from God to world:

It is possible for human beings, living, thinking, and acting in God, to think, see, and do, as God does. Instead of standing within the created world, looking in it for signs of a God who is outside it, we stand within God, and it is the world which now appears outside. When we stand within the world, God appears as totally transcendent and "other." When we stand within God, however, it is the world which appears as "other," but not by any means transcendent; on the contrary, we are greater than it. It appears as a pale and imperfect reflection of the dazzling and brilliant Truth in which we are living and making our home. (*The Way of Paradox: Spiritual Life as Taught by Meister Eckhart* [New York: Paulist Press, 1987]).

This "dazzling and brilliant Truth in which we are living and making our home" is the white clothes of Christ, whiter than any fuller could make them.

In the Transfiguration narrative Jesus radiates outward. This is the sign of his communion with God. God and he do not flee to a seventh heaven; God and he are moving in sync at the only earth there is. This is what the disciples are meant to grasp. This revelation is slightly different than the teaching embodied in this Sufi tale:

It is related that David was in the sanctuary. An ant passed in front of him. He lifted his hand with the intention of throwing the ant away from the place of prostration.

"O David," the ant protested, "what wantonness is this that you intend to inflict upon me? It is scarcely your task to lay hands on [human beings] in God's own house!"

David was grief-stricken and said: "O God, how should I deal with Your creatures?" A voice was heard: "Make it your habit to act out of fear of God so that none has to suffer on your account! Do not locate the true source of creatures in their bodies! Look rather at the mystery of their creation! If we were to order an ant to come out of its black robe, so many indications of divine unity would radiate from its breast that the monotheists of the whole world would be put to shame."

(Sharafuddin Maneri, in James P. Carse, *Breakfast at the Victory: The Mysticism of Ordinary Experience* [San Francisco: HarperSanFrancisco, 1994] 187)

The ant has to come out of its robe for the divine unity to be perceived. When the outer world falls away, the inner world is revealed. In the Transfiguration narrative the inner world is revealed in its transformation of the outer world. The disciples discover the presence of God not by stripping off the garments but by watching them turn beautiful.

Although theologians talk about sin and grace as two different states, I think they can also be appreciated as alternating experiences. I also think most people know the consciousness of both these experiences. Is there anyone who—feeling isolated and alone—has not reached out into the world and stuffed themselves with any excess available, only to find that the inner emptiness remained and even intensified? Is there anyone who, feeling grounded and at home, has not flowed out into the world with compassion and blessing only to find deeper compassion and more abundant blessing? In the second scenario we are transfigured with Christ.

Third Sunday of Lent

John 2:13-22

Getting beyond Deal

A Spiritual Commentary

Passover of the Jews was near, and Jesus went up to Jerusalem. In the temple he found people selling cattle, sheep, and doves, and the money changers seated at their tables. Making a whip of cords, he drove all of them out of the temple, both the sheep and the cattle. He also poured out the coins of the money changers and overturned their tables.

He told those who were selling the doves, "Take these things out of here! Stop making my Father's house a marketplace!"

His disciples remembered that it was written, "Zeal for your house will consume me."

The storyteller sets Jesus' actions and words in "the temple" (v. 14). However, when Jesus speaks, he calls the same space "my Father's house" (v. 16). This is the central conflict. The type of worship that goes on in the Temple is not appropriate for "my Father's house." It is this theological discrepancy that wields the whip, frees the animals, overturns the tables, and spills the coins.

The worship of the temple traffics in physical (animals) and social (money changing) life. In fact, physical and social life defines and restricts its mode of worship. Slaughtered animals are essential intermediaries between God and worshipers. Also, God and worshipers relate commercially. Exchange is the name of the game. Worshipers give God something; God gives worshipers something. The worshiper gives God a sacrificial animal and, in return, God gives the worshiper forgiveness for sins and help in various endeavors. This basic exchange is flexible enough to accommodate all the spinoffs of *quid-pro-quo* (this-for-that) living. For example, the more perfect the sacrifice (without blemish) the more assurance of forgiveness and help. In this way the mentality of the marketplace so permeates Temple worship that it degenerates into deal making.

Jesus' Father, however, is not a deal maker. He does not exchange favors for sacrifices. The Father is a free flow of spiritual life and love that cannot be bought, bartered, bargained, or bribed. Therefore, animals and money are inappropriate for two reasons. First, they belong to the physical and social spheres and so mask the spiritual nature of the relationship between the Father and worshipers. Second, they are gifts of the worshipers and so mask the priority of the Father's free gift of love. They give the impression of payoff. So set the zoo free and chase the moneychangers. They may be needed in the Temple, but they are not needed in "my Father's house" (2:16).

However, there may be a deeper implication of Jesus' actions and words. When the Samaritan woman asks Jesus about where to worship, on a mountain in Samaria or in Jerusalem (John 4:7, 20), he replies that "true worshipers will worship the Father in spirit and truth . . . God is spirit, and those who worship him must worship in spirit and truth" (John 4:23-24). This means worshipers do not have to travel to sacred places. Worship of the Father does not have to happen in the Temple. Worship can go on in an immediate and direct way. Whenever consciousness discerns, welcomes, and cooperates (truth as perception) with the activity of God (spirit), God is worshiped. Since Jesus is the fullness of grace and truth from whom all receive, his presence naturally initiates the acknowledgement of the divine (John 1:14, 16). In this sense, Jesus may be doing more than cleansing the Temple. He may be replacing it.

The disciples' recollection of Scripture does not catch the full theological revolution that is going on. But it does predict the effect of Jesus' words and actions. What Jesus has done is dangerous. His zeal will consume him but not in the sense of an endeavor so passionate it totally occupies his mind and heart. Rather in the sense that what he does will provoke conflict. He will be consumed by the anger of others who lead and profit from the Temple commerce. Those others are about to appear.

> **The Jews then said to him, "What sign can you show us for doing this?"**
>
> **Jesus answered them, "Destroy this temple, and in three days I will raise it up."**
>
> **The Jews then said, "This temple has been under construction for forty-six years, and will you raise it up in three days?"**
>
> **But he was speaking of the temple of his body. After he was raised from the dead, his disciples remembered that he had**

said this; and they believed the scripture and the word that Jesus had spoken.

To the religious authorities, Jesus' words and actions imply he is the Messiah. Only the Messiah has the right to cleanse the temple. But the Messiah will be accompanied by mighty signs that legitimate his actions. So they request a sign. Although the text does not say what type of sign they expected, most likely it would be a miraculous happening on the physical and social level. Their consciousness is confined to the physical and social dimensions of life. Therefore, what they want from Jesus is physical and social fireworks.

Jesus does articulate a sign, and on the level of words it suggests a miraculous happening in the physical-social world. But signs are always ripe for misunderstanding. In particular, literal minds that cannot move from physical-social language to spiritual perception will be confused. So the authorities are baffled when they hear that the Temple building that took forty-six years to build can be destroyed and rebuilt in three days. They take literally what is meant symbolically. Their only response is to be stunned by the incredibly short timeline. They are incapable of following the wordplay and so incapable of reading the sign as a spiritual revelation. In the next episode when Jesus tries similar wordplay with Nicodemus, Nicodemus will be perplexed and ask, How can these things be? (John 3:9). The authorities are in the same state of befuddlement.

Although the authorities miss the clues, the reader is given more help. When Jesus starts with the word "destroy," he is talking directly to the authorities. They will destroy the temple of his body, the dwelling place of God. "[I]n three days" does not designate a timeframe. It symbolizes the presence and power of God. Jesus' physical life will be reestablished through a process of resurrection, a process he is capable of because of his communion with the Father. Therefore, the overall meaning of this episode is that Jesus' restructuring of Temple worship evokes the ire of the religious leaders. They will kill him, but their malicious efforts will only reveal the Father's power of resurrection. This is both the sign they seek and the sign they cannot read.

It is also a sign that confused the disciples. It was only after Jesus died and rose that they remembered and grasped the fullness of what he had said. In the light of the Resurrection, they saw how the Scriptures and Jesus' words mutually illumined each other. The Scriptures foretold the Temple cleansing would lead to his death (see Ps 69:9; referenced in NAB from John 2:27), and Jesus foretold his death would lead to the Resurrection. Both predictions were fulfilled, so the disciples came to believe both in the Scriptures and in Jesus' word.

Teaching

Deal making is hardwired into the human condition. It permeates social arrangements. "If you do that, I'll do this" or "If you give me that, I'll give you this" is implicit in so much human interaction. Something for something is the air we breathe. Back scratching is just how we get through until Friday.

Therefore, it is no surprise that "dealing" is easily transferred from the social to the spiritual sphere. How we get what we want from one another is analogously how we get what we want from God, and how God gets what God wants from us. This is a crass way of talking about one of the most basic images of the Bible: covenant. God made covenants with Noah, Abraham, Moses, David, etc. This covenant tradition became a powerful interpretive tool for the vagaries of individual and social life. Applying the rules of covenant seemed to bring events under control. Bad things happened because the covenant was broken. Good things happened because the covenant was kept. Of course, it was not that simple. Covenant traditions were always changing and adapting in order to be persuasive. But the basic framework was deal making, deal breaking, and deal keeping.

There is a downside to using a persuasive social activity as the way divine-human relationships work. Its analogous character can be lost. We do not notice that the *quid-pro-quo* way we deal with one another is something like and something unlike how God deals with us and we deal with God. The "something unlike" drops out, and we think we are literally bargaining with God. This is more than an innocent theological error. It is a major obstacle to spiritual development.

Also, it can turn ugly. When religious elites negotiate the deals between God and people, theologically grounded oppression becomes possible. The religious elites prey on the fears of people, telling them what is needed to make amends to God or gain divine favor. They also provide the means of the transaction. The Gospel of Mark directly attacks this type of practice. "Beware of the scribes, who . . . devour widows' houses and for the sake of appearance say long prayers" (Mark 12:38, 40). The intermediaries are being paid to pray to God for poor widows. It is unscrupulous manipulation by callous people. But its legitimating context is the dealing-making God.

Christian reflection developed the implications of the cleansing of the Temple. The Letter to the Hebrews sees Jesus, the Lamb of God, becoming the once-and-for-all perfect sacrifice that ends the need for ongoing animal sacrifices (Hebrews 9). Paul sees the bodies of believers becoming temples of a "living sacrifice" which is a form of worship acceptable to God (Rom 12:1). Both these directions use Temple symbolism to undermine the actual building of the Temple and its animal sacrifices. They envision a relocation of the sacred. God is not found in the Temple building but in the body of Jesus and among the community of the dead and risen Jesus. However, the hard truth is that it is easier to repudiate the Temple than eradicate the deal making God.

In the movie, *A House of Sand and Fog,* the son of an Islamic man is shot. The father is distraught and instinctively begins to pray. He says at one point, "If you let my son live, I will lay in the park, put bird seed on my eyes, and let the birds eat my eyes out." This deal emerges out of the dark recesses of his being, wells up from a primordial space. That space dwells in all people. Stress and tragedy bring it out of hiding. For most of us, there is no eliminating this deep dealing-making tape. But we can slowly record another tape.

The Father of Jesus, who is often not at home in the images of the marketplace, is at home when we are simply grateful for life and serve life in whatever way we can. When we can receive and give and when we can find joy in both, we are at play in "the temple." In truth, we have been admitted into the "Holy of Holies" (see Heb 9:3). Our "sacrifice" is cooperation with the divine "sacrifice" that makes life holy by self-giving. The joy is not in making a good deal, but in getting beyond deal.

Fourth Sunday of Lent

See also the Second Sunday of Lent in *The Spiritual Wisdom of the Gospels for Christian Preachers and Teachers*, Year A, *On Earth as It Is in Heaven*.

John 3:14-21

Preferring Darkness

A Spiritual Commentary

[Jesus said to Nicodemus:] "[J]ust as Moses lifted up the serpent in the wilderness, so must the Son of Man be lifted up, that whoever believes in him may have eternal life.

After the Israelites escaped Egypt, they wandered in the desert and complained bitterly to God. God sent serpents into their camp. The serpents bit people and they died. God told Moses to make a bronze serpent, put it on a stick, and hold it high. The people who looked on it were cured of their snake bite (see Num 21:1-9). It is a form of homeopathic medicine. What brings the disease in one form cures the disease in another form.

Humans are bitten by death. The Son of Man, the one who comes down from above, becomes death, death on a cross. He is lifted up so the people can see him. If when they see him they can believe, eternal life will flow into them. What are they to believe? They are to comprehend how divine life has entered into human life precisely at that point where human life is failing (death) and at that point sustains the human person through the loss of temporal life. Eternal life both suffuses and transcends temporal life, and this truth is realized by looking on the crucified one. In one form death brings a loss of life; in another form—the crucifixion of the Son of Man—death brings a fullness of life.

For God so loved the world that he gave his only Son, so that everyone who believes in him may not perish but may have eternal life.

Indeed, God did not send the Son into the world to condemn the world, but in order that the world might be saved through him."

This is the inner truth, the truth at the center. Or, in another image, this is the highest truth, the truth above all other truths. Or in another

95

image, this is the revelation of the hidden actor behind it all. The revelations involved in this episode are progressive. It begins with what may be a stretch but what is definitely within our reach. We are beings who are grounded and sustained by an ultimate Mystery that we do not control or completely comprehend. Then we are gradually led to a spiritual knowing that blows our mind. The dynamite revelation is that the essence of that Mystery is a self-giving love completely dedicated to human fulfillment. This is what drives everything: "the Love which moves the sun and the other stars," as Dante said (*Paradiso,* 33.145).

The Son of Man was sent into the world by this love. Divine Love could not tolerate the sight of human perishing. Divine Love wants to fill people with a life that does not end. Even if the people in the world have strayed from their grounding in God and oppressed one another, God does not seek condemnation. The Divine desire is for salvation. The judgment of God is love and life.

However, the judgment of humans may be otherwise.

Those who believe in him are not condemned; but those who do not believe are condemned already, because they have not believed in the name of the only Son of God.

Freedom is always operative. If people enter into this revelation and integrate it into their lives, they will be grounded in the divine love that sustains and renews creation. Therefore, condemnation cannot reach them. But if they refuse this love and the one who reveals it, they separate themselves from the source of life. The inevitable outcome is condemnation. But why would people refuse the love of God revealed in the Son?

And this is the judgment, that the light has come into the world, and people loved darkness rather than light because their deeds were evil. For all who do evil hate the light and do not come to the light, so that their deeds may not be exposed.

You cannot know light and darkness until you are in the light. Before the light appears that illumines consciousness, everything is normal, conventional, just the way things are. You are in darkness, but you do not know it. The light, an alternate way of knowing and doing, exposes the present way of knowing and doing as alienated. This alienation is the darkness of the world, and it only appears when the light comes into it.

However, once the light reveals the darkness for what it is, it creates the conditions for a decision. Those who have a history of doing evil immediately grasp that their wickedness will be exposed. At a deep level, they encounter enough light to see their wrongdoings, and they understand this "seeing" is an invitation to repent. But they refuse the invitation, turn away from the light and embrace the darkness. Although the full reasoning behind their fear of exposure is not developed, a major influence seems to be the accumulated weight of wicked things, the longstanding habit of evil doing.

But those who do what is true come to the light, so that it may be clearly seen that their deeds have been done in God."

On the other side, a history of living the truth, doing good deeds, predisposes one to come to the light. As strongly as those doing evil avoid exposure, those living the truth seek exposure. The ultimate energy and inspiration of their good deeds has always been God. They have always known that they were not the source of any goodness that occurred through their actions. But this ultimate authorship is often hidden, difficult to discern. The light will bring this truth into heightened visibility. It will be clearly seen. This is what they want, so they move toward the light.

A Teaching

Preferring darkness, self-condemnation, is both easier and more mysterious than we think.

When we first hear that God does not condemn, there may be a sigh of relief. On the social level, we are used to being judged by other people. We are continually being put on the scales of someone else's mind and found wanting. Our boss, our spouse, our family, and our neighbors have mastered the look and language of "Sorry, Charlie . . ." (Some readers may recall the "Charlie the Tuna" commercials.) Since negative appraisals are the air we breathe, we may have projected this chronically evaluative mindset onto God. When we hear that God is a love who has abandoned judgment in favor of salvation, we may find a "Yes!" coming forth from the center of our being. We feel off the hook.

Actually, we are on the hook in a whole new way.

At first, we think that no one would be stupid enough to walk away from salvation. If it is all love and no condemnation, what is the problem? The problem is that we individually are not all love, and the world in which we live is not all love. The presence of all love makes this painfully clear. We might have glimpsed our persistent lack of love in the twilight zone between light and darkness. But we have kept it there, pushing it back toward darkness but never beckoning it toward light. Now this strategy is threatened. The light has arrived. And it instantly engenders in us an inner panic. Something we have hidden for so long might come screaming out into the open. There will be individual and social consequences. We cannot face exposure. We seek the shelter of night.

There is a story in St. John's Gospel (8:1-11) that captures the painful exposure of the light and the sulking preference for darkness. The Pharisees have brought a woman caught in adultery to Jesus. They seek to trap him by pitting him against Moses. The Pharisees claim that Moses taught them to stone such women. What does Jesus have to say?

Jesus bends down and writes with his finger on the ground. When they keep on questioning him, he stands up and says, "Let anyone who is without sin be the first to cast a stone" (v. 7). Then he bends down and writes on the ground a second time. These symbolic actions and words are the light coming into the alienated world. Suddenly evil doing is exposed and darkness is seen.

Jesus writing twice is reminiscent of YHWH writing twice. God wrote the Ten Commandments with the divine finger (Exod 31:18), just as Jesus writes on the ground with his finger (John 8:6, 8). Moses took the tablets down from the mountain into the camp of Israelites. He found the people worshiping a golden calf, and he threw and broke the stone tablets (Exod 32). When he returned to the mountain, God said to him, "Cut two tablets of stone like the former ones, and I will write on the tablets the words that were on the former tablets, which you broke" (Exod 34:1) God always writes twice. Merciful compassion is the nature of God.

The impact of this symbolism is not lost on the Pharisees. They have claimed that their desire to stone the woman is motivated by what Moses taught. But Jesus, the true interpreter of the Mosaic law, shows that the Ten Commandments are essentially about mercy because after Moses' angry outburst that led to his stoning the people, God wrote the commandments again. This strips the Pharisees of their cover. If it is not Moses and God who have authorized their violent behavior, where has it come from? Could it be that it comes from the dark spaces of their hearts that the Light of the World has now made visible?

The Pharisees have lost their identity as righteous enforcers of God's unforgiving law. In its place is full insight into their repressed darkness. This is what Jesus offers them as a new identity. They are sinners like everyone else. They can live the compassionate life of forgiven sinners who do not have the luxury of casting stones. But they have been casting stones a long time, and the older they are the more they are attached to that identity. So "they went away, one by one, beginning with the elders" (John 8:9). The invitation of the light is no match for the comfort of the darkness. And they go away "one by one." Each one lives for a moment on the edge of freedom—but only for a moment. The light has exposed their acceptable way of doing things as darkness. So now continuing doing things the usual way has become a preference for darkness, and this preference for darkness has become the free choice of self-condemnation.

This is why preferring darkness, self-condemnation, is both easier and more mysterious than we think. We did not always know it as darkness. It was just business as usual. We went about life making decisions and pursuing our well-being in an unthinking way. Only with the arrival of the light did the racist, sexist, classist, character of our thoughts and deeds become evident. However, by this time, we were attached to our thinking and behaving. It was easier to create a cover story than to engage in painful self-examination. Other people seem eager to buy this cover story and become accomplices in our deceit. They will willingly not look at what we will not look at, if we return the favor and not look at what they will not look at. The light is unwelcome, shining on too much. More accurately said, it puts everything in a new light, a harsh light. Quite simply, the darkness is preferable.

Fifth Sunday of Lent

John 12:20-33

Dying before You Die

A Spiritual Commentary

[A]mong those who went up to worship at the festival were some Greeks.

They came to Philip, who was from Bethsaida in Galilee, and said to him, "Sir, we wish to see Jesus."

Philip went and told Andrew; then Andrew and Philip went and told Jesus.

Greeks who worship the liberating power of God (Passover) are seeking Jesus. But they have to go through intermediaries. Their contact people are Jews with Greek names (Philip and Andrew) who come from towns close to Gentile territory (Bethsaida in Galilee). This procedure is more than protocol. Gentiles have to go through the Jews who have direct access to Jesus. Although salvation is not restricted to Jews, it does come "from the Jews" (John 4:22). And Jesus is a Jew, the full embodiment of God's covenant with Israel. Therefore, Philip and Andrew are the Greeks' access to Jesus.

Their simple request "to see Jesus" entails more than a casual meeting. "To see Jesus" means to enter into his revelation. However, in the word-play of John's Gospel, Jesus must be "lifted up" (John 3:14; 12:32), crucified, in order to be seen. Therefore, the Greeks seek the full revelation of the cross, divine-human love entering into and transforming death.

Jesus answered them, "The hour has come for the Son of Man to be glorified. Very truly, I tell you, unless a grain of wheat falls into the earth and dies, it remains just a single grain; but if it dies, it bears much fruit.

Jesus understands the arrival of the Greeks as a sign that the time of universal revelation is at hand. The Son of Man is the essential human being, the one who connects the divine and the human. His glorification manifests the flow of divine-human life. The path of this manifestation, however, is paradoxical. The agricultural image of single grain of wheat that enters the ground and dies in order to grow into "much fruit" (v. 24) provides the key. The revelation will entail the death of Jesus, the Jewish individual. But this death is not construed as loss. Rather it is seen as the beginning of a transformative process that will yield greater results than individual life.

Jesus will become more through death, not less. An aspect of this more is greater availability. To come to Jesus in his historical form entails a journey to where he is at and some contacts to get to meet him. To come to Jesus in his resurrected form is an immediate possibility. As the Gospel of Thomas images it:

> Split a piece of wood; I am there.
> Lift up the stone, and you will find me there. (GT 77)

Those who love their life lose it, and those who hate their life in this world will keep it for eternal life. Whoever serves me must follow me, and where I am, there will my servant be also. Whoever serves me, the Father will honor.

This path of Jesus' revelation contains crucial instructions for his followers. It illuminates a universal spiritual process, a process with which people are to consciously cooperate. If people identify with their individual lives as separate beings, they will lose that life. Death will eventually take it from them. But if they do not identify with separate individual life, the death of that life becomes a stage in a process of transformation. Death is not a loss but a transition into eternal life. The actual death, resurrection, and ascension of Jesus will definitively reveal this truth.

But this truth is already present in the consciousness of Jesus. He has disidentified with his separate life and centered himself in double communion with his Father and his followers. Although in another text these followers will be called friends, not servants, because Jesus tells them "everything I have heard from my Father" (John 15:15), in this text they are designated as servants because they are still in the learning process. This learning process is how to manifest divine love by disidentifying with separate life and centering themselves in the holy communion between God and people. When they engage this process and make it happen, Jesus, who revealed this way, is present to them, and the Father will honor them by acting through them.

> **Now my soul is troubled. And what should I say—'Father, save me from this hour'? No, it is for this reason that I have come to this hour. Father, glorify your name."**

The prospect of losing individual selfhood always produces fear and anxiety. Jesus is not an exemption. His troubled mind pushes him to ask for an exemption. But he resists this temptation to "love his life in this world." He was born to die; his whole life was geared to reveal the Father's love that transforms human life through death. Instead of a plea for rescue, Jesus asks for the revelation to be enacted.

> **Then a voice came from heaven, "I have glorified it, and I will glorify it again."**

> **The crowd standing there heard it and said that it was thunder. Others said, "An angel has spoken to him."**

This prayer is answered because it coincides with the perennial activity of the divine. This is the glory of the Father: to bring greater life out of lesser death. Divine love has been doing this in the past and it will do this in the future. It has been doing it throughout the ministry of Jesus, and it will do it throughout the ministry of his followers. But the crowd cannot comprehend this mystical truth. They reduce it to thunder, an event confined to the physical world. Or they interpret it as an angelic consultation, not the Father's presence but the help of a lesser spiritual intermediary.

> **Jesus answered, "This voice has come for your sake, not for mine. Now is the judgment of this world; now the ruler of this world will be driven out. And I, when I am lifted up from the earth, will draw all people to myself."**

> **He said this to indicate the kind of death he was to die.**

Although the crowd cannot accurately decode the voice from heaven, it came for their benefit. In order for the spiritual to enter into their consciousness, it needs to be manifested through physical occurrences: a sound coming from the sky. Jesus' consciousness is beyond that restriction. He is directly in touch with the spiritual. He is not dependent upon its physical manifestations. That is why the voice did not come for his sake.

Even more, the outer appearances of the physical-social world will no longer restrict human consciousness. The dominance of the physical-social world in its alienated state, unconnected to God and disunified in itself, has come under judgment. Death has ruled this world, claiming everyone within it. But its hegemony is over. Jesus' death will not entail the universal fate of going down into the earth. In his death he will be "lifted up from the earth" (v. 32; see also John 3:14). It is this kind of death, death as a transformative process, that will attract all people to Jesus. Death as extinction will give way to death as exultation. This will be the kind of death Jesus will die, and this kind of death will draw all people to him.

Teaching

"The grain of wheat that falls into the ground and dies in order to produce much fruit" is one of many images that suggest death is a transformative process. There is the acorn that needs to be cracked open in order to become an oak; the cocoon that needs to be split in order for the butterfly to emerge; the candle whose flaming wick melts the wax in order that light and heat happen. Embracing this vision— that death is a transition that leads to higher and greater being—might be essential for peaceful living. At least the last lines of Goethe's "The Holy Longing" seem to suggest this:

> And so long as you haven't experienced
> This: to die and so to grow,
> You are only a troubled guest
> On the dark earth.

> (trans. Robert Bly; see below)

If this is how death is, perhaps people should be in the dying business while they are alive. In another poem called "The Time before Death," Kabir writes:

> What you call "salvation" belongs to the time before death.

> If you don't break your ropes while you're alive,
> do you think
> ghosts will do it after?
> . . . .

> What is found now is found then.
> If you find nothing now,
> you will simply end up with an apartment in the City of Death.

If you make love with the divine now, in the next life you will have the
face of satisfied desire.

(Both poems from *The Soul Is Here for Its Own Joy: Poems from Many
Cultures*, ed. Robert Bly [Hopewell, N.J.: Ecco Press, 1995])

There is a code phrase for this project: "Die before you die so when you
die, you won't die."

But what does this enigmatic code mean?

This code phrase is often associated with a story. This story has
many renditions ("Until You Die," in Osho, *Journey to the Heart*. Element, 1995, 3; Kabir Edmund Helminski, *Living Presence: A Sufi Way to
Mindfulness and the Essential Self* [New York, N.Y.: Jeremy P. Tarcher/
Perigee Books, 1992] 127–28; Coleman Barks, *Delicious Laughter: Ram-
bunctious Teaching Stories from the Mathnawi of Jelaluddin Rumi*, [Athens,
Ga.: Maypop, 1990] 55–57). Its basic plot begins with a rich and generous man who freely gives gold to various groups of people. On one day
it would be widows; another day it would be invalids; another day it
would be poor students, etc. The only requirement was that the recipi-
ents should wait in silence. Not all could meet that requirement.

When it was the day for lawyers to receive gold, one pleaded his
case with great gusto before the rich and generous man. The rich and
generous man simply passed by. The next day the designated group
was the lame. So the lawyer wrapped splints around his legs and
posed as a cripple. The rich and generous man recognized him immediately and passed by. The following day the group was widows. The
lawyer disguised himself as a widow. However, he did not fool the
rich and generous man who passed by him without bestowing gold.

So the lawyer found an undertaker and concocted a plan. The undertaker would wrap him in a shroud and put him in the path of the
rich and generous man. The rich and generous man would surely
throw gold coins on the shroud for proper burial. The lawyer and the
undertaker would split the money.

The rich and generous man did throw coins on the shroud. The
lawyer's hand quickly broke through the shroud and grabbed the
coins before the undertaker could run away with them. Then he
emerged from his burial cloths and said, "Do you see at last how I have
received from your generosity?"

"Yes," said the rich and generous man, "but first you had to die."

The story suggests there are two dimensions to human beings. There
is a surface dimension that is scheming and conniving to get what it

wants by promoting itself and disguising itself. There is an argumentative lawyer in all of us. There is no end to our machinations on this level. We are continually exerting our will to get what we want.

But there is a deep dimension that is able to receive gold from someone who is both rich and generous by simply being silently present. The rub is that we must die to the schemer to become the receiver. It is the posture of silence that allows us to receive the gold that the rich and generous One wants to give. As Rumi says; "the mystery of 'Die before you die' is this: / that the gifts come after your dying and not before. / Except for dying, you artful schemer, / no other skill impresses God" (*Mathnawi* 6.3837-40 in Helminski, 128).

The thrust of this teaching is: if death is a transformative process, get a head start. At death the scheming and conniving self who manipulates the world to get its desires will fall away. The deeper self who in its very being is receiving love from God and passing it on to others will emerge. As St. Paul might say, "now is the time" (see 2 Cor 6:2) to practice letting go of the schemer and surrendering into the receiver. Why wait?

Second Sunday of Easter
John 20:19-31

Resurrecting with Questions

A Spiritual Commentary

When it was evening on that day, the first day of the week, and the doors of the house where the disciples had met were locked for fear of the Jews, Jesus came and stood among them and said, "Peace be with you."

It is still the first day of the week because the processes of the new creation are still unfolding. Earlier on this first day of the week the disciples, in the persons of the Beloved Disciple and Mary of Magdala, realize that Jesus is with God (John 20:1-18). Now on the evening of that same new day of creation, the disciples discover that he is simultaneously in their midst. Jesus is both with God (ascension) and with them (resurrection). This simultaneous presence emphasizes that he is a bridge, connecting the disciples with God and God with the disciples. He is the mediator between the divine and the human. That was what he was in his incarnate life, and that is what he is in his resurrected life. "And there was evening and there was morning, the first day" (Gen 1:5).

However, there is a major difference between the pre-Easter and post-Easter presences of Jesus. The post-Easter Jesus does not enter through doors, as people with physical bodies must do. The doors are locked, yet he was in their midst. This strongly suggests that the disciples have a spiritual realization of the presence of Jesus. He does not appear as an outer form as he previously did, but he manifests himself as a presence emerging from within and allaying their inner panic. His presence is known by the fact he brings peace in the midst of fear.

This peace is the fulfillment of his promise. "Peace I leave with you; my peace I give to you. I do not give to you as the world gives. Do not let your hearts be troubled, and do not let them be afraid" (John 14:27). Jesus leaves them peace, and this giving of peace is contrasted with how the world gives. The text does not go further with this contrast. But the overall sense is that the world gives and takes away. The security of one moment is replaced by the anxiety of the next moment. The world cannot sustain an abiding peaceful presence. Yet that is precisely how Jesus sees himself, an abiding presence that transcends the vagaries of the world. Jesus does not stop the chaos of the world. Rather he is present within it, calming and untroubling the heart, bringing peace.

After he said this, he showed them his hands and his side. Then the disciples rejoiced when they saw the Lord.

The showing of his hands and feet accompanies and makes real his word of peace. The disciples are able to read these signs of his wounded and opened body, and so they see the Lord. "Seeing the Lord" does not mean a physical sighting of the resuscitated body of Jesus. Rather it is a code phrase for knowing the revelation of Christ at such a depth that life is changed. This knowing happens when the disciples see the opened wounds.

But what is it they know? How do they read the signs in the hands and side?

Jesus is interiorly united to the Father. But this interior unity is not a private possession. It is meant to flow forth, bringing divine life to all who are disposed to receive it. This flowing forth is how Jesus glorifies the Father. The crucifixion is the supreme hour of this glorification. It is the time and place when divine life and love are most powerfully visible and available, present and transcendent in and through physical death. The throes of death reveal the greater flow of life.

The symbolic carrier of this spiritual truth is the lancing of the side of Jesus from which flows blood and water (John 19:34). Although this image triggers many interpretations, the gushing of blood and water is universally connected to the process of birth. And that this gushing comes from the side of Jesus recalls the birth of Eve from the side of Adam. Therefore, the opening in the side of Jesus is how his interior union with God becomes available as a life-giving birth for others. The openings in his hands perform the same symbolic function. They are channels that make available his interior life with God. This is what constitutes "seeing the Lord," receiving divine life through the symbols that mediate his "love that lays down its life for his friends." This is the truth of his death, and its realization leads them to rejoice.

They are living out the situation Jesus described earlier:

> [S]ome of his disciples said to one another, "What does he mean by saying to us, 'A little while, and you will no longer see me, and again a little

while, and you will see me'; and 'Because I am going to the Father'?"
. . . [Jesus said] 'Very truly, I tell you, you will weep and mourn, but the
world will rejoice; you will have pain, but your pain will turn into joy.
When a woman is in labor, she has pain, because her hour has come. But
when her child is born, she no longer remembers the anguish because of
the joy of having brought a human being into the world. So you have
pain now; but I will see you again, and your hearts will rejoice, and no
one will take your joy from you. (John 16:17, 20-22)

The sorrow they had at the loss of Jesus' physical presence is now replaced by a joy that cannot be taken away. The reason this joy cannot
be taken away is that it is grounded in a spiritual presence that is not
subject to loss the way physical presence is. In this sense, this new
situation is superior to the old situation. It is a never-ending presence.
Therefore, this joy "no one will take . . . from you" complements a
"peace the world cannot give" (see John 14:27).

**Jesus said to them again, "Peace be with you. As the Father has
sent me, so I send you."**

**When he had said this, he breathed on them and said to them,
"Receive the Holy Spirit. If you forgive the sins of any, they are
forgiven them; if you retain the sins of any, they are retained."**

Jesus offers them peace a second time. The beloved disciple had to
look twice into the tomb before he came to belief. Mary Magdalene
had to turn twice before she recognized the gardener as the teacher.
Now the disciples hear the word of peace twice. It brings them into the
fullness of revelation. The first time Jesus' word of peace expelled
fear because it was the reception of perfect love, the love of God for
God's children. "There is no fear in love, but perfect love casts out
fear" (1 John 4:18).

Now that the disciples are grounded in the peace that perfect love
brings, Jesus confers peace a second time. This time peace is the power
of mission. The disciples have received the divine life that is stronger
than death mediated through the open wounds of Christ. However,
divine life cannot be possessed. It can only be received and given
away. Therefore, they are immediately sent, commissioned by Jesus in
the same way the Father commissioned him. They have to give the life
they have received to others. The chain is established: from the Father
to Jesus, from Jesus to the disciples, and—by implication—from the
disciples to whomever the disciples will commission.

The key to this mission is the capacity to receive the Holy Spirit. Just as in the Genesis story God breathed into the clay of the earth and the human person became a living soul (see Gen 2:7), so now the Risen Lord breathes into his disciples and they become a new creation, a creature living by the breath of God. Living by the Spirit, they join the work of the Spirit. The work of the Spirit is to make things one.

The path to this oneness is through the forgiveness of sins. Sin is what separates God from the world and people from one another. Jesus has taken away the sin of the world, replaced the fundamental separation between God and the world with communion. The communion with God is the condition for the possibility of people forgiving one another and coming into unity. However, people must realize and engage this responsibility. If they hold onto the sins that separate, then separation will continue. If they let go of (forgive) those sins, unity will develop. The Holy Spirit enlivens people to co-create the human condition. This is the power of the resurrection, the freedom to overcome separation and bring unity.

> **But Thomas (who was called the Twin), one of the twelve, was not with them when Jesus came.**
>
> **So the other disciples told him, "We have seen the Lord."**
>
> **But he said to them, "Unless I see the mark of the nails in his hands, and put my finger in the mark of the nails and my hand in his side, I will not believe."**

The story line shifts. Thomas, who is called the Twin, was not present when the other disciples "saw the Lord." The other disciples bear witness to what they have seen, but it is not enough for Thomas. Taking the word of another does not suffice. He has his own criteria for believing, and community attestation is not among them. He wants to probe the flesh. In particular, he wants to probe the marks of Jesus' death. Presumably, this physical confirmation will convince him it is really Jesus. The one who was crucified and the one whom he once knew in the flesh will be confirmed as alive. This is sense knowledge, the type of knowledge most people rely on as an indication of reality.

This demand for physical verification is misplaced. Jesus is not a resuscitated corpse and resurrection is not a return to earthly life. However, there is irony in what he wants. The only way he will see the Lord is if he enters into the wounds. But these wounds are not available for his intrusive probing. These wounds are ones that Jesus shows to people so they may receive God's life and realize his true identity. The criteria for knowing the ultimate truth about Jesus are the same after his death as before his death. The person must go beyond the physical level and open himself or herself to the communication of divine life and recognize Jesus as God's incarnate presence. This is spiritual knowledge; the type of knowledge most people think is too subtle and evasive.

> **A week later his disciples were again in the house, and Thomas was with them. Although the doors were shut, Jesus came and stood among them and said, "Peace be with you."**

The coming of Christ into their midst is a regular happening. Every first day of the week Jesus is with them. When they gather, he gathers with them. Once again, he is not there physically because the doors were locked. He is in the midst of the disciples, emerging from within, as the communication of peace and the presence of joy. This time Thomas is present. More importantly, Thomas is with the other disciples. He is part of the community, and it is as part of the community that he will experience the risen Lord.

> **Then he said to Thomas, "Put your finger here and see my hands. Reach out your hand and put it in my side. Do not doubt but believe."**

> **Thomas answered him, "My Lord and my God!"**

Jesus invites Thomas into his wounds, into the correct understanding of his death and through that understanding into the reception of divine life. Although Jesus uses words similar to what Thomas said—which was essential for him to believe—he is not complying with Thomas' demands. The meaning is quite different. Jesus is encouraging Thomas to reach for the divine life that flows through him. It plays upon a line from the Adam and Eve story of Genesis: "See, the man [sic] has become like one of us, knowing good and evil; and now, he might reach out his hand and take also from the tree of life, and eat, and live forever" (Gen 3:22). Jesus is asking Thomas to reach out and live forever. Thomas must have obeyed Jesus' command for his cry, "My Lord and my God," signals both the reception of divine life and the recognition that Jesus and the Father are one. It might also signify that Thomas now knows he is not the twin of Jesus, not on the same level as the Son.

But there is a large omission in the story. What Thomas does not do is physically probe the wounds. He does not get his flesh and blood verification, but he does come to belief. The message, a consistent message in the Gospel of John, is that believing is not a matter of physical observation but of realizing spiritual truth. In fact, it is in the community of believers enlivened by the presence of the risen Christ that Thomas comes to know Jesus at a level that eluded him when he knew Jesus in the flesh.

In John's Gospel the character of Thomas has an ongoing difficulty in grasping the true meaning of Jesus' death. In the Lazarus story, when Jesus decides to go back to Judea where he will be in danger from the authorities, Thomas enthusiastically speaks to and for the other disciples, "Let us also go, that we may die with him" (John 11:16). It is a statement of bravado, perhaps even loyalty. But it is without understanding. They are not to die with Jesus; their task is to learn to receive the divine life that will come to them through Jesus' death. Jesus is not a reckless revolutionary courting death, and they are not kamikaze disciples.

Thomas' ignorance of the meaning of Jesus' death continues during the Last Supper conversations. Jesus is reflecting on his transition from this world to the Father. He insists that his upcoming separation from his disciples is only to prepare a place for them. Then he will come and take them to himself "so that where I am, there you may be also" (John 14:3). In other words, Jesus predicts a brief separation followed by a permanent, life-giving communion.

Then he tells them, "And you know the way to the place where I am going" (John 14:4). Although Jesus says they know, Thomas speaks for the group and says they do not know: "Lord, we do not know where you are going. How can we know the way?" (John 14:4). Jesus responds, "I am the way, and the truth, and the life. No one comes to the Father except through me. If you know me, you will know my Father also. From now on you do know him and have seen him" (John 14:5). We are not told whether Jesus' response to Thomas brought him from not knowing to knowing. But the whole context suggests that it did not. Although Thomas has seen Jesus in the flesh and talked to him, he does not know him in his theological identity as being both the path to God and the very presence of God. In particular, he does not know that the way to this simultaneous knowing of Jesus and the Father is through grasping the spiritual truth of Jesus' death.

Therefore Thomas' interactions with the incarnate Jesus, the Jesus available for physical probing, did not facilitate the deepest truth about him—namely his oneness with the Father and communication of divine life through his death. Thomas learns this truth through Jesus' spiritual presence within the gathered community. There is an important implication of this path of belief. The fact that Thomas knew Jesus in the flesh is not an extraordinary privilege to understanding the revelation of Christ. Common sense would seem to suggest that those who saw Jesus in the flesh have a great advantage over those who did not. But Thomas' experience suggests that the spiritual presence of Christ within the community is the way to come to a correct understanding of the pre-Easter Jesus. Thomas moves from darkness into light only on the evening of the first day of the week.

> **Jesus said to him, "Have you believed because you have seen me? Blessed are those who have not seen and yet have come to believe."**

How would the literary character of Thomas answer Jesus' question, "Have you believed because you have seen me?" "Seeing the Lord" in the sense of probing his wounded flesh was how Thomas thought he would come to belief. That was his condition for believing, and that condition kept his consciousness on the level of the flesh. However, he never did probe the wounds, and yet he came to belief. So physically seeing Jesus is not how belief comes about. The answer to the question is no. Thomas did not come to faith through physical sight.

Thomas came to belief by spiritually grasping the meaning of Jesus' death and, through that understanding, he received the divine life that is stronger than death. He expressed and communicated this experience by exclaiming Jesus as *his* Lord and *his* God, the one who "took him to himself" (see John 12:32) and in the process took him into God. This experience is available within the community of disciples who gather each week and who find that Jesus is among them offering them the life that flows through his open wounds. It is not necessary to physically see him in the flesh. In fact, even those like Thomas who saw him in the flesh in his pre-Easter days only understood him and believed when they contacted his spiritual presence within the believing community. This experience of the risen Lord is not relegated to the past. It is present and available when the disciples gather "next week." The time and date of the gathering is "evening on that day, the first day of the week."

Now Jesus did many other signs in the presence of his disciples, which are not written in this book. But these are written so that you may come to believe that Jesus is the Messiah, the Son of God, and that through believing you may have life in his name.

The life of Jesus is a life of signs—words and deeds that were capable of pulling people into the mystery of Spirit. His disciples were present for these signs, only some of which have been written down. Therefore, the disciples know much more than is written in this book. The living Christ of the community supercedes any written material.

However, this writing is important. It is not only that these signs have been committed to written form and therefore can outlast the death of the disciples. It is also the way these signs were written. They were written in a way that reflects the signs in the actual historical dynamics of Jesus' life. In particular, the writing reflects the complex interplay between the physical and spiritual dimensions of life.

Therefore, this writing is itself a sign. It is meant to draw the reader into full belief that Jesus is God's Son and Messiah. This belief will open the reader to the flow of divine life that comes from Jesus. Readers, even though they have not met Jesus in the flesh, will experience the imparting of divine life through this written text within the community of disciples.

Teaching

Rainer Maria Rilke, the German poet, is often quoted as encouraging us not to excessively prize answers but to live questions. Behind this advice is a sense that we, as human beings, have not completely explored who we are and who we might become. One way this adventure in self-discovery could be pursued is by paying close attention to the questions that emerge in human consciousness. Sometimes these are questions about the adequacies of old ways of thinking and behaving. Sometimes these are questions that are tied to inklings in the present, or flashes of insight, or intuitions that challenge the dominance of rational logic.

Whenever I ponder St. John's Gospel in general and the stories of Christ's resurrection in particular, a number of questions enter my mind. I usually dismiss them because they threaten the comfortable boundaries of my confined consciousness. I sense that even asking them in a sustained way will take work, and living them will demand stepping off the edge of security-consciousness into a night of trust. Ordinary people may hold unexamined opinions about these questions or entertain them after a third beer. But they are seldom seriously pursued. However, once you accept that humans are only aware of a small fraction of what they are experiencing, the door is opened into a world where people can be present even though the doors are locked.

I wonder: what kind of a barrier is death? While people are alive, we often talk of a spiritual presence to one another. At least part of what that means is that we sense a reality deeper than body and mind that is crucial to the identity of a person. We presume that this deeper reality is mediated through body and mind. Therefore, when body and mind have fallen away, this deeper reality is inaccessible. Body and mind constitute "remains"; spirit goes into another world, the spirit world. The deceased is with God and at rest, i.e., inactive. However, in St. John's Gospel ascension and resurrection are distinguished. Ascension means Jesus is with God; resurrection means he is still present to the ones he loved. His love relationships are intact. The disciples do not have to go on without him. They have to go on with him in a new way.

Is Jesus a special case? Or is the disciples' experience of the death, ascension, and resurrection of Jesus a revelation of the spiritual structure of reality, a spiritual structure in which all participate? Do all who have given and received love in this incarnate life continue to do so after the death of the body? Is love really stronger than death?

Perhaps our advice to those grieving the loss of a loved one is too influenced by the powerful, yet limited, capacity of physical sight. We expect those left behind to grieve their loss and then get on with life, accepting the absence of the one they once loved. Is it crazy to think that they should assume a spiritual presence that cannot enter fully into most human consciousnesses and then get on with their life? If so, how should we think about this in such a way that consciousness may eventually open to it?

When we are impressed with the power of death to sever ties, we often seek signs that something of the person has survived. The person may not be with us in the way they once were, but we want some indication that they are somewhere and they are at peace. It seems that we will accept the loss if we know the person is happy in another reality. Separation is presupposed. But we would like a word from beyond that everything is all right. When it comes our time to die, this loved one is often imagined as someone who has gone ahead and prepared a place and will be waiting for us. We have all heard stories of people who are close to death seeing visions of deceased loved ones. It is assumed that they are a welcoming committee, guiding the about-to-die person to the other side. Death means reconnecting with those whom we have loved and lost.

This rendition is often the way Christian faith in life after death is characterized. However, it is not the spiritual consciousness of resurrection in John's Gospel. John's "Good News" is not impressed with the separation power of death. Jesus may be going to God, but that does not mean he is leaving his loved ones on earth—just the opposite. His death will bring about a condition in which the disciples will be able to see his abiding love clearly: "I will not leave you orphaned; I am coming to you. In a little while the world will no longer see me, but you will see me; because I live, you also will live. On that day you will know that I am in my Father, and you in me, and I in you" (John 14:18-20). The world that sees with physical eyes will no longer see Jesus after his death. But the disciples, the ones whom he loves, will see him because they will perceive him with spiritual eyes. This will happen "On that day," the day when he physically dies.

Why will the death day of Jesus be also his resurrection day, and the day the disciples will grasp the communion between God, Jesus, and themselves? The human person is a composite being. In classical language, we are body and soul, material and spiritual. When we appreciate ourselves as physical, we know what it means to say we are *with* someone or *beside* someone or *above* someone or *below* someone. Physical realities are separate from one another. When they come together, they do so only to break apart again. This sense of separation is so pervasive that even the moments of togetherness are haunted by thoughts of future separation. Most of us are very aware of this combination of together and separate. When we love someone very deeply, we instinctively fear they will die and leave us: the stronger the sense of togetherness, the stronger the fear of separation.

However, we can also appreciate ourselves as spiritual beings. When we do this, we know what it means to say we are *in* someone. Spiritual beings interdwell. They can be in one another without displacing anything of the other within which they dwell. "Inter-dwelling" is the essential spiritual condition—"I am in the Father, you in me, and I in you" (see John 14:10; 15:4; 17:21). In spiritual consciousness togetherness holds sway with such force that separation is inconceivable. When the physical falls away, this spiritual communion remains and takes "center stage." This is why Jesus says, "On that day," the day of his physical death, they will realize the truth of spiritual indwelling. When the physical is present, it monopolizes consciousness. When it is absent, the emptiness can be experienced not only as loss but also as possibility. There is a new form of presence. It is not waiting for us beyond death. Even though the doors are locked, he or she is "in our midst." On the spiritual level, we are never orphaned.

Can this be true?

How do we live this question of the resurrection?

Third Sunday of Easter

Luke 24:35-48 *LM* • Luke 24:36-48 *RCL*

Revitalizing Disciples

A Spiritual Commentary

For users of the *Lectionary for Mass:*

> [The two disciples] told what had happened on the road, and how he had been made known to them in the breaking of the bread.

For users of the the *Revised Common Lectionary and the Lectionary for Mass:*

> While [the eleven and their companions] were talking about this, Jesus himself stood among them and said to them, "Peace be with you."
>
> They were startled and terrified, and thought that they were seeing a ghost.
>
> He said to them, "Why are you frightened, and why do doubts arise in your hearts? Look at my hands and my feet; see that it is I myself. Touch me and see; for a ghost does not have flesh and bones that you see that I have."
>
> And when he had said this, he showed them his hands and his feet.
>
> While in their joy they were disbelieving and still wondering, he said to them, "Have you anything here to eat?"
>
> They gave him a piece of broiled fish, and he took it and ate in their presence.

When the two travelers who turned back from Emmaus returned to Jerusalem, they were greeted by the eleven and their companions with "The Lord has risen indeed, and he has appeared to Simon" (v. 34). However, they do not respond to this startling news. Instead they tell about "what happened on the road and how he had been made known to them in the breaking of the bread" (v. 35). This is what they were talking about as Jesus "himself stood among them" (v. 36).

In the Emmaus episode the risen Jesus is part of the narrative, but he is not the point of the narrative. (See the "Third Sunday of Easter," *The Spiritual Wisdom of the Gospels for Christian Preachers and Teachers,* Year A, *On Earth as It Is in Heaven.*) The point is that the two travelers come to understand the real identity of Jesus, an identity that is symbolized in the eucharistic gesture and embodied in how Jesus actually died. Although they previously knew the gesture and had information about his death, they comprehended neither the gesture nor his death. They were not able to answer the question the unknown risen Christ asked them, "Was it not necessary that the Messiah should suffer these things and then enter into his glory?" (Luke 24:26). The ancient Christian connection between Eucharist and Cross is what eluded them.

However, the unknown risen Christ interprets the Scripture for them, remains with them, and repeats the eucharistic gesture. With his help there is a breakthrough. Everything falls into place. They understand who Jesus is and the larger plan of which he was a part. Jesus is filled with God's life; and he gives God's life to others so that they can grow strong on it. As bread nourishes the physical level, Jesus nourishes the spiritual level. This eucharistic truth inspired and directed how he died. He forgave those who were crucifying him, offered salvation to one of the criminals, and handed his spirit over to God (Luke 23:34, 43, 46). He was always giving divine life to others, even as he was dying. That is what was "made known to them in the breaking of the bread" (v. 35).

Therefore, the Emmaus episode is a teaching on how to interpret the Eucharist as the meaning of the Cross, and how to interpret the Cross as the embodiment of the Eucharist. Although it is called an appearance story, it hardly qualifies. When Jesus appears among them, he is not recognized. When he is recognized, he disappears. In between he is definitely in the "Teacher" mode, from listening to their unenlightened rendition of what happened in Jerusalem, to upbraiding their slowness, to patiently showing them the true interpretation of his suffering and dying. His risen status is assumed, but it is not the focus. In fact, could the unknown Christ who suddenly fades in and just as suddenly fades out be a ghost? The misinterpretation of Jesus' death has just been corrected. Now it is time to correct a misinterpretation of his resurrection.

Ghosts are the disembodied presence of people who have died and are still considered dead. They haunt the earth terrifying its inhabitants. If you have perceived the presence of someone who had died, it was a ghostly presence. Many scholars suggest that the storm at sea stories in both Matthew (14:22-33) and Mark (6:45-52) are resurrection episodes read back into the life of Jesus. In these stories Jesus manifests his power over evil and death by walking on the tumultuous seas. However, the disciples mistake him for a ghost. He has to correct this impression and assure them, "It is I" (= "I am"). It is Jesus who is sustained by the power of God, and they do not have to be afraid. The same assurance is present in this appearance story.

Peace connotes the restoration of relationships, relationships between God and people and people among themselves. When Jesus stood among them with the word, "Peace," he restored them to relationship with himself. The barrier of death has been overcome. Jesus and his disciples are united. He is not a ghost, and they do not have to be afraid. He is alive and real. The criteria of his reality and aliveness are their seeing him and touching his hands and feet, and the fact he eats some cooked fish. Flesh and food are sure signs this is not a ghostly presence.

These criteria of reality and aliveness cause some problems. The overall conviction of the New Testament is that the resurrection is not resuscitation. Jesus does not return to the same space-time continuum that he inhabited before his death. However, this language seems to say just that. Warm flesh is the physical life we know and warm food is how we keep it going. But the language should be taken analogously, somewhat like and somewhat unlike the reality. Jesus is truly real and alive, just as we are truly real and alive by flesh and food. However, this reality and aliveness is not like flesh that constitutes physical life and the food that contributes to it. This is all the imagery intends. To go further, and Christian theologians have always gone further, is to allow the symbols of flesh and food to give rise to thought (as St. Paul does in 1 Corinthians 15).

> Then he said to them, "These are my words that I spoke to you while I was still with you—that everything written about me in the law of Moses, the prophets, and the psalms must be fulfilled."

> Then he opened their minds to understand the scriptures, and he said to them, "Thus it is written, that the Messiah is to suffer and to rise from the dead on the third day, and that repentance and forgiveness of sins is to be proclaimed in his name to all nations, beginning from Jerusalem. You are witnesses of these things."

The risen Jesus is not a ghost who haunts, but the Living One who revitalizes his disciples. The two on the road "stood still looking sad" (Luke 24:17). Now Jesus is teaching and commissioning them. Luke began his Gospel with the intention of giving an "orderly account of the events that have been fulfilled among us" (Luke 1:1). He ends his Gospel with Jesus explaining to the disciples how the promises of the Law and the Prophets, and the experience of God in the Psalms have come to completion. In him God's plan for the salvation of the world has been revealed and inaugurated. It must go out to all people. Of course, it begins right where they are, in Jerusalem. They are witnesses who now know the story and must live the reality.

Teaching

It was a wind-blasted winter evening, close to midnight, and the doors of the apartment were locked. Inside the disciple was eating popcorn and riffling through the Gospels. He was reading at top speed, flipping pages, hoping a word, a sentence, a story would make him stop. He was looking for something, but he wasn't sure what it was.

Suddenly Jesus appeared and sat down in the chair opposite him. The disciple blanched. He shook his head, rubbed his eyes, looked away, and then looked back. Jesus stubbornly stayed put. Finally Jesus said, "Got anything to eat?"

"I get it," said the disciple. "That's what you did after you rose. When the disciples thought you were a ghost, you asked for something to eat. It reassured them you were real."

"I was hungry. What is this stuff?"

"Popcorn." The disciple passed the bowl over to Jesus. "Try some, Lord," he said; and the words sounded absolutely ludicrous. He consoled himself with the thought that he didn't say, "Mister Lord."

Jesus took one piece of popcorn and looked at it as though he were examining a diamond with an eyepiece.

"Wonderful shape," Jesus said; "and each one is just a little different. I like them."

The disciple became uneasy. He had never heard popcorn referred to as "them." And how did he know he liked them if he hadn't tasted them?

Jesus put one piece in his mouth and chewed it carefully for close to a minute. The disciple grabbed a handful.

"Not enough salt," Jesus finally said.

"Salt is not good for you," warned the disciple.

"I was always one for a lot of salt," said Jesus. "Hey!" Jesus raised his finger in the air like he was about to give a teaching. "Has anyone tried putting butter on this stuff?"

"It's been done. But butter's not good for you either."

"You are a very careful person," said Jesus.

"Thanks," said the disciple. "Here, have some more." The disciple raised the bowl of popcorn off the table and offered it to Jesus.

"No thanks."

"You are the only person I know who can eat only one piece of popcorn and stop."

"Of course. I'm God," Jesus said, and laughed.

The disciple did his best to chuckle.

"How come when *you* eat popcorn?" Jesus said as he stroked his chin, "you try to get as much into your mouth as possible, and it spills out, and you have to pick it off your shirt, and put it back in your mouth?"

"Oh God, I knew this was going to happen."

"Why does everybody say that when I'm around?" asked Jesus, a bit irritated. "What did you know was going to happen?"

"You notice everything and make remarks."

"Don't you like to be noticed?"

"As a matter of fact, I don't."

The disciple closed his eyes. When he opened them, Jesus was still there, smiling.

"Why did you come?"

"To teach you how to eat popcorn." Jesus looked pleased with himself.

The disciple looked down at the bowl of popcorn on the table. "Are you going to toy with me?" he said, haughtily.

"I am not toying with you. I always come to seek what is lost; and when people are searching through my story at midnight like it was a medicine cabinet, it is usually a sign they are lost."

"Like hell I'm lost!" the disciple shouted.

"Like hell you're not!" Jesus shouted back.

Their eyes locked. The disciple was the first to look away.

"It's a mild case of midlife crisis. I'll be over it in a couple months." The disciple gave a "what can I tell you" shrug of his shoulders.

"Is that what they are calling temptation these days—midlife crisis?"

The disciple laughed in spite of himself.

Slowly Jesus reached over to the bowl of popcorn, took one piece, and popped it into his mouth. Jesus' obvious enjoyment made the disciple shake his head.

"Even God can't eat only one piece of popcorn," said the disciple.

"Especially God," said Jesus. "Try some."

The disciple instinctively took a handful of popcorn, but then let some fall back into the bowl. He put the pieces in his mouth two or three at a time.

When both of them had finished chewing, Jesus said in a very gentle voice, "You have been with me now a long time, and you are wondering whether it is all worth it. You are thinking of divorcing me quietly, aren't you?"

"It has crossed my mind."

"My friend, you need more chutzpah. Blessed are those who are not embarrassed by me."

Jesus waited, but there were no words for a long time.

Then Jesus said, "There was a bank robber who planned a heist for a long time. He had worked out the details and was ready to go. But when he got to the bank teller's window, he suddenly panicked and asked directions to the washroom."

"Hah! You're saying I can't carry through what I set out to do."

"I'm saying risk the salt on the popcorn."

"Jesus," the disciple said in an exasperated tone, "I'm going to lay it on the line. You walk too fast: I can't keep up."

"Better to be out of breath behind me than ahead of everyone else."

"I want a more moderate master so I can be a better disciple."

"You are a perfect disciple. You're having second thoughts."

"That may be accurate, but it's hardly perfect."

"My friend, that is the way of the earth beyond the earth. Why live out of something as small as you are? Love me because I am large enough to betray. But I do not think you are happy in the land of mercy."

"God, you are a bittersweet experience. Why do you say things so harshly?"

"Peter used to say that I was the only one who could say, 'God loves you' and get everybody mad."

The disciple laughed. So did Jesus.

"You laugh at the right places," said Jesus. Then suddenly he asked, "So, are you going to stick around?"

"Where will I go? 'You have the words of eternal life'" (John 6:68).

"No fair stealing Peter's lines."

"Will *you* stick around with someone like me?" The disciple sighed like some great build up of pressure had been released.

"Is that what this is all about? asked Jesus. "[Y]ou know everything; you know that I love you" (John 21:17).

"No fair stealing Peter's lines. Why did you say that?"

"When Peter said it to me, it blew me away. I hoped it might do the same for you."

"But I don't know everything."

"You know enough."

"I know that even when I want you to go away, I don't want you to go away."

"East of Eden we call that love," said the Master, and tears ran freely down his face.

In imitation of his master, the disciple cried.

For a long time there were no words, only the silence of communication.

"You know," Jesus finally said, "after Lazarus came back to life, he told me that what woke him up in the tomb was the sound of my tears" (see John 11:35).

"I can believe it," said the disciple.

Jesus smiled and reached for a third piece of popcorn. The disciple also took a piece. Jesus closed his eyes to savor better. The disciple did likewise. When the disciple opened his eyes, Jesus was gone. But there was such an incredible lightness to his being, such a revitalization of his heart, that the disciple knew where he had vanished to.

Fourth Sunday of Easter

John 10:11-18

Loving Unconditionally

A Spiritual Commentary

[Jesus said to the Pharisees:] "I am the good shepherd. The good shepherd lays down his life for his sheep. The hired hand, who is not the shepherd and does not own the sheep, sees the wolf coming and leaves the sheep and runs away—and the wolf snatches them and scatters them. The hired hand runs away because a hired hand does not care for the sheep.

Jesus is in an essential and unbreakable communion with his disciples. This communion is constituted by Jesus giving his life into the life of his friends. This giving is an unconditional caring that has the safety of his friends as its core value. It does not recede when trouble arrives. In fact, Jesus dies so that his friends might live. This unbreakable communion that is characterized by his total self-giving is the quality that makes him a good shepherd. The shepherd dies: the sheep are safe.

Other teachers and leaders (hired hands) abandon their disciples when trouble arrives. They do this because they are concerned primarily about themselves and motivated by external rewards. Danger brings out their true colors. The appearance of the wolf reveals only a tenuous connection between the Teacher and the disciples. They do not care for their friends; they care for themselves. The sheep die: the shepherd escapes.

I am the good shepherd. I know my own and my own know me, just as the Father knows me and I know the Father. And I lay down my life for the sheep.

Jesus' relationship with his friends is built on mutual knowledge that is intimately related to the mutual knowing of the Father and the Son (see also John 14–15). This mutual knowledge entails a complex flow of life. The Father's life, which is essentially love, flows into Jesus, and the life of the Father and Jesus flows into Jesus' friends. So the

Father's self-giving into the Son results in the Son's self-giving into his friends. The completeness and transcendence of this self-giving is revealed when the Good Shepherd gives himself totally in the act of dying. In his death the love of the Father is revealed as sustaining and transforming the friends of Jesus through their own death.

> **I have other sheep that do not belong to this fold. I must bring them also, and they will listen to my voice. So there will be one flock, one shepherd.**

Jesus will predict that when he is "lifted up," he "will draw all" (other sheep) to himself (John 3:14-15; 12:32). This drawing will happen because his "voice" is attractive. What he reveals—the steadfast love of God that transforms death into life—will be the magnet. All humans who are awake and hungry will flock to this fold. The power of this revelation will create a single people from the vast varieties of the earth.

> **For this reason the Father loves me, because I lay down my life in order to take it up again. No one takes it from me, but I lay it down of my own accord. I have the power to lay it down, and I have the power to take it up again. I have received this command from my Father."**

This is how the Father's life and love works in and through Jesus. Jesus freely enters into the realm of death. On a surface level, it may look like he is at the behest of his enemies and they put him to death. But at a deeper level, a process of "laying down" and "taking up" is at work. His resurrection will be his continued life in the community of friends who have received his sacrificial dying into their hearts. This is how the other sheep will hear Jesus' voice. They will come in contact with those who are now listening to Jesus and through them contact his risen presence. This is the Father's plan for the revelation of divine love and the unity of all peoples. Jesus, the Good Shepherd, is enacting it.

Teaching

Two lovers look at one another and say without any reserve in their hearts: "I promise to be true to you in good times and in bad, in sickness and in health. I will love you and honor you all the days of my life" (*Rite of Marriage* [Roman Catholic] §25).

A father holds his newborn daughter and from some vastness within him says, "I would die for you."

A woman holds the hand of her terminally ill friend and says, "You know, I'm not going away."

When we first hear the phrase, "unconditional love," it seems a beyond-reach ideal, almost ominous. But actually we all have moments of unconditional love. In these moments we open ourselves unreservedly to another and commit ourselves totally to the the others' well-being. Like Jesus in the Gospel, we often reach for "laying down our life" language to express what, at the moment, seems so clear and undeniable to us. Unconditional love means everything and forever.

Of course, it may be difficult to make good on these passion-filled outbursts of love. In the rough and tumble of day-in day-out living, many conditions arrive. Our absolute statements of "all and forever" begin to be peppered by conditional clauses, "If you don't. . ." We are a combination of unconditional and conditioned. We have preferences, cautions, habits, and needs. This can become the classic standoff of an unconditional "irresistible force" and a conditioned "immoveable object." However, few of us think our failure to achieve one hundred percent "unconditionality" refutes our visionary moments of "all the days of my life" and "till death do us part." There was a truth in what we said when we said it.

Actually, there is more truth than we know in what we said when we said it. When we are swept up in the consciousness of unconditional love, it does not appear as something we choose. It is simply something we are. When this happens, we can glimpse the meaning of Jesus' "I am" statements. These are assertions of Jesus' fundamental being, his ultimate grounding in the Father. Therefore, his love, his identity as the Good Shepherd, is neither a personal achievement nor a moral preference. In philosophic language, unconditional love is a metaphysical condition that all participate in, a condition that has been revealed in the life, death, and resurrection of Jesus. And sometimes metaphysics, the ultimate structure of the real, sweeps us along so forcefully that our cooperation, which always has to be there, is barely noticed. We cannot boast of this love, since it does not appear as something of our making. We can only humbly accept it as what is.

Stephen Levine tries to describe this situation: "You cannot unconditionally love someone. You can only *be* unconditional love. It is not a dualistic emotion. It is a sense of oneness with all that is. The experience of love arises when we surrender our separateness into the universal. It is a feeling of unity . . . It is not an emotion, it is a state of being . . . It is not so much that "two are as one" so much as it is 'the

One manifested as two'" (*Who Dies?: An Investigation of Conscious Living and Conscious Dying* [Garden City, N.Y.: Anchor Press/Doubleday, 1982] 75).

In the language of the Good Shepherd, it is the Father's knowing and loving of the Son in which the friends participate. This participation engenders a knowing and loving among themselves which creates the "one fold."

Beatrice Bruteau develops this ground of unconditional love in dynamic relational language. She begins by asserting that the spiritual reality of the human person is a "free act of self-giving." Jesus' statement that no one takes his life from him but he freely lays it down (v. 18) reflects this identity: "Each member of the person-community is a sheer 'I am,' beyond anything that can be said about me, beyond my descriptive attributes that can be predicted *of* me. I am simply my process, my activity. But what activity? This same naked "I am" is, simultaneously and equally, basically a radiant 'May you be—that is, the will (and the act) to extend being and life" (*The Grand Option: Personal Transformation and a New Creation* [Notre Dame, Ind.: University of Notre Dame Press, 2001] 67).

Jesus, the Good Shepherd, is most himself, completely at home in his identity as "I am" when he is laying down his life for his sheep. His "I am" is simultaneously a "May you be."

So it is with us. This understanding of who we are may be far removed from our standard identifications with our body, our personality, and our social positions. But we glimpse it every so often. Is it not attractive? Is it not the magnet Jesus said it was? Does not this revelation draw you to itself? If it does, an alternate translation of "good" in "I am the good shepherd" (vv. 11, 14) might be appropriate. The word *kalos* in Greek can also be translated "beautiful."

Fifth Sunday of Easter
John 15:1-8

Abiding in the Big Picture

A Spiritual Commentary

[Jesus said to his disciples:] "I am the true vine, and my Father is the vinegrower. He removes every branch in me that bears no fruit. Every branch that bears fruit he prunes to bear more fruit.

A vine connects the nutrient earth with the flowering branches. It is a medium, a conduit between a greater reality and the fruit that greater reality is able to produce in its derivative forms. In a similar way, Jesus is also a vine, a mediator, the connection between the divine source and creation. The divine-creation connection is always present, but it is not in the consciousness of all people. Jesus is true because he is conscious of this connection. The word for "true" in Greek means a lack of forgetfulness. The True Vine remembers at all times the communion between "all there is" and the "Source of All There Is." This means that the True Vine lives simultaneously in the flux of time and in the Eternal Now.

If the comparison between a vine and Jesus were to be strictly applied, the Father would be the earth. But this Gospel—as do all mystic poets—uses language freely, beyond the constraints of logic, to express and communicate spiritual perceptions. "The Father" is ultimately directing the life and love that flows through Jesus. Therefore, the Father is the vinegrower whose ultimate goal is to produce vintage wine. With this goal in mind, he cuts away fruitless branches and prunes fruitful branches to produce more.

The laws that govern biological life are not the laws that govern spiritual life. But there are similarities. The poet W. H. Auden succinctly described the dynamics of spiritual growth: "If we really want to live, we'd better start at once to try; if we don't, it doesn't matter, but we'd better start to die (in Mihaly Csikszentmihalyi, *Finding Flow: The Psychology of Engagement with Everyday Life* [New York: Basic Books, 1997] 1).

In spiritual development there is a need for desire (If we really want to live) and effort (we'd better start at once to try). If desire is missing, biological life goes on under its own steam. But spiritual life—the passion, pleasure, and purpose that suffuses biological life—recedes. A death is occurring, not of the biological organism but of the spiritual vibrancy that can bring out its full potential.

The vinegrower knows these laws of spiritual development. His cutting away of dead branches is not a whim or lack of compassion. It is a recognition that if desire or effort is missing, the dying process is under way. But if people are trying, and trying is the operative word, then pruning is opportune. Spiritual development is just that, development. Although a definite end is often envisioned (for example, union with God and the producing of good works), it is more an adventure in becoming than a step-by-step march toward a goal. There is always the possibility of more and better fruit. This is what guides the scissors of the vinegrower.

You have already been cleansed by the word I have spoken to you. Abide in me as I abide in you. Just as the branch cannot bear fruit by itself unless it abides in the vine, neither can you unless you abide in me. I am the vine, you are the branches. Those who abide in me and I in them bear much fruit, because apart from me you can do nothing. Whoever does not abide in me is thrown away like a branch and withers; such branches are gathered, thrown into the fire, and burned.

The disciples who are at supper with Jesus know the pruning process. Jesus' word has "cleansed" them. It has stripped away whatever would block the flow of life between them and Jesus and the Father. This "cutting away" makes them unencumbered, ready for the next step. The possibility of a mutual and reciprocal indwelling emerges. This is a very subtle and nuanced experience, but it is the essence of discipleship.

Although the text simply says, "Abide in me as I abide in you" (v. 4), I see Jesus making the first move, so to speak. His consciousness enters into their consciousness. It does not replace their consciousness. Rather it complements and elevates it. It does this by situating the contents of their consciousness within the permeating presence of the flow of life and love from the Source into Creation. This forms a new horizon to everything they see, and consequently changes everything they see. But this is not an automatic mental transformation. They must personally welcome and cooperate with the consciousness of Jesus. They have to freely abide in him as he is freely abiding in them.

Jesus is pointing to a spiritual possibility. But this possibility depends on the highest levels of human participation.

Consciousness illumines and directs action. If spiritual consciousness is present (mutual abiding), then the acting person is able to discern the divine direction in all things and act in accord with its intentions. If spiritual consciousness is not present, then the acting person stumbles along with many competing agendas, unable to focus on essentials. This is a hard truth. Inner work is as much needed as outer creativity. The contrasting images of "branches bearing much fruit" and "withered and burned branches" set out the options.

If you abide in me, and my words abide in you, ask for whatever you wish, and it will be done for you. My Father is glorified by this, that you bear fruit and become my disciples."

There is a subtle saying, "Make all your cares into a single care and God will see to all your cares." If you are abiding in the true vine, your desires will be purified. The words of the true vine will have created in you a single wish. That wish will be to glorify the Father, to mediate divine life and love into the world. Since this desire coincides with the divine will, it will be achieved. In its accomplishment you will bear fruit. It is through this fruit bearing process that you become disciples-in-the-making. Discipleship is not a status; it is a never-ending process.

Teaching

In *Holy the Firm*, Annie Dillard relates a vision of Christ emerging from the waters of baptism:

> [Christ] lifts from the water. Water beads on his shoulders. I see the water in balls as heavy as planets, a billion beads of water as weighty as worlds, and he lifts them up on his back as he rises. He stands wet in the water. Each one bead is transparent, and each has a world, or the same world, light and alive and apparent inside the drop: it is all there ever could be, moving at once, past and future, and all the people. I can look into any sphere and see people stream past me, and cool my eyes with colors and the sight of the world in spectacle perishing ever, and ever renewed. I do; I deepen into a drop and see all that time contains, all the faces and deeps of the worlds and all the earth's contents, every landscape and room, everything living or made or fashioned, all past and future stars, and especially faces, faces like the cells of everything, faces pouring past me talking, and going, and gone. And I am gone. (New York: Harper & Row Publishers, 1977] 67)

Annie Dillard sees all time and space being carried in drops of water on the back of Christ. She is lost in that vision. But if she could remain in it and become clear-eyed, she would grasp the true vine's plea to "Abide in me" (v. 4).

The one who says "I am the true vine" (v. 1) is the Word, of whose reality it is said, "In the beginning was the Word" (John 1:1). This does not mean "way back there at the dawn of time" was the Word. It means "always and everywhere is the Word." This Word is essential to God: "the Word was with God, and the Word was God" (John 1:1), and The Word is essential to Creation: "All things came into being through [this one], and without [this one] not one thing came into being" (John 1:3). It is this larger whole of God and creation that provides a different perspective on everything that is happening within creation. The big picture always changes the small picture.

Many people think the spiritual transformation of life begins with a breakthrough into big-picture seeing. Ordinary consciousness is acutely aware and highly invested in physical and social reality. In an image from a Native American story, we are like mice, our noses sniffing the earth, arranging and rearranging stuff on the ground. But then something happens. An event forces us to look up and see more than we had previously considered. This larger vision forces us to evaluate our previous preoccupation. Perhaps there is more to life than rearranging earth stuff.

Here begins the pruning that is the work of the vinegrower. Pruning is a matter of cutting away what might obstruct further growth. If we want to grow in the larger vision and the works it inspires, most probably we have to engage in a process of letting go. Spiritual traditions name this process "detachment." Detachment leads to emptiness. Emptiness leads to openness and receptivity. Consciousness is more spacious. The big picture—the continual flow of life and love from the Source into Creation—is accommodated and becomes more and more persuasive. Abiding in the vine begins to happen. Can fruit be far behind?

Sixth Sunday of Easter

John 15:9-17

Living in the Love Chain

A Spiritual Commentary

[Jesus said to his disciples:] "As the Father has loved me, so I have loved you: abide in my love. If you keep my commandments, you will abide in my love, just as I have kept my Father's commandments and abide in his love. I have said these things to you so that my joy may be in you, and that your joy may be complete.

This is my commandment, that you love one another as I have loved you.

Some philosophers are convinced that the human person is naturally religious. This is not the same as belonging to a religion or being thoroughly convinced of a personal God. It means that an examined life discovers an intuitive sense that there is a higher order of things, and that human well-being depends on people aligning themselves with that order. To be separated from this higher order is to be lost; to positively participate in this order is to be found.

In the Christian revelation this higher order is a proactive love that is embodied and revealed in Jesus. People do not have to search for it as if it were not searching for them. Also, its rules are simple. People must learn to live in their sphere in the way this proactive love lives. There is a story about a king riding in a coach on a rainy day. He sees a poor man walking on the road and desires to give him a ride and keep him out of the rain. But the man is leery. "What must I do to get this ride," the man says. "Only accept it," says the King. The key to relating to the higher order is to learn to receive its love.

But the King's response is only half accurate. Once the love is accepted, a chain effect takes place. As Jesus received the love of the Father, he loved his disciples with that same love. This is not an isolated moment but a steady state of affairs. Jesus abides in the love of the Father because he keeps his commandment to pass that love on to the disciples. The disciples will abide in Jesus' love if they keep his commandment. His commandment is the same as the Father's commandment: love as you have been loved.

The purpose of this revelation of how the higher order works is joy. Jesus' joy, the activation of his essential nature, is to pour the love he has received from the Father into his disciples. Therefore, they share not only the love but the joy of the love giver. But this communicated joy of Jesus is only an initial taste. The law of completion means that you only understand what you have received when you give it away. Therefore, the disciples will enter into the fullness of joy when they love one another as Jesus has loved them. Living the life of the higher order entails experiencing its mode of fulfillment. It enters more deeply into its own joy when the love it gives is received and then given to another. This is eternal life: the endless receiving and giving of love.

> **No one has greater love than this, to lay down one's life for one's friends. You are my friends if you do what I command you. I do not call you servants any longer, because the servant does not know what the master is doing: but I have called you friends, because I have made known to you everything I have heard from my Father.**

If people grasp and understand themselves as links in the love chain—from the Father to Jesus, from Jesus to them, from them to one another—they move from anxious, separate living into holy communion. There is no need to grab, or hold, or possess this life, as if it were a scarce commodity. It is abundant beyond measure. God does not measure the Spirit. If you know this, in the deep sense of having comprehended and enacted this law of the love chain, you have grasped what Jesus is ultimately about. And if you know what Jesus is ultimately about, you will know what the Father is ultimately about. This thoroughly realized and integrated knowledge collapses the separation of the higher order from the lower order. There are no more servants who are ignorant of the ways of the higher order. There are only friends moving effortlessly in the Father's love.

> **You did not choose me but I chose you. And I appointed you to go forth and bear fruit, fruit that will last, so that the Father will give you whatever you ask him in my name. I am giving you these commands so that you may love one another."**

When anyone in the lower order begins to grasp the laws of the higher order, they are immediately overwhelmed. Living the love chain of the higher order in the tumult and tension of the lower order seems impossible. In the face of this quaking, Jesus reminds his friends of some basics. They are not intruding with lower order arrogance on higher order excellence. They are not overreaching, puffed up with pride. They have been chosen by Jesus and the Father to enact the love chain. And the Father does not ask people to do things for which they are unprepared. Therefore, if they ask the Father for what they need to make this happen in the way Jesus made it happen, the Father will respond. After all, it is an adventure that the Father started—this loving one another.

Teaching

In the beginning we were both the storyteller and the "storylistener." In the end we will be both the storyteller and the storylistener. Right now, we are both the storyteller and the storylistener.

A constant inner dialogue accompanies our outer comings and goings. In the inner depths of ourselves we are carrying on a conversation. Sometimes this secret exchange slips out the lips. Someone within ear shot says, "What did you say?" We are unembarrassed and simply explain, knowing the person will understand, "Oh, I was just talking to myself." As a friend of mine says, "Sometimes it is the best conversation you can get." Whether it is the best conversation is debatable. But it is an influential conversation. What happens in the depths shapes what appears on the surface.

A good deal of this inner conversation is telling ourselves a story to which we avidly listen. As we wake, wash, work, love, and play, we are telling ourselves the story of who we are. "I am someone who does not do well on Monday mornings so I have to go slow . . ." "I am someone who works at a job that does not maximize my talents . . ." "I am someone who probably married too soon and am stuck with someone who doesn't excite me . . ." "I am someone who is getting older and I'm not getting out of life all I wanted . . ." In the inner depths the story lamp is always lit, and neither storyteller nor storylistener fall asleep.

This inner storytelling and storylistening process can take a negative turn. We remember and replay within ourselves events that have made an impact. These events come together to tell us the story of who we are. However, often memorable events are times when we have been shocked and humiliated, when our shortcomings and mistakes have broken into our consciousness with such force they cannot be expelled. Therefore, the story we learn to tell ourselves is a skewed version of who we are. We may even know that these are lopsided stories, but they are persuasive tales. The strange thing about negative stories is that they always promote themselves as the real picture. They appear as the raw, unvarnished truth before any "spin."

Can we tell ourselves the story that Jesus tells his disciples and that he wants them to tell to others? Can we tell our story as a link in the love chain? If we do, will it be persuasive enough to modify our negative interior stories that are so prevalent that they seem to tell themselves? In the language of the Gospel, can we actually experience ourselves as chosen for love?

A predictable way to proceed would be to shine the flashlight of memory into darkened corners of the past, to retrieve forgotten moments of love. Then we would tell these moments to ourselves until we became convinced we had been loved and that this love is foundational to who we are. Identified as receivers of love, we would recall all our own efforts to love. If failures appeared more often than successes, we would note that we continued to try and, still today, so much of what we do is our attempt to love and give life to others. And if consciousness is supple, we might become aware of a higher order of support for receiving and giving, the ground of the whole process and the endless energy of its operations. We would be retelling our story to ourselves and shifting the weight from negative and neutral experiences to times of love.

But there might be a shortcut.

James P. Mackey has some interesting things to say about how Jesus passed on the experience of the Father's love:

> In the end the only way to give people the experience of all life and existence as enabling and inspiring grace, the only way to give them the experience of being themselves grace and treasure, is to treat them as treasure and to be gracious to them . . . The sun may indeed rise on the evil and the good, and the same rain refresh the just and the unjust (Matt 5:45), but the lesson will likely be lost on me unless the warmth of another human being envelops me, unless some other human person refresh the weariness of my defeated days. I simply will not feel my own life, my own self, as grace or gift of God, unless someone values me. [This reverses logic] . . . The logic should surely read: first feel all life and existence as gift or grace, then feeling the grace of God, be gracious to others. Not, first feel the grace of some human presence, feel forgiven,

accepted, served, then begin to feel all life and existence as grace, and then feel inspired to be gracious to others. But it is really a universal human idiosyncrasy that is operative here, not a matter of logic. It may well be that some rare individual, perhaps Jesus himself, followed the former logic, having a power of perception and evaluation and acceptance far beyond the ordinary. Indeed in the case of Jesus, it is very likely that his power to value went far beyond anyone's ability to value him. But for the rest of us, we can only sense ourselves and our world valued and cherished by God when we feel cherished and valued by others. (*Jesus: The Man and The Myth: A Contemporary Christology* [New York: Paulist Press, 1979] 170).

This reflection opens up two more doors to the possibility of living in the love chain. First, choose one person who has loved you, cherished you, treated you like treasure, and see in that person a revelation of the universal love of God. Do not treat all people and events equally. Some people are sacramental carriers of divine love. Their human ability to love is highly developed, and it has tapped into a divine grounding and communicates more than just the care of one individual. Recall those people and meditate on their presence and words. Do not write them off as a lone voice of respect in a chorus of indifference and neglect. They are the voice in the wilderness (see Mark 1:3 and parallels) that not only prepares for the love of the Lord but provides it.

Second, do not think Jesus is so special that he is an exemption. Some people sense love at the center of life and existence in a direct way. They know the "Father in heaven" (Matt 6:9) even when the "father on earth" is either missing or dismissive. Just hearing of the Father in heaven may ignite the fire of love and bring people into full participation in the love chain. It does not matter how we enter into the love chain. It only matters that we enter into the love chain.

Seventh Sunday of Easter

John 17:11-19 *LM* • John 17:6-19 *RCL*

Uniting and Separating

A Spiritual Commentary

For users of the *Lectionary for Mass* and the *Revised Common Lectionary:*

[Jesus looked up to heaven and prayed: "Father,]

For users of the *Revised Common Lectionary:*

I have made your name known to those whom you gave me from the world. They were yours, and you gave them to me, and they have kept your word. Now they know that everything you have given me is from you; for the words that you gave to me I have given to them, and they have received them and know in truth that I came from you; and they have believed that you sent me. I am asking on their behalf; I am not asking on behalf of the world, but on behalf of those whom you gave me, because they are yours. All mine are yours, and yours are mine; and I have been glorified in them. And now I am no longer in the world, but they are in the world, and I am coming to you.

For users of the *Lectionary for Mass* and the *Revised Common Lectionary:*

Holy Father, protect them in your name that you have given me, so that they may be one, as we are one. While I was with them, I protected them in your name that you have given me. I guarded them, and not one of them was lost except the one destined to be lost, so that the scripture might be fulfilled. But now I am coming to you, and I speak these things in the world so that they may have my joy made complete in themselves. I have given them your word, and the world has hated them because they do not belong to the world, just as I do not belong to the world. I am not asking you to take them out of the world, but I ask you to protect them from the evil one. They do not belong to the world, just as I do not belong to the world. Sanctify them in the truth; your word is truth. As you have sent me into the

**world, so I have sent them into the world. And for their sakes I
sanctify myself, so that they also may be sanctified in truth.**

The mystical vision of St. John's Gospel is caught in this swirl of
language. Although there is a careful structure to this prayer for the
disciples, the unyielding logic of going from a first thought to a second
thought to a third thought is frustrated. The overall impression is a
spiral rather than a straight line. The words fall over one another. They
forge ahead, and then retreat to savor again what they savored before.
They are a river, opening tributary after tributary. As each flow of
thought and feeling moves away, it somehow mysteriously returns.
Everything is in everything else.

To the hyper-rational part of our minds, this language may seem
repetitious and incoherent, a basket of interlocking and squirming
snakes. But to the starving mystic in each of us, they are a feast. They
struggle to express the intuited truths of spiritual indwelling. If we
would engage these words, we should turn off our computer. Instead,
remember our first kiss and times we were sure we could touch the sky
if we stood on our toes and stretched.

When Jesus looks up to heaven and prays, he reflects the traditional
description of prayer as "raising the mind and heart to God." He clears
consciousness of its clamoring concerns and cultivates a steady awareness of what is essential and everywhere—divine reality. "Looking to
heaven" does not mean leaving the earth. Rather it is an appreciation
of the earth from heaven's perspective. It sees, hears, smells, touches,
and tastes the earth as a creation sustained and transformed by its
Source and Destiny.

This Source and Destiny is imaged as Father, a generative love. To
unfold the image further, this generative love supplies the seed, as all
fathers do. But the seed must be received and nurtured if it is to grow.
Therefore, the seed is looking for good ground in order to produce
fruit. In other words, generative love is a lure in the comings and goings of people and seeks acknowledgment and loyalty. The prayer of
Jesus will reveal the desires of an ultimate generative love and the way
those desires are engaged in the tumultuous affairs of earth.

Jesus the revealer has whispered the inner name of the Father
(Love) into the waiting ears of those whom Father has sent to him. This
coming together of Jesus and those who are attracted to him was not a
chance happening. Those who have come to Jesus and received him
already knew his loving Father in an inchoate way. In fact, they had

kept the Father's word, a word that readied them for the incarnate Word, the full manifestation of divine love. When the words poured forth from the mouth of Jesus, they were a love letter from the generative power they had already intuited. They immediately knew who had sent Jesus, and they remained in him. In doing so, they welcomed divine generative love in a full and intense way and brought it to birth on the earth.

Therefore, the glue between Jesus and the disciples has always been the revelation of divine love, a divine love that created all things and has become flesh in Jesus. But now a new situation is imminent. Jesus is returning to the Father. The great fear is that the loss of Jesus will mean the loss of the revelation. Jesus was the mediator; and without the mediator how will the disciples and the Father remain in touch? Said another way, have the words that Jesus has spoken been fully received? Have they transformed the consciousness of the disciples into the same consciousness that was in Jesus? If they have, then the loss of Jesus will not mean the loss of the revelation. The disciples will maintain the consciousness of being in Jesus and in the Father, even without the physical presence of Jesus to support and guide them. In short, they will "believe without seeing." Near the end of the gospel this inner state is declared "blessed" (John 20:29).

However, even if the disciples have temporarily realized the generative love of the Father and integrated it into their lives, they may not persevere in this spiritual work of incarnating divine love. They are in the world, surrounded by darkened consciousness. This darkened consciousness only knows how things are separate from one another. It does not know the generative love that sustains all things. Therefore, it flails about in violence and hatred. In fact, it has a particular animus against those who know and live the revelation. Their light threatens the darkness; and although the darkness cannot overcome the light, it never tires of trying. In this situation the Father and the disciples must stay exceptionally close. The competing consciousness of separation and violence is an active agent of evil. Only a stronger consciousness of divine love will protect the disciples.

Jesus has always been aware of the world's seductive pull, of the fall back into darkness after illumination, so he has exercised vigilance, protecting and guarding his disciples. None have been lost except the one whose character it was to be lost. However, even that tragedy fits into a larger divine plan that could be discerned through a deep reading of the Scriptures. Therefore, after Jesus' departure, this special care must be continued directly by the Father. Of course, it will continue; generative love never ceases to be generative. The purpose of Jesus praying for its continuance is for the disciples to overhear this request. In hearing the prayer, they will know that they must open themselves to ever deeper realizations and integrations of divine generative love.

When the disciples are consciously centered in the indwelling unity of the Father and the Son, the threat of the world becomes a promise. Therefore, the disciples are not to leave the world in search of heaven. The world is precisely where the disciples belong. They are not to flee the darkness; but, as Jesus has done, they are to bring light into the darkness. But in order to do that, they must return again and again to the Father. They must be "sanctified in truth" (v. 17), indwelling with Holy Father and the Son. This sanctification will unfold into the energy of mission.

Where does this prayer lead?

The disciples are to become the body of Christ in the world when the body of Jesus is no longer physically available. When this happens, Jesus' joy (generated by his oneness with the Father and his mission in the world) may become full in the disciples who are one with the Father and Jesus and sent on mission into the world. This prayer of Jesus is a passionate plea that the purposes of eternal generative love may be served in the perpetually perishing affairs of time.

Teaching

In writing about sexual intercourse the poet, Anne Sexton, did not focus on desire, arousal, or orgasm. Rather it was the state of union between the lovers that fascinated her, a state of union that was doomed because God would "untie the knot." Her lament was that sexual communion could not be sustained. It breaks apart, and the ecstasy of union returns to a lonely state of separation.

This pattern of union and separation also applies to interpersonal psychological connections. For example, we have a conversation where the sharing is so profound we feel we are inside the other person, sharing life from his or her perspective. Then the dialogue ends, and we go our separate ways. The next time we see that person we realize there is a bond. Although the closeness was in the past, it can be remembered and drawn upon. The "something special" lingers.

These times of togetherness are usually highly prized. We remember them as times when we were really alive and we entertain them in memory, daydreaming against isolation. We often go further than that. We seek out conditions that will allow them to happen again. However, these attempts to relive past intimate moments are usually ill advised. We find that times of togetherness are not capable of being planned. We cannot manipulate situations, or even create optimal conditions and wait. So we settle for an inner alertness, a readiness for union. When the possibility opens, we want to be responsive. We want to receive the gift when it arrives. But even if we do learn to flow with the lures of union, the pattern will prevail. God will untie the knot.

This is the way of things in the world of time. In his conversation with the woman at the well, Jesus points to this inevitability in another image. "Everyone who drinks of this water will be thirsty again" (John 4:13). In other words, the slaked thirst returns, and the pattern is established: thirst/slaked, thirst/slaked. Life in time is characterized by repetition. But Jesus quickly contrasts this pattern with a much different state: "but those who drink of the water that I will give will never be thirsty" (John 4:14). This points to a spiritual dimension that is not subject to alterations. The reason is: "The water that I will give will become in them a spring of water gushing up into eternal life" (John 4:14). The spiritual dimension is a giving that keeps on giving. In terms of the pattern of union and separation, it is a union that unfolds into greater and greater intimacy and never breaks apart into separation. In the spiritual dimension of life God does not untie the knot.

The metaphysical structure of reality may be a continuous flow of spiritual life from the Source into its creation. This flow is always looking for participation from creation according to its varied capacities. Plants have the capacity to cooperate more than rocks; animals more than plants; humans more than animals. Human participation presupposes consciousness and freedom. It is this consciousness and freedom that the Gospel of St. John targets. The law might have come through Moses, but "grace and truth came through Jesus Christ" (John 1:17). Jesus revealed the free flow of Spirit into creation. He called others to that same consciousness and to make free choices in the physical and social realms influenced by that consciousness.

However, we are only intermittently aware of this spiritual dimension. As the Sufi poet Rumi says, "It is a secret we sometimes see and then not." In other words, we alternate between "unitive consciousness" and "separation consciousness." For most of us separation consciousness dominates. When we open to grace and find ourselves in unitive consciousness, we can hardly believe it. We are tempted to dismiss the experience. "It must be something we ate." When we put this fleeting sense of union against our persistent sense of separation, it is rarely persuasive.

But perhaps it should be. Maybe the darkness has been pushed back; maybe dawn has broken the long reign of night. We might have glimpsed the ground of our other experiences of union. Our moments of sexual and psychological union might be reflections in temporal life of our eternal union with the generative love of Spirit. We are not isolated monads. Rather we are people connected to an ultimate spiritual Source; and through that Source we are connected to one another and the earth in the social, psychological, and physical dimension. If we can entertain this possibility, we may answer Jesus' prayer with a more convincing "Amen." Jesus always knew that God answered him because he spoke divine words from God's heart and not human words to God's ears. He was not pleading; he was revealing. I imagine the intensity of this prayer for us, his disciples, was because he was less certain about us.

Tenth Sunday in Ordinary Time

Proper 5

Mark 3:20-35

Belonging to the Will

A Spiritual Commentary

[T]he crowd came together again, so that Jesus and the disciples could not even eat.

When his family heard it, they went out to restrain him, for people were saying, "He has gone out of his mind."

Flocking and fallout!

People continue to be attracted to Jesus. They are so eager to hear him that they push into Jesus' home and keep him and his disciples from eating. This assertive behavior may simply show how fervently the crowd desired to be with Jesus. But it may also signal that they sought to share in the food of Jesus and his disciples. This food, of course, is the experience of the kingdom, its preaching, teaching, and deeds of power. At the end of this section Jesus will look at them and say, "Here are my mothers and brothers!" (v. 34). Obviously, they have been eating something.

Yet at the same time as some people are attracted, others are repelled. They see him as deranged, someone who has so contradicted the mores of society and offended powerful people that he must be "out of his mind" (v. 21). The mind he is out of is the conventional societal mind that accepts the present social arrangements and their theological justifications. This "not playing by the established rules" alarms his family. Since he belongs to them, they decide on an intervention. If they can keep him from saying and doing what is so confrontational, they will at least have exercised some damage control. They make their way toward the house that holds their offensive son and brother (see v. 31).

And the scribes who came down from Jerusalem said, "He has Beelzebul, and by the ruler of the demons he casts out demons."

At least one of the reasons Jesus is judged as out of his mind is that he has angered the religious leaders of Jerusalem. Scribes have arrived with a more serious charge than momentary mental maladjustment. Their contention is that that Jesus' ability to cast out demons is because the prince of demons inhabits him. This attempt to discredit him is intrinsically connected to what most offends them about Jesus. Their deeply felt need is to remain pure. Their logic is: contact with demons makes one impure, so demons should be avoided. Of course, demons do not appear naked. They need bodies to inhabit. So avoiding demons entails avoiding people who manifest signs that they are in contact with unclean spirits. Therefore, many people are ostracized and shunned.

Jesus is diametrically opposed to this theological accommodation with the demons, leaving them free to harass whom they want. He engages demons; he does not walk around them. In the minds of the scribes this can mean only one thing: he contaminates himself. He cannot be considered holy or one who is seeking holiness. The fact that he casts out the demons and restores people to wholeness does not mitigate this basic impurity. It only means he has power in the demonic world. In fact, given the fact that he can order demons around suggests that it is the prince of demons who works through him.

> **And he called them to him and spoke to them in parables, "How can Satan cast out Satan? If a kingdom is divided against itself, that kingdom cannot stand. And if a house is divided against itself, that house will not be able to stand. And if Satan has risen up against himself and is divided, he cannot stand, but his end has come. But no one can enter a strong man's house and plunder his property without first tying up the strong man; then indeed the house can be plundered.**
>
> **Truly I tell you, people will be forgiven for their sins and whatever blasphemies they utter; but whoever blasphemes against the Holy Spirit can never have forgiveness, but is guilty of an eternal sin"—for they had said, "He has an unclean spirit."**

Jesus not only engages demons, he also engages spurious scribal theology. He calls them into the house because many of the people who crowd in to see Jesus have heard their charges. If those attracted to Jesus are going to remain attracted, Jesus has to undercut the scribal reasoning and propose another interpretation of his demon-ridding activity.

The scribal rendition is seriously flawed. If what they propose is true, it goes counter to a universal experience. "If a kingdom is divided against itself" (v. 24), it will fall. Since the demonic agenda is to inhabit people, it is hardly likely that Satan would decide to expel his minions. Satan is not known for self-defeating behavior. So the power at work in Jesus is not the power of Beelzebul.

What is really happening is a test of strength. Satan is a powerful adversary. He possesses people, holds them captive, locks them in his house. But Jesus is more powerful than Satan. He overcomes him. The strong one is bound by one stronger (Mark 1:7). Once bound, Jesus takes back Satan's captives. He plunders his possessions. The scribal theology is so frightened of demons that it abandons people. Jesus' theology is so solicitous of people it never backs off liberation. Jesus is able to "release to the captives" (Luke 4:18) because his strength comes from the Holy Spirit (Mark 1:8; 10).

There is a great deal at stake in these conflicting interpretations of Jesus' demon-ridding actions. If the religious leaders and those whom they convince interpret the exorcisms as Satan redeploying his forces, they may be irretrievably lost. Most surely, God is infinitely forgiving. But under certain circumstances this forgiveness may not be able to be accessed. If people are so benighted that they see good and call it evil, they simply will not ask for forgiveness. Why should they? They think they are opposing evil, although in reality they are opposing the work of the Holy Spirit. They mistake the presence of the Holy Spirit for the presence of an unclean spirit. They are in the grip of 360-degree confusion that the Gospels call hardness of heart. This confusion may be permanent.

> Then his mother and his brothers came; and standing outside, they sent to him and called him. A crowd was sitting around him; and they said to him, "Your mother and your brothers and sisters are outside, asking for you."
>
> And he replied, "Who are my mother and my brothers?"
>
> And looking at those who sat around him, he said, "Here are my mother and my brothers! Whoever does the will of God is my brother and sister and mother."

Jesus' family finally arrives, but they do not go into the house. They are not open to listening to Jesus' proclamation and teaching. Instead, they ask Jesus to come out of his house, to come back to them and their conventional way of thinking and acting. But things have gone too far. Jesus cannot go back home.

In a very dramatic scene Jesus starts a new family. He has been told by the people sitting around him, those inside the house, "Your mother and your brothers and sisters are outside" (v. 32). If people are outside the house, if they refuse to hear the teaching and engage the work of the kingdom, even though they are related by blood, they are not Jesus' family. So Jesus' question, "Who is my mother and my brothers?" (v. 33) sets the stage for a radical consciousness shift. He answers his own question with his eyes. He looks at all those who are with him and startlingly states that they are his family. But there is nothing automatic about this new family; the bond is not the accident of blood. It is their shared commitment to and cooperation with the will of God. They belong to Jesus by doing the will of God as he does it.

Teaching

I have often been one of the insistent crowd, pushing into the intimate space between Jesus and his disciples, putting my own need for a spiritual teaching before their recurrent physical need for food. Perhaps better said, I did not want them to eat without me. I have opened their story again and again, hoping to find them at table and sit with them, to break the bread of understanding and to drink the wine of love. Jesus always obliges. He cannot refuse a beggar.

But every time I am in the house of Jesus and he gazes around at the people he has silenced with a question, I sense the stirrings of a new community. This community includes all those I see face-to-face, all those I love and sacrifice for, and who love and sacrifice for me. But it grows beyond that. It includes those I merely hear about. But when I hear about them, I intuitively know we have eaten together. Then it goes beyond even that. In this community there are those I have never heard about but whom I know have existed and could not resist the lure. It is all the people who belong to the "Will of God."

The family of belonging to the Will is an invisible and universal community that spans space and time. These people—past, present, and future—act in consort with God. This co-acting with God often begins with a flickering intuition. Alfred North Whitehead identified this intuition when he described religion as

> the vision of something which stands beyond, behind, and within, the
> passing flux of immediate things; something which is real, and yet wait-

ing to be realized; something which is a remote possibility, and yet the greatest of all present facts; something that gives meaning to all that passes, and yet eludes apprehension; something whose possession is the final good, and yet is beyond all reach; something which is the ultimate ideal, and the hopeless quest. ("Science and the Modern World," trans. R.F.C. Hull and Alan Crick in *20th Century Philosophy and Religion* [Chicago: Encyclopædia Britannica, 1990] 275)

This intuition creates a desire to participate in this reality. Some call this desire the "quest for salvation." But no matter what it is called, once it is activated, it nags us to go further. And we find ourselves interrupting the meals of one who says he knows what that something is and what that something is doing.

In the house of Jesus that something is revealed as the Holy Spirit, the liberating presence of God to all the peoples of the earth. The Holy Spirit is at work alleviating, accompanying, and transforming physical and social suffering.

Holy Spirit,
giving life to all life,
moving all creatures,
root of all things,
washing them clean,
wiping out their mistakes,
healing their wounds,
you are our true life,
luminous, wonderful,
awakening the heart
from its ancient sleep.

(Hildegard of Bingen in *The Enlightened Heart:
An Anthology of Sacred Poetry*, ed. Stephen Mitchell
[New York: Harper & Row, 1989] 42)

This is the something we sense: a Holy Spirit restoring life and calling us to cooperate. Wherever and whenever we hear and respond to this lure, we enter into the family of Jesus. Joining the work of the Holy Spirit is what makes us a brother, sister, and mother to Jesus. The mission creates the family.

Sometimes I talk this way in public, and what I say is often translated into "people sharing the same values." I guess this is true as far as it goes. But it must be stressed that these values are not arbitrary. They are the effulgence in time and space of what is eternal and ultimate.

Also, when we talk about a community of shared values, we instinctively move toward social organization. We naturally want to lift up saints and to handicap favorites. But in this community of those who belong to the Will, we should avoid comparative measures. We should even avoid ascribing permanent status to those who belong to the Will, for that will quickly devolve into the split between those who do and those who do not.

Instead, we should simply tell stories of times when our rebellious and obedient wills became more obedient, when the Spirit worked through us. I have heard it said that strictly speaking there are no enlightened people, only enlightened behavior. And Flannery O'Connor, the Southern, Gothic-short-story writer and novelist, once remarked, "When the sun hits the trees a certain way, even the meanest of them sparkles." I like "belonging to the Will" to be open ended and surprising.

There is a man in Rwanda who kept people alive during a genocide; a woman who held the hand of a dying man so tenderly he found peace; a ten-year-old insider who reached out to a ten-year-old outsider; a grandmother who keeps in loving contact with the children her son abandoned; that same abandoning father helping a coworker in depression; the depressed coworker thanking a cleaning lady so profoundly that she cried. Everyone gets to belong to the Will at one time or another; and when we hear of another's momentary belonging, we know the answer to Jesus' question, "Who is mother and brother and sister to me?"

Eleventh Sunday in Ordinary Time

Proper 6

Mark 4:26-34

Growing Mysteriously

A Spiritual Commentary

[Such a large crowd gathered around Jesus that he got into a boat and began to teach them using parables.] Jesus said, "The kingdom of God is as if someone would scatter seed on the ground, and would sleep and rise night and day, and the seed would sprout and grow, he does not know how. The earth produces of itself, first the stalk, then the head, then the full grain in the head. But when the grain is ripe, at once he goes in with his sickle, because the harvest has come."

[Jesus] also said, "With what can we compare the kingdom of God, or what parable will we use for it? It is like a mustard seed, which, when sown upon the ground, is the smallest of all the seeds on earth; yet when it is sown it grows up and becomes the greatest of all shrubs, and puts forth large branches, so that the birds of the air can make nests in its shade."

With many such parables he spoke the word to them, as they were able to hear it; he did not explain to them except in parables, but he explained everything in private to his disciples.

We have to take seriously the concluding, summary comment of the storyteller. Jesus used parables to teach about the kingdom of God. People on the outside heard the parables and interpreted them as best they could. But the disciples on the inside received private instructions. Jesus unpacked the imaginative language and went into greater depth. Therefore, parables are spoken in two interpersonal contexts: Jesus and casual listeners, and Jesus and serious apprentices. Casual listeners represent ordinary awareness, stubbornly attached to the surface of events. Serious apprentices represent spiritual awareness, willing and eager to find deeper meanings.

Why are parables difficult to understand?

Parables take situations from the material and/or social dimensions of life and imaginatively describe them so that they illumine the spiritual dimension of life. What happens in the parable is "something like" what happens in the realm of the Spirit. But it is also "something unlike" what happens. The key is for the listeners to grasp the "something like." However, if they have no knowledge of the spiritual realm, they will be confused about the connection or take the "something unlike" and try to apply it. In minds that are only aware of material and social realms, these parables become comments on farming and agriculture.

The imaginative form of the parable deepens this foundational situation. Images are open-ended. They can be developed in many different ways. Parables open a territory, but they do not map it. They discipline the mind to look in a certain direction, but they do not tell you all you will see. This means that the teacher who uses parables almost certainly must provide further instruction. The odds that the casual listener will grasp the connection and develop it correctly are slim.

So why do spiritual teachers use parables?

Ordinary consciousness is familiar with the material and social realms, but it is unfamiliar with the spiritual realm. So it is useful to use the familiar to point to the unfamiliar. Also, when listeners initially grasp the connection between the parable and the spiritual realm, it has the impact of both a discovery and a revelation. It appears to be both something we have found and something that has been given to us. And it bursts into consciousness as an "aha" moment that has the possibility of changing consciousness in a permanent way.

This change of consciousness, however, will probably not happen unless the teacher is present to celebrate, promote, and extend the new awareness. The teacher has a profound grasp of the consciousness that the parables are meant to serve. Although each person who has "eyes to see and ears to hear" (see Matt 13:15-16; Mark 4:9, 23) can take some spiritual food from the parable, greater growth takes place only with the guidance of the teacher. So to say, Jesus "taught them . . . in parables" (Mark 4:2) is a compressed statement of an ongoing interpersonal process by which Jesus transferred his own consciousness to his disciples.

In a previous passage Jesus told the parable of the sower, seeds, and soils. Then when he was alone with his disciples, they asked him about the parable (Mark 4:3-10). He said to them, "To you has been given the secret of the kingdom of God, but for those outside, everything comes in parables" (Mark 4:11). Then he explained the parable, especially he unraveled the spiritual dynamics of the first three soils (Mark 4:14-20). So the disciples and the readers were both privileged to hear the parable and to be instructed by the teacher.

However, the explanation of the fourth soil, the good soil, was not very illuminating: "hear the word and accept it and bear fruit, thirty and sixty and a hundredfold" (Mark 4:20). This remark is enigmatic and needs exploration. The parables of the productive earth (seed growing secretly) and the transformative earth (mustard seed) do this work of further elaboration. They unpack how the good soil works, how an accepting and fruitful consciousness is developed and sustained. However, we, as readers, are told Jesus continued to privately instruct his disciples on these parables. But we are no longer privy to those instructions. We are on our own—not an optimal place to be with parables.

The first parable about seed and soil urges us to trust a natural growth process. Once contact is made between the seed (the word) and the good earth (the receptive human heart), a process of development will begin. This process is more mysterious than we know and we should not interfere in it. The sower sleeps and rises "night and day," not knowing how sprouting and growing are happening (v. 27). "Sower control" will not contribute to growth.

There is a parable about a man who sowed seed in his field and every day uncovered the soil to see how the seed was doing. He wanted to catch each moment in the interaction between seed and soil and intervene in their natural lovemaking. He did not trust the seed and soil to produce growth without his ongoing adjustments. Nothing grew.

However, the trusted growth of seed and good earth together has a pattern. It is a pattern of unfolding augmentation. The seed and good earth produce "first the stalk, then the head, then the full grain in the head" (v. 28). Finally, there will be ripeness, harvest, and the seed will have become bread. If interfering with the process is discouraged, cooperating with the process is prescribed as noticing the mystery. The greater is contained in the lesser and will emerge out it. In other words, the whole growth process is not known at once and should not be envisioned at once. The full grain is in the head, and the head is in the stalk. The hundredfold is in the sixtyfold, and the sixtyfold is in the thirtyfold.

This is a consoling teaching to those who have heard the parable of the sower, seed, and soils and know only too well the failure of the first three soils. (See the interpretation of the Lukan rendition of this parable in *The Spiritual Wisdom of the Gospels for Christian Preachers and Teachers, Year A, On Earth As It Is in Heaven,* 16–20.) Becoming good earth that produces fruit does not mean directing the whole process or even understanding it completely. Rather it involves trust and cooperation. In particular, it entails paying patient attention to each increment. Once the seed is sown you will learn about the stalk; once the stalk appears you will discover the head; once the head is known the full grain will emerge. Of course, the goal of the whole process is not individual development, but how your ripeness will be harvested and become bread for others.

The second parable is also reassuring. Their initial grasp of Jesus' teaching is minimal. As many episodes in Mark's story attest, there is more confusion and incomprehension than there is light. What they now know is as small as a mustard seed. But the greater is contained in the lesser. What is important is that the lesser is sown in the good earth. It is the act of sowing that stimulates the unfolding. This has happened, so the seed will grow. Once again, the outcome will not be individual development, but an enhanced ability to be shade and comfort for others.

The Gospels make it clear that correctly responding to Jesus, accepting his invitation, is a stretch for ordinary consciousness. Our minds are pedestrian; his words are wings. He sees more in us than we see in ourselves. It is not easy to know yourself as mustard seed and be in the presence of someone who sees you as the sheltering tree of life. Paul Murray's poem, "Know Yourself," captures some of this tension:

> There is a world within you
>   no one has ever seen,
> a voice no one has ever heard,
>   not even you.
> As yet unknown
>   you are your own seer,
> your own interpreter.
>   And so, with eyes and ears
> grown sharp for voice or sign,
>   listen well—
> not to these words
>   but to that inward voice,
> that impulse beating in your heart
>   like a far wave.
> Turn to that source, and you
>   will find

what no one has ever found,
a ground within you
no one has ever seen,
a world beyond the limits
of your dream's horizon.

(*The Absent Fountain* [Dublin: Dedalus Press, 1991] 12)

Teaching

Sometimes spiritual teachings are given in direct discourse. At other times, parables can be clustered together, each one illuminating and extending the other. In that spirit, the following story is offered as complement to the two parables of Jesus:

> Three men who lived along a caravan route in the desert. They made their living buying and selling trinkets and goods from the caravan passengers. However, they dreamed of being gardeners. But how could they be gardeners in a desert?
>
> Then they heard the master gardener would be coming through on the next caravan. They decided to invite him to teach them the art of gardening. The master gardener heard about these aspiring gardeners. So when his caravan arrived, he decided to visit them.
>
> He arrived at the house of the first man and asked him, "Do you wish to grow something in this deserted place?" The man knew this question would be asked and he had given it considerable thought. He realized that he liked to daydream about gardening and read books about gardening. But he did not really want to be a gardener. He told the master gardener, "No."
>
> The master gardener smiled and said, "Fine." Then he left and proceeded to the home of the second man.
>
> The second man had also envisioned what the conversation with the master gardener would be like. They would begin with the practicalities of the gardening—how to open the earth, how to plant the seed, how to close the earth, how and when to water it, what to do when it began to grow. Then they would soar from practicalities to philosophy and talk about gardening as a way of life, finishing with a prayer to the Great Gardener in the Sky. This is what the second man expected.
>
> However, when the master gardener arrived, he asked, "Do you want to grow something in this deserted place?" The man replied, "Yes" and was about to go further when the master gardener held up his hand and simply said, "Wait here. I will be back."

The master gardener returned two days later and said, "There is a wheel in the back of your future garden. Turn it one full turn every afternoon." Then the master gardener left.

The man was disappointed. He went to the site of his future garden and saw the wheel. He turned it one full turn. He did the same the second and third day. However, the fourth and fifth day he was too busy to turn it. So it continued; some days he turned the wheel and some days he did not. After two months his neighbors arrived, saw nothing had grown in his garden, and asked him why. He said it flatly, "The master gardener is a fraud. If you want to grow something, do not ask him."

Meanwhile, the master gardener had arrived at the home of the third man. He asked him, "Do you want to grow something in this deserted place?" The man said he did, and the master gardener told him to wait and he would return. Two days later he returned and said, "There is a wheel in the back of your future garden. Turn it one full turn every afternoon."

What the man did not know was the master gardener had installed an underground irrigation system. With each turn of the wheel it released hidden waters that nourished the earth deep down inside itself.

The third man was also disappointed by these terse instructions, but he followed them faithfully. Then one day something happened that disturbed him greatly. Something began to grow. Green shoots shot up through the cracked and parched earth. At the sight of the green growth the man became anxious. How would he keep the plants alive and flourishing? The master gardener had given him no detailed plan. The man was beside himself with worry.

Then one day he made a remarkable discovery. Instead of worrying about how to keep the green growth alive, he looked at the plants themselves. On each leaf were instructions about what to do next. The man followed the instructions and soon his home was surrounded by a lovely garden.

The neighbors came and exclaimed, "How did you ever grow this beautiful garden in this deserted place?"

The man shrugged and said, "It seemed to happen naturally. I persevered and tried not to have too many expectations."

(enlarged from the shortened version in
Harry R. Moody and David Carroll,
*The Five Stages of the Soul: Charting the Spiritual
Passages That Shape Our Lives*
[New York: Anchor Books/Doubleday/Random House, Inc., 1997] 197)

Twelfth Sunday in Ordinary Time

Proper 7

Mark 4:35-41

Passing on Fearlessness

A Spiritual Commentary

[When evening had come, Jesus said to his disciples:] "Let us go across to the other side."

And leaving the crowd behind, they took him with them in the boat, just as he was. Other boats were with him.

Jesus' long day of teaching is over. The impact of the teachings has yet to be determined. The crowd is left behind because they did not have the parables explained to them, and so they did not receive the secret of the kingdom of God (Mark 4:11, 33). They have heard the public teaching, but they have not received private instructions (see last Sunday's commentary). Therefore, they are not ready for the next step.

However, the disciples have been personally coached: "he explained everything in private to his disciples" (Mark 4:34). So Jesus invites them to join him in crossing over to the other side. As the episode develops, the meaning of "crossing over" will become clear. It is a symbolic interior journey from fear to faith. If the teaching and explanation has taken, the disciples will be able to cross over to the other side with him. They will have put on "the mind of Christ" (1 Cor 2:16) and become his disciples not only in desire but in actuality. But it is one thing to hear "everything" explained, and quite another thing to understand and integrate what has been heard. This boat trip will show the need for more understanding and integration.

The disciples do not hesitate. Although it was Jesus' invitation, the disciples take the initiative. They take him into *their* boat, symbolizing this crossing over will be basically their adventure (v. 36). Also, they take Jesus, "just as he was" (v. 36). This is a mysterious comment. Jesus has been teaching the crowds and the disciples seated in a boat on the sea (Mark 4:1). This is appropriate for he "fishes for people" (Mark

1:17; Matt 4:19) and his teachings are nets to catch people. To take him "just as was" into their boat means their sea journey will be a continuation of his teachings. The point of the teachings is a transformation from fear to faith. Other boats were with Jesus because hearing the teachings naturally unfolds into this spiritual opportunity. Every generation will be invited to cross over to the other side.

> **A great windstorm arose, and the waves beat into the boat, so that the boat was already being swamped.**
>
> **But he was in the stern, asleep on the cushion; and they woke him up and said to him, "Teacher, do you not care that we are perishing?"**
>
> **He woke up and rebuked the wind, and said to the sea, "Peace! Be still!"**
>
> **Then the wind ceased, and there was a dead calm.**
>
> **He said to them, "Why are you afraid? Have you still no faith?"**
>
> **And they were filled with great awe and said to one another, "Who then is this, that even the wind and the sea obey him?"**

The disciples cannot make the crossing. The transfer of spiritual wisdom from Jesus to them is incomplete. The storm makes them doubt. So they awaken Jesus the Teacher and he models faith, a response to the storm rooted in the love and power of God. But the disciples respond with fear, and while the Teacher asks them to look at themselves, they persist in puzzling over him. Although they accepted the invitation to cross over, they could not get to the other side.

The Letter of James gives this advice: "If any of you is lacking in wisdom, ask God, who gives to all generously and ungrudgingly, and it will be given you. But ask in faith, never doubting, for the one who doubts is like a wave of the sea, driven and tossed by the wind; for the doubter, being double-minded and unstable in every way, must not expect to receive anything from the Lord" (Jas 1:5-8).

Temporal life is constantly harassed by physical and social dangers. When we are in the midst of them, our minds identify with what threatens us. They mirror the winds and the waves, making us as driven and tossed as they are. In this state, we cannot receive from God. We cannot make the wisdom of Jesus' teachings work.

However, Jesus' mind is not storm tossed. He sleeps, resting on a cushion no less, a picture of abiding peace during turbulence. But the disciples are "double-minded and unstable in every way" (Jas 1:8). They cannot still the storm of their minds by themselves. They resort to waking Jesus, and their question to him reveals the root of their inability. "Teacher, do you not care that we are perishing?" (v. 38). They are doubters. The dangers make them question if God loves them. The storm has split their minds between Jesus' teachings about the love of God and the very real waves that beat upon and swamp their boat. They vacillate, and this vacillating keeps them from receiving from God, the one who gives "generously and ungrudgingly" (Jas 1:5).

The awakened Jesus shows them the power of a steady mind open to God and mediating God's power into the storms of life. He rebukes the pretentious power of fear. He gives commands of silence and peace, and the winds and waves have no option but to obey. The storm is not on the same level as God's love for his people. Does God care? The answer to the disciples' vacillation is, "Yes!" But this care can only be received by the non-doubting mind. It is this teaching they must continue to understand and integrate. Jesus, the Teacher, directs them to this task. "Why are you afraid? Have you still no faith?" (v. 40).

However, now a different type of fear grips them. The NRSV translation says "they were filled with great awe," but the literal Greek is "they feared a great fear." This fear is conventional religious trembling in the presence of a manifestation of divine power. People prostrate themselves and quake whenever God's power appears. But even this type of fear can work against faith. It generates wonder and worship, but it does not encourage imitation. It pushes the disciples to talk to themselves about Jesus and his ability (v. 41). But what Jesus wanted was for them to talk to him about how their fear was still overriding their faith. Curiosity and speculation about Jesus' identity does not substitute for the disciples' failure to realize and integrate his spiritual teachings into their own lives. When Jesus the Teacher cannot be received, Jesus the Savior is born.

Teaching

I once told a woman I saw mystics and prophets as pioneers, charting new territories for the rest of us. She looked at me and shrugged, "Or else they just tell what we know." I do not think these options—pioneer of the new or revealer of what we know—are mutually exclusive. But my penchant is to honor what Baron von Hugel called the "great tradition," and to admit as he did, "I have never learnt anything myself by my own nose" (in Timothy Jones, *Finding a Spiritual Friend:*

How Friends and Mentors Can Make Your Faith Grow [Nashville: Upper Room Books, 1998] 29).

But what have I learned from the great souls who have preceded me and whose writings I have pondered? In particular, what have I learned from studying and praying the Gospels? As this episode attests, spiritual wisdom is notoriously difficult to pass on. Even if I had an older and wiser spiritual director to help me, as I did once, I sympathize with the disciples. I feel more comfortable worshiping Jesus than following him.

For myself, I have noticed three guideposts along the way of receiving the spiritual wisdom of another. First, I hear about the wisdom someone has articulated for the purpose of passing it on. For example, "perfect love casts out fear" (1 John 4:18). I mull this over, connect it with other things, test it for coherence, wonder what it might mean. All this is highly rational activity. But it is necessary. It helps me hone in on the mystery to which the words point.

Second, somewhere along the way I have to move from rational appreciation to realized understanding. Spiritual teachers are famous for trying to provide occasions for realized understanding to happen. Edmund Helminski tells this story:

> At one point in my journey, my teacher's teacher, an eighty-year-old man, had been in a serious car accident that had brought him near death. For months the master's condition was uncertain, causing all those who loved him to become acutely aware of what his living flesh-and-blood friendship meant to them. Eventually he would recover. When he was well enough to barely walk, he phoned my teacher to tell him that he would have a special lesson if he could come to his apartment on a certain night. Since this was the first opportunity for the two of them to be together in months, my teacher was full of expectation.
>
> They took a walk that evening, so slow and deliberate that it emphasized the attention for each painful step. They walked as far as one of the most elegant drinking establishments of that great city. My teacher's teacher opened the door of that tavern and they entered. It was as if they were perfectly invisible, while the patrons, the most fashionable men and women, continued in their loud, intoxicated conversations. "See?" he simply said. (*Living Presence: A Sufi Way to Mindfulness and the Essential Self* [New York: Jeremy P. Tarcher/Perigee, 1992] 23–24)

Moments of realization are often serendipitous. They happen when you least expect it. But what happens is you "see" the wisdom for yourself. Someone says "See," and you do. The wisdom is now your own. You get it. If the teacher stops a sentence, you can complete it. You have in-herited the tradition but not, as T. S. Eliot insisted, without great labor. Third, realized understanding, as important as it is, is not integration:

> The hard truth is that spiritual realization is relatively easy compared with the much greater difficulty of actualizing it, integrating it fully into the fabric of one's embodiment and one's daily life. By *realization* I mean the direct recognition of one's ultimate nature, while *actualization* refers to how we live that realization in all the situations of our life. When people have major spiritual openings, often during periods of intense practice or re-treat, they may imagine that everything has changed and that they will never be the same again. Indeed, spiritual work can open people up pro-foundly and help them live free of the compulsions of their conditioning for long stretches of time. But at some point after the retreat ends, when they encounter circumstances that trigger their emotional reactivity, their unresolved psychological issues, their habitual tensions and defenses, or their subconscious identifications, they may find that their spiritual prac-tices have barely penetrated their conditioned personality, which remains mostly intact, generating the same tendencies it always has. (John Wel-wood, *Toward a Psychology of Awakening: Buddhism, Psychotherapy, and the Path of Personal and Spiritual Transformation* [Boston: Shambhala, 2000] 194)

I fantasize that this is what happened to the disciples. Under Jesus' careful guidance, they had made great advances. They had realized for themselves the love of God that is greater than the troubles of the world. They were ready to cross over from fear to faith. But when the troubles of the world arrived, they could not "hang on" to faith. As Evelyn Underhill admitted, "It is far easier, though not very easy, to develop and preserve a spiritual outlook on life, than it is to make our everyday actions harmonize with that spiritual outlook" (*The Spiritual Life* [Harrisburg, Pa.: Morehouse Group, 1997] 78–60). The single-hearted may see God. But the double-minded see both God and the waves, and the waves win.

"Fear" and "faith" are code words for Mark. Although their mean-ing depends on the context in which they are used, they point to the dynamic challenge of discipleship. This challenge does not seem to have a final resolution. The Gospel ends with the disciples displaying fear rather than faith. "So they went out and fled from the tomb, for terror and amazement had seized them; and they said nothing to any-one, for they were afraid" (Mark 16:8). I believe this is because fear is an essential feature of discipleship. Integration is never over, especially if you are trying to inherit the wisdom of Jesus who realized and integrated a divine love that is stronger than death (cf. Song 8:6).

Thirteenth Sunday in Ordinary Time

Proper 8

Mark 5:21-43

Touching Our Loneliness

A Spiritual Commentary

When Jesus had crossed again in the boat to the other side, a great crowd gathered around him; and he was by the sea.

Then one of the leaders of the synagogue, named Jairus, came and, when he saw him, fell at his feet and begged him repeatedly, "My little daughter is at the point of death. Come and lay your hands on her, so that she might be made well, and live."

So he went with him.

Jesus stays close to the sea. It is his place of teaching. Crowds gather and he casts out his net. But Jesus teaches with authority (Mark 1:27). His words become deeds, and his deeds are embodied words. What he says indicates how he acts, and how he acts illustrates what he says. He is a unity of word and deed, so the sudden appearance of a leader of the synagogue is not an interruption. What Jesus was teaching will now take the form of a symbolic story. As the story unfolds, the teaching will gradually deepen and become more complex.

Jairus is uncharacteristic of synagogue leaders. Synagogue leaders do not beseech Jesus. They stand and watch disapprovingly. They discredit Jesus as a lawbreaker because he works on the Sabbath or as unclean because of his contact with people who have transgressed the purity codes. But Jairus is a suppliant, begging Jesus repeatedly. The story does not tell us how this synagogue leader broke ranks, how he came to find himself at the feet of Jesus. But the implication is that his dying daughter has made him desperate. There is nothing wrong in desperation, but often it is born out of fear and impotence. As the story unfolds, both he and his wife will be asked to move beyond fear and impotence.

Nevertheless, his request acknowledges that God is working through Jesus. He wants his daughter to live by the divine life that can come through Jesus' hands. That is true enough as far as it goes. But it might be too one sided. Jesus is not a wonderworker, miraculously touching and instantly curing. Divine love is not communicated by simply being physically touched by Jesus and healing is more than recovery from illness. A suffering woman carries this deeper teaching, a suffering woman whom Jesus and Jairus will meet on their way:

> **And a large crowd followed him and pressed in on him. Now there was a woman who had been suffering from hemorrhages for twelve years. She had endured much under many physicians, and had spent all that she had; and she was no better, but rather grew worse.**
>
> **She had heard about Jesus, and came up behind him in the crowd and touched his cloak, for she said, "If I but touch his clothes, I will be made well."**
>
> **Immediately her hemorrhage stopped; and she felt in her body that she was healed of her disease.**
>
> **Immediately aware that power had gone forth from him, Jesus turned about in the crowd and said, "Who touched my clothes?"**
>
> **And his disciples said to him, "You see the crowd pressing in on you; how can you say, "Who touched me?"**
>
> **He looked all around to see who had done it. But the woman, knowing what had happened to her, came in fear and trembling, fell down before him and told him the whole truth.**
> **He said to her, "Daughter, your faith has made you well; go in peace, and be healed of your disease."**

The limits of physical contact are stressed. On one level, physicians who use physical strategies to effect physical cures have not been able to help this hemorrhaging woman. In fact, they have made things worse, adding financial collapse to physical malady. On a more important level, the crowd is pressing in on Jesus. Physical contact is constant. But just physically touching Jesus does not lead to receiving divine love. When Jesus asks, "Who has touched me?" he does not mean it in the physical sense of skin against skin or clothes against clothes. His disciples take it in this crude sense. But this type of touching, rubbing against Jesus, is not spiritually significant.

The woman touches Jesus in a different way. She has heard about Jesus. We are not told what she heard, but she has obviously heard enough to develop an appropriate interior disposition. She has a cooperating consciousness, one that is able to receive the flow of divine power. This consciousness does not stress physical touch as if skin on skin contact produced healing. She knows that all she has to do is touch his cloak, just come into minimal contact with him. The spiritual love is coming through Jesus, and so some contact is necessary. But it is spiritual love, and so her interior openness to divine love is what is important. Jesus' desire to manifest divine, compassionate love is matched by her readiness to receive it.

Both Jesus and the woman know "it" has happened. Salvific power has gone out and salvific power has been taken in. And they know it immediately. It happened on a level deeper than the piecemeal and plodding way the mind works. But there is a need to make conscious the salvific work of divine love. Jesus' search for her enables her to come forward with the traditional set of feelings and thoughts that accompany divine presence, "fear and trembling" (v. 33). But this "fear and trembling" is turned into a conversation about the "whole truth." The "whole truth" goes beyond the physical laying on of hands to include a communion of consciousness between Jesus and the woman.

Jesus makes clear what has happened. She has never been an unclean woman with uncontrolled bleeding. She is a daughter of God who is suffering. She held onto that spiritual identity, and that deeper identity gave her courage to reach for God's love as it was manifesting itself in Jesus. God's love is for God's children, and she is one of God's children. That is her faith. And the healing that comes from that faith is more than physical. She can go in peace and enter back into the community. Since she has been spiritually touched by God, she can physically touch and be touched by others. She is re-included into interpersonal and community living.

Jairus asked that Jesus lays hands on his daughter (v. 23). By "daughter" he meant his biological offspring. However, to the ears of the Jesus he was pointing to a daughter of God who was being threatened by physical death. Jesus immediately went with him for the love of the Father is ever with his children. If people know and believe this, their consciousness cooperates, and the spiritual love enters the physical and social realms with healing.

But the teaching is not yet over.

> While he was still speaking, some people came from the leader's house to say, "Your daughter is dead. Why trouble the teacher any further?"
>
> But overhearing what they said, Jesus said to the leader of the synagogue, "Do not fear, only believe."
>
> He allowed no one to follow him except Peter, James, and John, the brother of James.
>
> When they came to the house of the leader of the synagogue, he saw a commotion, people weeping and wailing loudly. When he had entered, he said to them, "Why do you make a commotion and weep? The child is not dead but sleeping."
>
> And they laughed at him.
>
> Then he put them all outside, and took the child's father and mother and those who were with him, and went in where the child was.
>
> He took her by the hand and said to her, "Talitha cum," which means, "Little girl, get up!"
>
> And immediately the girl got up and began to walk about (she was twelve years of age). At this they were overcome with amazement. He strictly ordered them that no one should know this, and told them to give her something to eat.

Is divine love only about restoring people to physical health? If it is, then death means there is no need for the carrier of divine love. The people from Jairus' house are correct. The teacher should not be troubled further. His possible miraculous ability is no longer needed. But Jesus instructs Jairus not to let the fear that death always produces dominate his consciousness. He is to believe even in the face of death. He believed when his daughter was at the point of death. He has just witnessed how important interiorly holding onto the "daughter of God identity" is. God's love turns death into sleep. And sleepers can be awakened (see Eph 5:14).

But this teaching and the consciousness that accompanies it is not accessible to the crowd. Their level of spiritual awareness is not sufficiently developed to face the challenge of death. They are dismissed. Only Jairus (to be joined by his wife) and the inner circle of the twelve are allowed to go further. These must show a tenacity of consciousness, even come to a new level of development through what they are going to witness. They must hold onto the love of God that makes all things possible in the face of wailing and weeping. These are loud manifestations that death rules life. Only steadfast attachment to the love greater than death will quiet this awful din (cf. Song 8:6). Whatever mocks and ridicules this consciousness of greater love must be excluded. This means the people—and wailing—must be put out. But it also means the consciousness of Jesus, Peter, James, John, and the girl's parents must resist worshiping death with screams. Mourning and wailing represent the fear and ridicule inherent in darkened minds, darkened minds that all people share in to some degree.

Jesus does not pray to God to bring a dead girl back to life. Nor does he rigorously lay hands on her, as a miracle worker might. His consciousness has never wavered: "The child is not dead, but sleeping" (v. 39). So he takes her hand, and with the tender, intimate address and invitation of divine love—whose ultimate daughter she is—he awakens her. This happens immediately. The spiritual is not encumbered by time or space the way the physical is. In biblical thought, God owns blood. So God's love, working through Jesus, has stopped the twelve-year flow of blood in the hemorrhaging woman and started the flow of blood in the twelve-year-old girl. Divine love is geared to specific human situations and designed to bring them to betterment.

However, everyone that Jesus healed and brought back to life eventually became sick and died. These stories may reveal God's concern about improving the quality of life (stopping hemorrhaging) and reversing untimely death (the demise of a child). But their full import lies elsewhere. Since God created human physical life, divine activity could continue to create it. But this is not a mechanical process. Human consciousness is involved in complex and baffling ways. These stories give a glimpse of the necessary interior dispositions.

The interior disposition of Jesus is his awareness of himself as the Beloved (see the accounts of Jesus' baptism and transfiguration) who expresses and communicates divine love. At the request of Jairus, he immediately responds. A daughter of God is facing death; she should not face it without God's love which flows through him. His interior focus is consistently on this missionary identity. So when the hemorrhaging woman touches him, he is immediately aware that loving power has gone out. He instructs Jairus that a steady, believing consciousness is necessary, a consciousness that he possesses. When tumult and wailing want to distract him and ridicule dissuade him, he does not succumb.

Finally, he acts on what he understands. He brings the inside to the outside. Jesus stayed awake, and therefore he is able to awaken the girl.

The interior disposition of the hemorrhaging woman is revealed in what she says to herself. She is so convinced of the free and unsolicited love of God in Jesus that only the merest touch of the hem of his garment is enough. She does not have to petition him as if he would be unwilling (Mark 1:40) or be part of the jostling crowd who might mistakenly think physical touch by itself bestows blessing. Her interior openness is the key. Receiving consciousness is critical.

An interior disposition is also demanded of the inner circle of the twelve and Jairus and his wife. They are not merely observers. They are asked to consciously cooperate as divine love reveals that "one stronger" than death has arrived (Mark 1:7; 3:27). This means they must resist the way death parades as ultimate and not be carried away by weeping and wailing or cowed by ridicule. This full unfolding of divine love is revealed in the death and resurrection of Jesus, so the observers are enjoined not to tell the story of the synagogue leader's daughter. Her life is really an eating, a sharing in the Christian eucharistic story. If she eats at the Christian table, she participates in the death and resurrection of Jesus. That is the whole truth, and it is that story that must be told.

Teaching

In terms of using the five senses analogously as ways of spiritual knowing and communicating, touch probably comes in third. We say, "We see God," and "We hear God," on a regular basis. Eyes and ears are what Jesus tries to open so that the spiritual might be perceived (see Mark 7 and Luke 4:18, for example). These are the most used analogies. Smell and taste are the least used. While we may "taste and see that the LORD is good" (Ps 34:8) and claim there is a "fragrance" to holiness, the nose and the tongue are not highly frequented analogies. Touch is in the middle, after sight and sound, and before taste and smell.

But there is a quality about touching that makes it an apt sense for experiencing Spirit. Rachel Naomi Remen, a physician who works on humanizing the world of medicine, tells a story that gets to the core of healing touch. She does workshops with other physicians and, at one point, has them touch one another with healing intent. It is always a moving exercise as the doctors reclaim aspects of themselves and others with which they have, to continue the metaphor, "lost touch."

One man described his experience in this way:

At first I thought I would just play it safe, but after Jane [his touching partner] told me about the pain she usually has in her back I decided to take a chance and tell her about my divorce. How hard it had become for me to trust women. She asked me where I felt this pain, and I couldn't actually say it, so I touched by heart. She nodded . . . Then Jane put the palm of her hand on my chest. I was really astonished by how warm her hand was, and gently and tenderly she touched me. A little at a time the warmth of her hand seemed to penetrate my chest and surround my heart. I had a strange sort of experience. For a while there, it seemed to me as if she were holding my heart in her hand rather than just touching my chest. That's when I felt the strength in her hand, how rock-steady she was, and in a funny way I could feel that she was really *there* for my pain, committed to being there, and suddenly I was not alone. I was safe. That's when I started to cry. (*Kitchen Table Wisdom* [New York: Riverhead Books, 1996] 240)

The temptation of this man at the start of the experience, to play it safe and not tell his touching partner, is a universal human tendency. We keep our pain to ourselves and, in the process, isolate ourselves from the human companionship that is so necessary.

In the same book Remen tells a story she calls, "Kissing the Boo-Boo." Jessie had suffered a temporary bowel obstruction from adhesions that had been caused by the radiation used to treat her cancer. When the pain began, she packed a small overnight bag and drove herself twenty-five miles to the hospital. She had to pull over several times to vomit. Then, she spent one full day in the emergency room. When Rachel asked her why she did not call any of her friends, she said they were all working and besides,

"None of my friends know[s] a thing about intestinal obstruction."
"Then why didn't you call me?"
"Well it's not really your field either," she replied.
"Jessie," I said, "even children instinctively run to others when they fall down." With a great deal of heat she said, "Yes, I've never understood that. It's so silly. Kissing the boo-boo doesn't help the pain at all." I was stunned. "Jessie," I said, "it doesn't help the pain, it helps the loneliness." (59–60)

Pain and loneliness are often co-companions.

When we see another person in pain, it can increase the sense of distance, even if the seeing is compassionate. When we listen to another person in pain, they can be comforted because their words are being received. But touching seems to be special. It has the capacity to bridge the separateness and create a non-abandoning sense of presence. In the story of the woman who touched the man's chest, the touching woman seemed to reach through the man's skin and actually hold his heart with such a rock-steady sense that he knew he was not alone—and that he was safe. From a theological point of view, if this is what was communicated, then the touching person had become a vehicle for divine love. In some cases the flow of divine love may cure. Physical maladies may become better. But whether it physically cures or not, human touch that communicates divine care and inclusion always heals. The isolated person is no longer alone and, here the mystery deepens, unexplainably safe.

Fourteenth Sunday in Ordinary Time

Proper 9 (Part 1)

Mark 6:1-6 *LM* • Mark 6:1-13 *RCL*

Overcoming Familiarity

A Spiritual Commentary

For users of the *Lectionary for Mass* and the *Revised Common Lectionary:*

[Jesus] came to his hometown, and his disciples followed him. On the sabbath he began to teach in the synagogue, and many who heard him were astounded.

They said, "Where did this man get all this? What is this wisdom that has been given to him? What deeds of power are being done by his hands! Is not this the carpenter, the son of Mary and the brother of James and Joses and Judas and Simon, and are not his sisters here with us?"

And they took offense.

Then Jesus said to them, "Prophets are not without honor, except in their hometown, and among their own kin, and in their own house."

And he could do no deed of power there, except that he laid hands on a few sick people and cured them. And he was amazed at their unbelief.

Astonishment at Jesus' words and deeds may be the first step toward belief. If people trace their astonishment and pursue their perplexity to its source, they will discern a transcendent power at work in Jesus. Even though they may know him on an ordinary level, this knowledge will not block their appreciation of his transparency to God. They will welcome and cooperate with the God who is working through him. This cooperation will result in deeds of power: revelations, healings, and exorcisms. Jesus' revelation will be matched by faith.

However, in Jesus' hometown, astonishment and perplexity are the first steps toward rejection. The people of his native place know him too well. They know his work and his family; and since origins determine destiny, they know he is overreaching himself. They "put him in his place," reminding themselves of what they know only too well. He is one of them, an ordinary human being who should be doing ordinary things. He should be making tables, not speaking wisdom, curing the sick, and casting out demons. In their minds his ordinariness undercuts and refutes the greatness they have heard about and have themselves witnessed. Therefore, they cannot explain or "stomach" Jesus' wisdom and power. His prophetic speech and action may be honored elsewhere, but among his own it only produces offense. Consequently, his revelation is not matched by faith, so the cooperation that is needed for mighty deeds is not available.

This short episode begins and ends with astonishment. The hometown people are amazed at Jesus' ability to reveal God, and Jesus is amazed at their inability to respond enthusiastically to this revelation. The root of both amazements may be theological. The townspeople are stunned because they believe the ordinary excludes the extraordinary. God only works through special people or learned people or official people. This carpenter son of Mary simply is not eligible. Jesus is stunned because if God can work through him, one of them, God can also work through them. His words are a mirror for their own ability to enter into God's remaking of creation. How can they turn away from the potential that is being offered them? How can they resist the invitation of God? The Son of Man is amazed. But the Son of Man is not deterred. He leaves the dust of his feet in Nazareth and moves on to other villages (see Mark 6:11). The teaching that is rejected in his hometown will be accepted elsewhere.

For users of the *Revised Common Lectionary:* Proper 9 also includes Mark 6:7-13. A spiritual commentary on those verses and a corresponding teaching is developed on the Fifteenth Sunday in Ordinary Time.

Teaching

One of Mark Twain's memorable lines was, "Familiarity breeds contempt and . . . children." But the process by which familiarity produces children is much better known than the process by which it creates contempt.

Familiarity with people results in increased knowledge about them. This knowledge is about their bodies: how they look, how they talk about their health, how old they are, what they like or do not like to eat, etc. It also includes their work and leisure histories: where they have traveled, what hobbies they have, what social successes and failures they have endured. Finally, we gather in our minds predictable features of their personalities: their introverted or extroverted styles, their persistent fears, their penchants, their values, etc. What happens is we have them "nailed down" or, in another image, we have them "in a box." In both cases, they cannot move.

It is difficult to hold lightly the knowledge of another we think is dead-on accurate, especially when it is confirmed again and again by what they say and do. Yet we may be blessed by the experience of overhearing the box that other people have put us in. We will almost certainly be offended. Their box is really a Procrustean bed. They have simply lopped away everything of us that did not fit into the paltry categories their meager minds have managed. We are infinitely more than they have nailed down.

If we have had this experience of overhearing our box, we may find a considerable inconsistency looming into consciousness. We are always more than other people think. But other people are exactly as we depict them. At Nazareth they will not let Jesus out of the box they have put him in. But my bet is they think that they themselves are beyond boxes. Everybody can be reduced but the reducer.

The way out of this tendency to box other people is to stay aware of how tightly we fit, if we fit at all, into the box others have made for us. Whenever we are confidently analyzing people and predicting their behavior, we should realize that, not too far away, we are being analyzed and predicted. If we do not dismiss this thought, it will unfold into a "Do unto others as you would have them do unto you" invitation (the Golden Rule; see Mark 12:31 and parallels). The key word is "do." We are to start the reciprocity. We should grant transcendence to others because we know we are transcendent, and if they would grant transcendence to us, it would be a real and just thing to do. This inner reasoning can be tricky, but it gets the ball rolling.

As noted above, I like to think of this largesse as "granting transcendence." It begins a faith conviction. But if we pay attention, it will be borne out in experience. Faith tells us we are ultimately a mystery because we are inescapably related to Ultimate Mystery. Therefore, we are always more than what we manifest and, by extension, always more than the boxes that have been made for us. That is a given. But beyond that, our transcendence may burst into imminence. It may enter into and elevate the dimensions of us that are observable. When this happens, as it happened to Jesus in Nazareth, everyone is surprised. They have to face the fact that their boxes are inadequate, or they have to reject the one who broke them. Humility is always preferred to rejection.

I like to think we all break the boxes of mediocrity that others put us in. They did not think we had it in us. But, as one sage put it, strictly speaking there are no enlightened people, only enlightened behaviors. They look at us as if we were strangers. But really we were truly ourselves. Familiarity has been overcome.

Fifteenth Sunday in Ordinary Time

Proper 9 (Part 2)

Mark 6:7-13 *LM* • **Mark 6:1-13** *RCL* (continued)

For users of the *Revised Common Lectionary,* the following completes the Gospel for Proper 9, begun on the previous Sunday.

Following Injunctions

A Spiritual Commentary

For users of the *Revised Common Lectionary:*

Then he went among the villages teaching.

For users of the *Lectionary for Mass* and the *Revised Common Lectionary:*

[Jesus] called the twelve and began to send them out two by two, and gave them authority over the unclean spirits. He ordered them to take nothing for their journey except a staff; no bread, no bag, no money in their belts; but to wear sandals and not to put on two tunics.

He said to them, "Wherever you enter a house, stay there until you leave the place. If any place will not welcome you and they refuse to hear you, as you leave, shake off the dust that is on your feet as a testimony against them."

So they went out and proclaimed that all should repent. They cast out many demons, and anointed with oil many who were sick and cured them.

Preaching, teaching, and deeds of power (healings and exorcisms) are three expressions of the single activity of kingdom making. One stream breaks into three tributaries. However, in the organic relationship among the three, teaching holds a special place. Sheer proclamation ("Repent, for the kingdom of heaven has come near" [Matt 4:17]) may attract attention, but it necessarily unfolds into greater explanation and direction. If proclamation works, teaching follows. Deeds of power may lead to astonishment, as it did in Jesus' hometown. But unless their meaning is understood and their revelation pursued, healings and exorcisms can feed into hardened ways of thinking. These ways of thinking not only block access to the kingdom, but they also create opposition to it. Ultimately, it is Jesus the teacher who travels from village to village (v. 6b, not part of *LM*).

When we read that the twelve were given "authority over the unclean spirits," we immediately think of them grappling with possessed people and somehow restoring them to full functioning in their families and communities. In a sense, this is accurate. But the emphasis is not on the sudden and positive change of the afflicted or on the disciples displaying miraculous curative abilities. Rather both communities and individuals are urged and instructed to rethink the taboos and restrictions around clean and unclean boundaries. "[T]hey went out and proclaimed that all should repent" (v. 12). The twelve, symbolizing the twelve tribes of Israel, are sent out primarily to create an alternative community based on a new teaching about divine holiness.

It is this "new teaching—with authority!" (Mark 1:27) that Jesus has given the twelve. This is what they have assimilated, and this is what they are asked to share with others. Instead of fearing uncleanness and pushing away people who show "unclean signs," they are to have faith, to emulate the God who is mercy and compassion. The flip side of driving out unclean spirits, expelling demons, and curing the sick is their reentry of the cured into the community. This reentry is only possible if people have developed a new consciousness that supports this type of kingdom activity.

Jesus teaches the disciples; the disciples teach other people. In order for the disciples to be successful, the new way of thinking and acting they have learned from Jesus must be integrated. The way they present themselves must be "of one piece" with the new teaching. How they work with people to create a more inclusive sense of community is as important as healing and exorcising. Therefore, Jesus gives them instructions.

The instructions are both practical and symbolic. They must go out two by two, complementary witnesses to the new way of life Jesus has inaugurated. Walking stick and sandals both facilitate travel and remind them that they are to spread the Good News from place to place. They are not to settle down. Their single tunic captures this single-mindedness: they are men on a mission. (See Eugene LaVerdiere, *The Beginning of the Gospel: Introducing the Gospel According to Mark* [Collegeville, Minn.: Liturgical Press, 1999] 155.) Without bread, bag, and money, they become part of those in need. Their lack of provisions elicits the compassion that is the cornerstone of the new community. Welcoming the disciples is the first step toward welcoming those whom the disciples welcome—the ones excluded because of their illnesses. Hospitality is an essential part of kingdom living.

This welcoming is the crucial aspect of the hospitality—not the "richness or extent" of it. The twelve are not to behave as travelers looking for the best accommodations. Also, they are not to wrangle with those who do not accept their kingdom activity. They do not have to retaliate. They are to leave the dust of their feet there. In that way, the refusing people will know the invitation of God has moved on. There are other people and other villages. The Good News must be preached in word and deed.

Teaching

Injunctions have an honored place in spiritual teaching. We are told to do or not to do something. "Do not be afraid of that which can kill the body and do no more" (see Luke 12:4). "Do not identify with the fruits of your labor" (see Luke 10:17-20). "Take a staff but no bread on your journey" (see Mark 6:8 and parallels).

Although there are many injunctions, there are not corresponding detailed instructions. We are told what to do or not to do, but we are not told exactly how to do it or not to do it or, for that matter, why we should do it. For example, how does one go about not being afraid of the death of the body when the mind is filled with pre-rational tapes about how to protect our bodily identities at all costs? Or how does one go about disidentifying with the fruits of one's labor when wanting to be recognized for what we have done is one of our strongest driving forces? Or why should we take a walking stick but not bread on the journey?

The spiritual texts are often silent about how to deal with these difficulties. This may be a regrettable lack of specificity on their part, or it may be a deliberate ploy. Injunctions without explanations or instructions may combine to point spiritual seekers in a particular direction and yet allow them the surprise of discovering a truth for themselves.

As we struggle to carry out the injunctions, we learn what we need to know. We encounter obstacles and allies both in ourselves and in our situations. We have to work with these blocks and openings, these resistances and desires. If we are patient and persevere, we will develop spiritually through this work. This means we will coincide with ourselves as spiritual people dynamically living in physical, psychological, and social reality. It also means our lives will become an invitation for others to undertake their spiritual adventure. All this can come about from following the injunctions. We come to see injunctions not primarily as goals to be accomplished but as paths to be walked, paths that will lead us to deeper levels of consciousness.

Jack Kornfield tells the story of following an injunction to bow. As a young man and the only Westerner in a Buddhist monastery in Thailand, he was instructed to bow to every monk that was older than he was. If he respected an older monk, there was no problem. But when he had to bow to a "twenty-one-year-old monk full of hubris" or to a sloppy old rice farmer of a monk "who never meditated a day in his life," he was conflicted. Nevertheless, he bowed.

> He also began to realize how he could make this bowing work.
>
> I began to look for some worthy aspect of each person I bowed to. I bowed to the wrinkles around the retired farmer's eyes, for all the difficulties he had seen and suffered through and triumphed over. I bowed to the vitality and playfulness in the young monks, the incredible possibilities each of their lives held yet ahead of them.
>
> (*After the Ecstasy, the Laundry: How the Heart Grows Wise on the Spiritual Path* [New York: Bantam Books/Random House, Inc., 2000] ix–xi)

From following the injunction to bow to everyone he learned how to be open to whatever life brings and to learn from it. He quotes a poem of Rumi that he now knows from the inside because of his experience of bowing:

> This being human is a guest house,
> Every morning a new arrival.
>
> A joy, a depression, a meanness,
> some momentary awareness comes
> as an unexpected visitor.
>
> Welcome and entertain them all!
> Even if they're a crowd of sorrows,
> who violently sweep your house
> empty of its furniture,
> still, treat each guest honorably,
> He may be clearing you out
> for some new delight.
>
> This dark thought, the shame, the malice,
> meet them at the door laughing,
> and invite them in.

> Be grateful for whoever comes,
> because each has been sent
> as a guide from beyond.

("The Guest House" in *The Illuminated Rumi,*
trans. Coleman Barks [New York: Bantam Books/
Broadway Books/Random House, Inc., 1997])

This profound spiritual approach to life became available to Kornfield because he followed the injunction of bowing.

Someone who might have glimpsed what the disciples experienced by following the injunctions of Jesus is a woman named Peace Pilgrim ("Peace Pilgrim" by Ann and John Rush in *Peace is the Way: Writings on Nonviolence from the Fellowship of Reconciliation,* ed. Walter Wink [Maryknoll, N.Y.: Orbis Books, 2000). For thirty years she walked across America teaching the importance of peace. "I shall remain a wanderer until [humankind] has learned the way of peace, walking until I am given shelter, fasting until I am given food." What her shelterless and foodless condition did was allow people to be hospitable. She was always given shelter and food. She created the conditions for the goodness of people to come forth and for them to acknowledge their deep desire to hear the message of peace. This spiritual wisdom about people and peace was not speculation. She came to it by following a path, a path, I think, that was close to the one Jesus gives his missionary disciples.

Having been at many debriefings, I can see it now: The disciples return with walking stick, sandals, and one tunic, but still without bread, bag, or money. As they tell Jesus what they did and what they taught, he asks, "[D]id you lack anything?" (Luke 22:35).

They say, "Nothing" (Luke 22:35; NIV).

"Ah!" he says.

Sunday between 10 and 16 July

Proper 10

Mark 6:14-29

Saving Our Lives

A Spiritual Commentary

For users of the *Revised Common Lectionary:*

King Herod heard of [the healings and other miracles] for Jesus' name had become known.

Some were saying, "John the baptizer has been raised from the dead; and for this reason these powers are at work in him."

But others said, "It is Elijah."

And others said, "It is a prophet, like one of the prophets of old."

But when Herod heard of it, he said, "John, whom I beheaded, has been raised."

For Herod himself had sent men who arrested John, bound him, and put him in prison on account of Herodias, his brother Philip's wife, because Herod had married her.

For John had been telling Herod, "It is not lawful for you to have your brother's wife."

And Herodias had a grudge against him, and wanted to kill him. But she could not, for Herod feared John, knowing he was a righteous and holy man, and he protected him. When he heard him, he was greatly perplexed; and yet he liked to listen to him. But an opportunity came when Herod on his birthday gave a banquet for his courtiers and officers and for the leaders of Galilee.

When his daughter Herodias [or the daughter of Heriodias herself] came in and danced, she pleased Herod and his guests; and the king said to the girl, "Ask me for whatever you wish, and I will give it."

And he solemnly swore to her, "Whatever you ask me, I will give you, even half of my kingdom."

She went out and said to her mother, "What should I ask for?"

She replied, "The head of John the baptizer."

Immediately, she rushed back to the king and requested, "I want you to give me at once the head of John the Baptist on a platter."

The king was deeply grieved; yet out of regard for his oaths and for the guests, he did not want to refuse her. Immediately the king sent a soldier of the guard with orders to bring John's head. He went and beheaded him in the prison, brought his head on a platter, and gave it to the girl. Then the girl gave it to her mother.

When the disciples heard about it, they came and took his body, and laid it in a tomb.

Mark is usually a sparse storyteller. But in this episode he creates a complex psychological portrait. Although scholars agree that this picture of Herod and the banquet is historically unreliable, it expresses a theological-social truth at the heart of the Gospel. Weak people kill; strong people suffer under their weakness but do not retaliate in kind. John, Jesus, and those who follow them will be persecuted by people in power who are weaklings and who succumb to pressure (Mark 15:15). But John, Jesus, and those who follow them will not cave in to persecution. Strengthened by faith and unafraid to die, they will preach repentance to the political and religious leaders.

Rumors are swirling. No one denies Jesus' preaching, teachings, healings, and exorcisms are extraordinary. But what is underneath it all? Is he another irritating prophet attacking existing social arrangements? Is he Elijah ushering in the end time? Or is he John the Baptist come back to life?

When Herod hears of Jesus, he has no doubt. "John, whom I beheaded, has been raised" (v. 16). This is a self-centered and eerie estimate of what is happening. In Herod's mouth these are words of guilt and foreboding. He has done something (beheading John), and now it has returned to haunt him. The storyteller is bursting with gossip. Here is the skinny.

Herod is caught in the middle. On one side is John who fascinates Herod. Herod recognizes that he is a holy person and likes to listen to him talk. But one of the things John likes to talk about is Herod's marriage, an adulterous tumble with his brother's wife. But Herod's interests are more superstitious than moral. John has not converted him to his favorite topic: repentance. Herod is dabbling in John.

On the other side is Herodias. She is not sure Herod is dabbling in John. As the prize grabbed by both Herod and Philip, she is at the center of John's call to conversion. She has the most to lose, and she wants John killed. But Herod will not comply. He imprisons John, but he will not put him to the sword. Will one day Herod listen too long and too attentively to John? Herodias knows Herod is weak, and the first one to apply enough pressure will win him over. Will John's rhetoric break him down? Will Herodias be handed a bill of divorce and become an ex-royal, having to fend for herself outside palace protection? She cannot let this happen. She must increase the pressure from her side. An opportunity presents itself, and she seizes it.

Herod's weakness is now mercilessly displayed. He throws himself a self-serving birthday banquet and invites those he wants to impress. His lust is publicly tweaked by the dance of Herodias' daughter. He goes over the top and boasts his pleasure is worth up to half his kingdom. But the dancing girl's mother has been watching in the wings, and she knows what she wants. Herod orders the beheading of John reluctantly, but he does order it. He does not want to lose face, to break his promise in front of the guests he wants to impress. His own self-image pressures him into an act he regrets and whose supernatural consequences he fears. Herod is no longer in the middle. A man who could stand up to nobody kills a man who stood up to everybody.

The world thinks that kings are strong, powerful rulers who impose their will on others. Their wealth, power, and fame are to be envied. That is a fantasy. They are superstitious people who secretly are attracted to the revelations of John and Jesus, but they do not have the courage to repent. They are manipulated by clever women to do evil things. But it is really their boastful, lustful, and fearful selves that eventually bring them to grief and guilt. They are without inner substance, obsessed with prestige, and constrained by what others think of them. Herod is an exemplar, someone who saves his life in this world, his social position, at the cost of killing a holy and righteous man (see Mark 8:35; Luke 17:33). He harms another to save his own face.

Teaching

I spend the majority of my time saving my life, the life of my family, and the life of my friends and neighbors. Maintaining life in this world is full-time activity. The law of entropy applies. If I do not give attention and care to relationships, they become routine and begin to atrophy. If I do not give attention and care to work, I become bored, and the people who hire me no longer call. If I do not give attention and care to my material surroundings, they fall apart. I feel responsible for the conservation of the physical-social world in which I live.

I know this temporal world is not permanent. One of my spiritual practices is to meditate on my death as a way of purifying my priorities and relishing my life. I try not to overly attach myself to the present form of things. However, I am not sure how successful this effort is. When I think of some losses, especially the loss of relationships, a terrifying emptiness swallows me. Emerging from this howling void, I vow to love and contribute to eternal values. But these values manifest themselves in what I know best: relationships, work, and neighborhood. While I am incarnate, I tend the garden of the flesh.

Within this commitment to saving my life, the short story of Herod's undoing is a real warning. This pathetic king is so weak he kills a holy and righteous man because he fears he will lose the respect of other political and religious leaders. I would like to treat him as a past historical figure, a species of regal scum. But I think he is the inner temptation of everyone who loves their life and wants to save it. Since I am one of those people, I want to notice what went wrong.

I think it began with Herod's strange combination of interest and inaction. He likes to listen to John, but he pays him no heed. He does not convert to the eternal values John's offers. If he did, he might have been more modest in his reward to the girl whose dance excited him. Also, he would have found the strength to refuse Herodias' vicious scheme. Having learned repentance from John, he could repent of his promise and tell his guests he had no intention of staying committed to a mistake. But he did not have the resources of conversion, so he could not call on them when forces came together to crush this man in the middle.

It could be said that the life Herod was saving was a false life, a social reputation based on a boast. Also, the extent he went to in order to protect that life, taking the life of another, was the type of power kings could wield in those long ago days. But I do not think that makes him exceptional. It makes him typical. We read every day of politicians and corporate executives, people at the top, who harm the lives of others to protect their lavish lifestyles. They exhibit the same quick and easy way with every life that is not their own. They have never converted from ego to soul, from love of self to love of others (see Mark 12:13 and parallels). They may have sat through a thousand sermons, but they are so attached to their social image that they become desperate whenever it is threatened. The heads of others are a small price to pay for the maintenance of their life in their world.

Herod is the dark brother to all who want to save their life in the world. Paradoxically, his darkness shows the path of light. We will only know how to correctly save our life in this world if we convert and value the eternal world. We must move beyond listening and not acting. No one knows what the future holds. Events are conspiring to bring us into situations where the only way to save our life will be to lose it, the only way to move justly and honestly forward will be to access the resources of conversion.

Sixteenth Sunday in Ordinary Time

Proper 11

Mark 6:30-34 *LM* • Mark 6:30-34, 53-56 *RCL*

Resting in Compassion

A Spiritual Commentary

The apostles gathered around Jesus, and told him all that they had done and taught.

He said to them, "Come away to a deserted place all by yourselves and rest a while."

For many were coming and going, and they had no leisure even to eat. And they went away in a boat to a deserted place by themselves.

Now many saw them going and recognized them, and they hurried there on foot from all the towns and arrived ahead of them.

As Jesus went ashore, he saw a great crowd; and he had compassion for them because they were like sheep without a shepherd; and he began to teach them many things.

It is tempting to read this passage from the point of view of harried, overworked missionaries. The apostles have just returned from the front lines of mission and debriefed with the person who sent them. Now, as Jesus said, it is time to go away by themselves and rest. After a tour of duty, they deserve some "rest and relaxation." They cannot get it where they are. There is "a revolving door" of people coming and going in such numbers and with so many demands that the apostles cannot even eat. So they get in a boat to get away, to rest and eat by themselves in "a deserted place" (v. 31), that is, a place without other people. But the demanding people continue to harass them. They go on foot to the place that Jesus and the apostles are journeying to by boat, and the feet of the people are faster than the oars. They arrive before the apostles. When Jesus goes ashore and sees the crowds, his compassion trumps his plan for eating and resting in a deserted place. He discerns that the people do not have the teaching they so desperately need. So he responds by teaching them "many things" (v. 34). No rest for the apostles. The mission is back on.

But this passage is peppered with spiritual symbols, and they tell a different story. After the apostles tell Jesus about their teaching and deeds, *it is not time for a break from mission. It is time for a deeper teaching about the nature of the mission and how it is to be carried out.* They are invited to "come away to a deserted place" to "rest" and "eat" (v. 31). A deserted place, as the disciples will emphasize later on (Mark 6:35), is not where food is normally found. Therefore, the desert becomes a symbol for learning how to be fed by God. (See also Jesus' time in the desert after his baptism.) To come away to that place means to return to the Source, to be nurtured by God.

Also, rest should not be taken in a conventional sense. It does not mean more time to sleep and play and less time to work. Rest is Sabbath rest, learning how to be sustained by the goodness of Creation, a Creation rooted in God. Rest does not mean inactivity but acting in consort with Creation, with the Spirit of the Creator who is already acting. The overall project is to learn how to receive divine energy and nourishment, energy and nourishment that drives the mission.

This is not an easy lesson to learn. The ability to receive from a transcendent Source entails interior adjustments. A shift in consciousness is required. Therefore, they must "go in a boat," cross over to another way of thinking. This other way does not leave people behind. Wherever the apostles go, people will recognize them and be there before them. The problem is not people but the "coming and going" that prevents eating. In other words, the way their activity takes them away from the sustaining Source is the problem. On the other shore, in the new consciousness, everything begins with compassion, with noticing and identifying with unmet spiritual needs. The mission is rooted and sustained by divine compassion, and the apostles must stay in touch with this compassion.

For users of the *Revised Common Lectionary:*

> **When they had crossed over, they came to land at Gennesaret and moored the boat. When they got out of the boat, people at once recognized him, and rushed about the whole region and began to bring the sick on mats to wherever they heard he was. And wherever he went, into villages or cities or farms, they laid the sick in the marketplaces and begged him that they might touch even the fringe of his cloak; and all who touched it were healed.**

Jesus is a magnet. His healing power draws people. As soon as he is recognized, they bring their sick on mats and lay them before him. In the midst of commerce where nobody has any time for those who cannot buy and sell, they beg to touch the fringe of his garment. Healing inevitably happens.

But are they afraid to ask for more from the great man? Do they grasp the depth of what is happening through him? Do they understand his wandering ways as the divine embrace and restoration of Creation? Do they understand they are not stealing a healing, but entering into a compassion that welcomes all?

Teaching

The scoop on compassion is that it is tiring. In both our work and personal lives, people arrive with myriad needs. It is not enough to perfunctorily meet these needs. We must empathize with the people who have them. Compassion entails an interpersonal exchange in which one person feels and suffers with another. It is not a matter of keeping our distance. It is a matter of overcoming our difference. But this living in the need world of another, sharing their suffering, can be draining. That is why so many service professionals complain about compassion fatigue.

But the hint in the text is that compassion is a form of rest. How can that be?

When we try to be compassionate from a self-understanding of difference, we can quickly become worn out. We view ourselves as in a superior position and the other in a needy position. We are called upon from our greater health or knowledge or expertise to help. In order to help we must understand the person from the inside. The effort entails bringing our greater being into their lesser being and lifting it up. This is heavy lifting, and too much of it makes us exhausted.

But compassion can also come from a self understanding of sameness. We can find in ourselves the connecting link with the other. This cannot be manufactured. It must be genuinely perceived. We must refrain from identifying with the "edge" we may have, the possession, attribute, or knowledge that makes us a little bit better or luckier. This disidentification is not easy to do. All our life we have been taught to use our difference to gain advantage. In fact, we even see our originality not in closeness to the Origin from which all things come but in those aspects of ourselves that no one else shares. In order for a shift from difference to sameness to become a possibility, we must "come away to a deserted place to rest" (see v. 31). Compassion from a self-understanding of sameness is an alternate consciousness.

Bede Griffiths, a Benedictine monk who lived and worked in India for many years, worked to develop this alternate consciousness. He always prayed the Jesus prayer, repeating at every chance, "Lord, Jesus Christ, Son of God, have mercy on me a sinner." This meditation brought him into unity with all people who are suffering from the effects of alienation:

> I unite myself with all human beings from the beginning of the world who have experienced separation from God, or from the eternal truth. I realize that, as human beings, we are all separated from God, from the source of our being. We are wandering in a world of shadows, mistaking the outward appearance of people and thing for reality. But at all times something is pressing us to reach out beyond the shadows, to face the reality, the truth, the inner meaning of our lives, and so to find God, or whatever name we give to the mystery which enfolds us. ("Going Out of Oneself," *Parabola* 24 [Summer 1999] 24–25)

His prayer reminds him, despite a lifetime of spiritual development, that he is one with everyone else, wandering in a world of shadows.

Another example of developing this sense of sameness can be found in a remarkable reflection of Stephen Levine and others on their experience of working with a "cancer" patient named Katherine. She contacted their Dying Project and told them she had cancer. Over a period of time she met with many of them and attended their retreats. Finally, people became suspicious, and it was discovered that she was "faking it." She was not ill. In fact, she had a history of faking sickness and abusing morphine. Eventually, she disappeared. Levine and his associates reflected:

> Clearly, our work with Katherine as with all such beings is work on ourselves. Another teaching in helplessness, another opportunity to let go of ourselves, to be no one special, to gently watch the constant changes of the mind—going beyond hope and doubt until at last fear dissolves in the sense of endless being, in the connectedness that joins us all. Katherine's mind is no different from the minds of any of us. It was just that she held in fiery pain to her suffering. We can only wish mercy for such beings and for those parts of ourselves too that scream out for attention and in confusion rail against the way of things. Her suffering is as real as anyone's we have worked with. We wish her Godspeed.

(*Meetings at the Edge: Dialogues with the Grieving and the Dying, the Healing and the Healed* [New York: Doubleday/Random House, Inc., 1984] 189)

There are many profound observations in this reflection. But the recognition of sameness is one of the most startling. "Katherine's mind is no different from the minds of any of us. It was just that she held in fiery pain to her suffering. We can only wish mercy for such beings and for those parts of ourselves too that scream out for attention and in confusion rail against the way of things." It is this recognition of sameness that is the wellspring of their compassion. The title of the episode is "A Deeper Pain than Dying."

When we recognize our sameness, our actions come from a space of communion. They are not the willful efforts of a separate being trying to exert influence in the foreign territory of another. They become the coordinated work of united people who are grounded in what ultimately unites them: a common humanity and a common Source. Compassion is not an achievement but the recognition of the deeper truth of solidarity. The consciousness of this truth is a restful place from which action flows easily, without pressure and pushing, happening more by itself.

Seventeenth Sunday in Ordinary Time

Proper 12

John 6:1-15 *LM* • John 6:1-21 *RCL*

Restoring Our Soul

A Spiritual Commentary

For users of the *Lectionary for Mass* and the *Revised Common Lectionary:*

Jesus went to the other side of the Sea of Galilee, also called the Sea of Tiberias. A large crowd kept following him, because they saw the signs that he was doing for the sick.

Jesus has a permanent following. However, why the large crowd is following him is ambiguous. They see that he is healing the sick, and healing alone will always attract people. But the healings are signs more than they are mighty works. They are meant to be seen through more than to be looked at. If people come to gawk and gape, they will only be dazzled by the exterior. If they come to meditate, they will receive the revelation.

Jesus went up the mountain and sat down there with his disciples. Now the Passover, the festival of the Jews, was near.

The mountain is the earth's highest point, the closest it gets to the sky. People ascend the mountain; God descends to the mountain. The mountain is where the divine and the human meet. (See the stories of Moses and Elijah, as well as the Transfiguration accounts, for example.) Jesus is the meeting of the divine and the human. He is seated in the position of the teacher, and his disciples are around him. Therefore, what follows will be a teaching about how the divine and the human work together.

When he looked up and saw a large crowd coming toward him, Jesus said to Philip, "Where are we to buy bread for these people to eat?"

He said this to test him, for he himself knew what he was going to do.

Philip answered him, "Six months' wages would not buy enough bread for each to them to get a little."

One of the disciples, Andrew, Simon Peter's brother, said to him, "There is a boy here who has five barley loaves and two fish. But what are they among so many people?"

The teaching begins by distinguishing the spiritual and the physical. Jesus sees with the eyes of the Spirit, and so he "looks up" to see the large crowd coming toward him. He is the "Word made Flesh" (see John 1:14, esp. the KJV Bible). So if they are coming toward him, they must want to understand how the Spirit manifests itself in the flesh. This is who Jesus is and what he always reveals.

However, not all are attuned to this level of reality. Jesus, the Teacher, tests his disciples to see where they are at, to discern their readiness to receive the revelation. Since they are the primary ones who are to understand the teaching, they must be engaged.

Both Philip and Andrew are mired in the material. When they hear the word "bread," it means flour and water. When they see people, they count how many. And they know the unalterable law of the physical dimension: scarcity. There are too many people, and there is too little money and too little bread. What they see—with a mind restricted to the physical dimension—is an impossibility. They neither envision bringing the spiritual to the physical nor do they know how to do that.

Jesus said, "Make the people sit down."

Now there was a great deal of grass in the place; so they sat down, about five thousand in all.

Then Jesus took the loaves, and when he had given thanks, he distributed them to those who were seated; so also the fish, as much as they wanted.

When they were satisfied, he told his disciples, "Gather up the fragments left over, so that nothing may be lost."

So they gathered them up, and from the fragments of the five barley loaves, left by those who had eaten, they filled twelve baskets.

The physical law of scarcity that the disciples know is replaced by the spiritual law of abundance that Jesus knows. It is this spiritual law that the disciples must learn. Their learning activity is to gather up all that is left over so that nothing is lost. They must remember and integrate this spiritual teaching into their lives and the lives of their communities.

But what are the dynamics of this spiritual law of abundance that is so essential to the disciples and their communities?

Jesus has the disciples make the people sit down. The seated Teacher is about to feed the seated people. They are seated on green grass. This is the imaginative posture that the psalmist requires:

> The LORD is my shepherd, I shall not want.
>   He makes me lie down in green pastures;
> he leads me beside still waters;
>   he restores my soul.
>   (Ps 23:1-3)

The Lord Jesus is going to restore the soul of his people. When the divine and human meet, this is what happens. The Spirit of God enters into the human spirit, as food is taken into the body, fills that spirit to its capacity ("as much as they wanted" [v. 11]) and completely "satisfies" its innate hunger for spiritual nourishment. This process is never exhausted, as the twelve baskets of leftovers signify (v. 13).

The large crowd that so impressed and disturbed the consciousness of the disciples is not daunting to the spiritual agenda of Jesus. Physical consciousness can only do division. It divides five barley loaves and two fish into five thousand and panics, "[W]hat are they among so many people?" (v. 9). Spiritual consciousness works by multiplication. It sees the five barley loaves and two fish of the small boy as the spiritual starting point. As the combined number of seven symbolizes, these loaves and fishes point to the sacred potential of the initiate, the small boy or girl that is the embryonic beginning of mature spiritual development. To literal physical consciousness they are not enough; to spiritual symbolic consciousness they are already becoming too much.

How does the rough, raw material grow into satisfying food?

We acknowledge our spiritual selves as gifts from the Source. We are not our own, but we are sustained at each moment by the Spirit who is beyond us. This fills us with gratitude, and the gratitude overflows. We distribute from our brimming fullness (our "cup overflows" [Ps 23:5]) to others. It is in this distributing, in this giving away, that the growth occurs. The physical law of scarcity can only understand giving away as a process of diminishment leading to nothing at all. The spiritual law of abundance understands giving away as a process of expansion leading to a sacred fullness. This way of restoring the soul is what the seated Teacher on the mountain wants to impress on his disciples. Perhaps if they gather up the abundance, they will not be controlled by a consciousness of physical scarcity.

When the people saw the sign that he had done, they began to say, "This is indeed the prophet who is to come into the world."

When Jesus realized that they were about to come and take him by force to make him king, he withdrew again to the mountain by himself.

The people did not receive the spiritual teaching. They saw the sign, but they could not follow the sign to the Source. They identify Jesus as the Prophet who is to come into the world. No matter who that prophet is, one like Moses or one like Elijah, Jesus is more than a prophet. He is also more than a king. He will tell Pilate, "my kingdom is not from here" (John 18:36). When people experience the bread and respond with prophesy and kingship, they have not seen the sign. The giver of the sign withdraws into his true identity, a mountain dweller, where the earth and sky meet, where God and humankind hold conversations.

For users of the *Revised Common Lectionary:*

When evening came, his disciples went down to the sea, got into a boat, and started across the sea to Capernaum. It was dark, and Jesus had not yet come to them. The sea became rough because a strong wind was blowing. When they had rowed about three or four miles, they saw Jesus walking on the sea and coming near the boat, and they were terrified.

But he said to them, "It is I; do not be afraid."

Then they wanted to take him into the boat, and immediately the boat reached the land toward which they were going.

Jesus comes to people in their darkness and fear. When their consciousness is benighted and they are buffeted by menacing circumstances, it means "Jesus had not yet come to them" (v. 17). But what terrorizes the disciples does not inhibit Jesus. He walks on the chaos that threatens to engulf them. He announces to them his name, telling them he has the same name as God. Although the translation of the NRSV text says, "It is I," the literal translation of the Greek, as the NRSV note states, is "I am," the name of God from Exodus 3:14. Knowing this, they should not be afraid. And then they do the one thing they have to do to move from fear to peace: They want to receive Jesus into the boat.

The prologue of St. John's Gospel says "But to all who received him, who believed in his name, he gave power to become children of God" (John 1:12). This desire is crucial. They believe in his name, the name of God, "I am." This receiving and believing makes them one with Jesus, a child of God. And children of God walk on waves; they do not drown beneath them. In Genesis, God gathered the waters that were everywhere into one place and made dry land appear (Gen 1:9). This is the continual action of the present God. The divine gives people a place to stand so the terrors, symbolized by the tumultuous seas, do not overwhelm them: "Immediately the boat reached the land" (v. 21).

Teaching

I have been told of a tombstone that simply reads" "It's always something!"

And it always is. Our barn burns down; the job offer arrives but it means moving to another city; our taxes are raised at the same time as our salary is reduced; our son calls at one in the morning from the police station; our spouse is suddenly sad and cannot explain; our doctor's office calls and leaves a message on the answering machine that they want to redo the blood test—and on, and on, and on. Indeed, life may be quiet, but we always add, quite sure of our foresight, that it is a quiet before the storm.

When we face challenges, we instinctively reach for the resources we need. Usually this means marshalling finances and networking with fellow workers, fellow sufferers, and friends. When it is appropriate and serious enough, we go "the whole nine yards" and reach into the spiritual realm. We expect help from God and/or the collective prayers of others. Emails regularly arrive with requests for prayers. What the Spirit is supposed to do is often spelled out in precise detail.

But what exactly is spiritual help?

Although we tell ourselves it won't happen, sometime we hope against hope and expect divine intervention. This does not have to be an angelic revelation or even a full-blown theophany. It can be a behind-the-scenes manipulation of events. When things suddenly shift and go in our favor, we have no problem in saying, "Thank God!" Sometimes it is just a religious knee-jerk reaction, but other times it is a genuine conviction that the Great Puppeteer was at work. Spiritual help is construed as an outside agent changing the outer flow of events. As long as we feel helpless in the face of "it's always something," we will seek greater powers to get things done.

However, spiritual help may not be directly about problem solving, about effectively engaging "it's always something." It may be directly about restoring a foundational disconnect. We are always out of touch with our souls to some degree. Spiritual help reestablishes this connection. Once we are situated more fully in the home of our soul, we can engage "it's always something" with more thorough comprehension and more sustained will.

Ralph Waldo Emerson has an interesting perspective on soul and how it functions:

> All goes to show that the soul in [a human being] is not an organ, but animates and exercises all the organs; is not a function, like the power of memory, of calculation, of comparison, but uses these as hands and feet; is not a faculty, but a light; is not the intellect or the will, but the master of the intellect and the will; is the background of our being, in which they lie—an immensity not possessed and that cannot be possessed. From within or from behind, a light shines through us upon things and makes us aware that we are nothing, but the light is all . . . When the soul breathes through intellect, it is genius; when it breathes through will, it is virtue; when it flows through affection, it is love. And the blindness of the intellect begins when it would be something of itself. The weakness of the will begins when the individual would be something of himself [or herself]. All reform aims in some one particular way to let the soul have its ways through us. (Essays: First Series, Essay 9, "The Oversoul")

Emerson sees soul as an animating reality, a background immensity that cannot be possessed, a light that shines through and breathes through functions with which we are more familiar: memory, calculation, intellect, will, etc. When this happens, intellect becomes genius, will becomes virtue, and affection becomes love. This is quite a description of a person being restored to his or her soul.

When we are each restored to our soul, our potential for handling "it's always something" is maximized. But, according to the suggestion hidden in the story of the loaves and the fishes, the maximizing effect is incremental. It begins by taking what soul consciousness we have, however immature and undeveloped. Then we acknowledge the groundedness of our soul in the Source and open to its influence. This allows the qualities of the Source to pass through our souls into our intellect, will, and affections. Now our actions are soul informed. In symbolic language, we are now distributing our loaves and fishes. With each distribution more Spirit is released. Since it is the nature of Spirit to give itself, it grows and becomes more fully present in mind, will, and affections. Therefore, the first action unfolds into a second, the second into a third, and on and on. As Lao Tzu says about the

Spirit, "when you draw upon it, it is inexhaustible" (*Tao Teh Ching*, 6 [New York: St. John's University Press, 1961] 9).

Our soul is restored by exercise. With each exercise, its influence multiplies. Since it is our true identity, we feel satisfied. We need not worry about scarcity. There is no scarcity in the Spirit (John 3:34). We should be thankful to all the disciples who gathered up the abundant fragments. Otherwise, we may have forgotten how to cooperate with the Source who is restoring our soul.

Eighteenth Sunday in Ordinary Time

Proper 13

John 6:24-35

Adjusting Consciousness

A Spiritual Commentary

[W]hen the crowd saw that neither Jesus nor his disciples were [at the place where Jesus had given the bread], they themselves got into the boats and went to Capernaum looking for Jesus.

When they found him on the other side of the sea, they said to him, "Rabbi, when did you come here?"

Jesus answered them, "Very truly, I tell you, you are looking for me, not because you saw signs, but because you ate your fill of the loaves. Do not work for the food that perishes, but for the food that endures for eternal life, which the Son of Man will give you. For it is on him that the Father has set his seal."

The crowd that is looking for Jesus is in search of a wonder worker. They saw the disciples get into a boat, but Jesus was not with them (John 6:22-23). So they themselves got into boats, trailing the disciples. Can the master be far from the disciples? When they find Jesus, they are intrigued about when he arrived. Since he did not come by boat, how did he arrive? Perhaps there has been a wonder and they have missed it.

Jesus surmises the hunger for the miraculous beneath their trivial question about the time of his arrival. He tries to redirect their concerns, to refocus their inquiring minds. They are seeking him because they have filled their bellies on the loaves. But they have not understood the loaves as signs of God's care for people. They are well acquainted with their physical hunger and deeply attached to filling it. But they are less acquainted with their spiritual hunger and unsure how to fill it. Jesus tells them that he himself, as the Son of Man, is the one who feeds them with eternal food. The Father, the Source of this eternal food, has approved this path and this process of entering into the eternal order (v. 27).

Then they said to him, "What must we do to perform the works of God?"

Jesus answered them, "This is the work of God, that you believe in him whom he has sent."

Jesus adjusts the consciousness of the crowd a second time. They hear his concern with eternal food as the traditional emphasis on performing the works of God. The Law enjoins them to imitate God, to do as God does. But this is only possible if people are co-acting with God. They can only do the works (the many) if they are united to the work (the one). With clever word play, Jesus says that he is the work of God. Therefore, to do the works of God they must join the work of God, to enter into the identity and mission of "him whom he has sent" (v. 29). The external works have to connect with inner consciousness. Law (outer) and spirit (inner) must form a partnership. In the words of the prologue, "The law indeed was given through Moses; grace and truth came through Jesus Christ" (John 1:17).

So they said to him, "What signs are you going to give us then, so that we may see it and believe you? What work are you performing? Our ancestors ate the manna in the wilderness; as it is written, 'He gave them bread from heaven to eat.'"

Then Jesus said to them, "Very truly, I tell you, it was not Moses who gave you the bread from heaven, but it is my Father who gives you the true bread from heaven. For the bread of God is that which comes down from heaven and gives life to the world."

Jesus adjusts the consciousness of the crowd a third time. They think that signs attest to the truth and authenticity of the person. If Jesus is the work of God, what work is he performing that would lead people to believe in him? They know the Law is from God, for Moses, the lawgiver, provided manna in the wilderness. Where bread was not available by natural means, it was provided by supernatural means, that is, bread from heaven (v. 31). This miracle means the Law which Moses gave is from God. The manna constitutes outside validation.

Jesus wants them to think about both bread from heaven and how they come to judgments of truth in a different way. The bread from heaven in the past was pieces of manna scattered on the earth. It was physical food, but even as physical food it was not meant to validate Moses. It was meant to reveal God. Jesus' Father is the ultimate giver of the true bread from heaven, and he is giving it at all times. This true bread from heaven is spiritual life for the world. It is wider than the history and people of Israel. It connects alienated Creation to its Source. This bread is its own reality. It does not point to something else; it is not a piece of an argument for authenticity. The experience of this divine life is its own authentication.

They said to him, "Sir, give us this bread always."

Jesus said to them, "I am the bread of life. Whoever comes to me will never be hungry, and whoever believes in me will never be thirsty."

Jesus adjusts the consciousness of the crowd a fourth time. The crowd has not completely followed Jesus' attempt to restructure their thinking. All they have heard is the possibility of Jesus' Father providing bread in a continuous way. They envision manna on the ground every day. Jesus can do this for it is his Father who is the ultimate giver. So they politely ("Sir") make the request.

Since "the bread of life" (v. 35) is the spiritual nourishment that flows from God into the world, and since Jesus is the Word who connects God to creation (John 1), he himself is the bread of life. And he is meant for others. Whoever comes to him will enter into a relationship with the eternal and so they will never feel spiritual hunger or spiritual thirst.

In these exchanges Jesus is dealing with a conventional religious consciousness that is difficult to change. It values miraculous deeds because they provide for physical needs and authenticate what a person says. Conventional religious consciousness stops short of considering the deeds as signs that reveal the deeper world of Spirit. In a similar way, those persons with this consciousness are concerned about actions that can be seen but not about the interiority of the actor, the place that enables the actions to be performed. Their consciousness is locked into the visible, material, and temporal. The invisible, spiritual, and eternal elude them.

Teaching

At a retreat I gave many years ago, a woman stood up and quickly stated her problem: "I'm tired of being an apple giver." She had three children under the age of five. They were always on her. "Mommy, get me an apple." "Mommy, tie my shoes." "Mommy, put on my coat." "Mommy, take off my coat." Never ending. She was sick of it.

The group was instantly supportive. Many had been there, and there was no shortage of advice: daycare; part-time employment; more husband-father involvement, etc. In the midst of these suggestions, another voice was suddenly heard. An older woman spoke up, "Honey, you gotta learn to sing." Then she went on to explain that the "apple giver" had to change her whole attitude. None of these escapist suggestions were going to provide lasting help. Tinkering with the outer world was not a substitute for inner change. She had to make "apple giving" an event where she and her child met. Although this older woman was eloquent, I am not sure she was heard.

In most situations there is a need for adjustments in both the outer and inner worlds. But we tend to emphasize the outer world as the litmus test of change. If we are doing something, we feel we are addressing the challenge. If we are only discovering how our ingrained ways of thinking and feeling are contributing to our situation, we might be accused of procrastination.

I was at a planning meeting once where the convener began with, "I am sure this meeting will lead to a call to action." If it did, the supposition was that the meeting would be a success.

However, spiritual teachers value interior change as the forerunner to new and incisive action. They often tweak and tease the consciousness of their student to see things in new ways. They do not state timeless truths but complement or correct what they already see happening. Jack Kornfield tells this story of his teacher Ajahn Chah:

> "It's like this," he said. "There is a road I know well, but it can be foggy or dark. When I see someone traveling this road about to fall in a ditch or get lost in a sidetrack on the right-hand side, I call out, 'Go to the left.' Similarly, if I see someone about to fall into a ditch or get lost in a sidetrack on the left-hand side, I call out, 'Go to the right.' That's all I do when I teach. Wherever you get caught, I say, 'Let go of that too.'" (*After the Ecstasy, the Laundry: How the Heart Grows Wise on the Spiritual Path* [New York: Bantam Books/Random House, Inc., 2000] 168–69)

Adjusting consciousness is largely a matter of balance. It adds, subtracts, multiplies, and divides, depending on what is needed. The teacher knows the road well; she or he helps others in fog and darkness.

Although Jesus' conversations with people who challenge or disagree with him are often polemical, I like to think of him as a teacher calling out, "Go to the left" or "Go to the right." In his dialogue with the crowds, I hear him saying:

"Don't keep hungering after wonders as wonders, thinking the next miracle will solve your problems. Notice there is a deeper hunger in you, not for what perishes in time but for what lasts into eternity."

"Turn your mind from doing things to the inner space from which you are able to do things. God's work is always co-done with God."

"Don't ask, 'How will I know this is true?' Ask, 'Am I in communion with God and receiving divine life?'"

"Manna every morning will not solve the whole problem. Connect with me and be forever satisfied on a spiritual level."

These are not easy adjustments to be made. When they cannot be made, the villain is a hardened heart, an inflexible attachment to a surface way of being and thinking.

However, when consciousness does adjust to the spiritual, it can change the human life in profound ways. One of my favorite stories of adjusting consciousness (a story also used in the first volume of this set) I have titled, "Junk!" It goes like this:

God bless my mother, and God bless me. We made it through.

She had a stroke and long period or rehabilitation, and it was clear she was going to have to stay with us for a while. I had all these things in mind: it was a chance to pay her back for all those years. There were these things I was going to help her clear up, like the way she was thinking. I wanted to do the whole job very well, this big opportunity. We should all feel good about it at the end. Little things like that. Some "little"!

Fights? Classics, like only a mother and daughter can have. And my mother is a great fighter, from the Old School of somehow loving it and being very good at it and getting a kind of ecstatic look in your eye when you're really into it. I guess I'm exaggerating. It drives me a little crazy. I hate to argue. Oh, well . . .

But it got bad. Over a hard-boiled egg we had a bad fight. We'd both gotten worn out, irritable, and frustrated. Boom! I don't remember what about—just about how it was all going and why her stay had gotten difficult and all of us had become more and more irritable and short-tempered.

In the middle of it, she stopped short and said, "Why are you doing all this for me anyway?" It sort of hit me and I started to list all the reasons. They just came out: I was afraid for her; I wanted to get her well; I felt maybe I'd ignored her when I was younger; I needed to show her I was strong; I needed to get her ready for going home alone; old age; and on and on. I was amazed myself. I could have gone on giving reasons all night. Even she was impressed.

"Junk," she said when I was done.

"Junk?" I yelled. Like, boy, she'd made a real mistake with that remark. I could really get her.

"Yes, junk," she said again, but a little more quietly. And that little-more-quietly tone got me. And she went on: "You don't have to have all those reasons. We love each other. That's enough."

I felt like a child again. Having your parents show you something that's true, but you don't feel put down—you feel better, because it is true, and you know it, even though you are a child. I said, "You're right. You're really right. I'm sorry." She said, "Don't be sorry. Junk is fine. It's what you don't need anymore. I love you."

It was a wonderful moment, and the fight stopped, which my mother accepted a little reluctantly. No, I'm joking—she was very pleased. She saw how it all was. Everything after that was just, well, easier—less pressure, less trying, less pushing, happening more by itself. And the visit ended up fine. We just spent time together, and then she went back to her house. (Ram Dass and Paul Gorman, *How Can I Help?: Stories and Reflections on Service* [New York: Knopf/Random House, Inc., 1985] 191–92)

There is a deeper level where spiritual love elevates our efforts, and things are "easier, less trying, less pushing, happening more by itself." Anyone who does not need this, please raise your hand.

Nineteenth Sunday in Ordinary Time

Proper 14

John 6:41-51 *LM* • John 6:35, 41-51 *RCL*

Being Pushed

A Spiritual Commentary

For users of the *Revised Common Lectionary:*

> Jesus said to them, "I am the bread of life. Whoever comes to me will never be hungry, and whoever believes in me will never be thirsty."

For users of the *Lectionary for Mass* and the *Revised Common Lectionary:*

> Then the Jews began to complain about him because he said, "I am the bread that came down from heaven." They were saying, "Is not this Jesus, the son of Joseph, whose father and mother we know? How can he now say, 'I have come down from heaven.'?"

> Jesus answered them, "Do not complain among yourselves. No one can come to me unless drawn by the Father who sent me; and I will raise that person up on the last day. It is written in the prophets, 'And they shall be taught by God.' Everyone who has heard and learned from the Father comes to me. Not that anyone has seen the Father except the one who is from God; he has seen the Father."

The "complaining" of the Jews (religious authorities) is often translated "murmuring." Murmuring is an inner state of smoldering confusion that could, at any moment, erupt into anger and violence. It is that combustible combination of "I don't get it" but "I don't like it." What is causing this complaining is a perceived discrepancy in Jesus' self-understanding. Jesus' human origins are known to them and "now" he is saying something that is incompatible with these origins. He is saying, "I have come down from heaven" (v. 42; cf. v. 41). He cannot have it both ways. He may be a heavenly figure who has come down and lived as a human being, or an earthly figure who has received divine

201

revelations. But he cannot be, at the same time, born of the human and born of the divine.

This would seem to be an opportune occasion for Jesus to articulate the foundation for the later christological doctrine of "truly human and truly divine." However, he takes the conversation in another direction. Jesus did not only say, "I have come down from heaven." He said, "I am the *bread* that came down from heaven" (v. 41) and "I am the *bread* of life" (v. 35). His emphasis was not directly on his identity and therefore on his authority, a theme with which religious authorities are obsessed. He emphasized his role as the giver of divine life to others, as the invitation to eat bread that satisfies hunger forever. He corrects their truncated rendition of what he is about.

The Jews should not complain among themselves. They only compound their lack of understanding and increase their sense of outrage. The people who can illumine their misunderstanding are those who have come to Jesus to receive the "bread come down from heaven." They have come because they already knew Jesus' Father in an inchoate way and were led by the Father to the one whom the Father sent. This is basic spirituality. The ones whom God teaches recognize the fullness of God's life, the life that is everlasting, the life that will raise them up on the last day. They have heard God's word and learned from it, and therefore they are open and ready. But they have not seen God in the way that the one "who is close to the Father's heart" has (John 1:18). But in the divine plan this "heart mate" has made known the Father. Therefore, those of the truth seek this greater revelation of the truth.

> **"Very truly, I tell you, whoever believes has eternal life. I am the bread of life. Your ancestors ate the manna in the wilderness, and they died. This is the bread that comes down from heaven, so that one may eat of it and not die. I am the living bread that came down from heaven. Whoever eats of this bread will live forever; and the bread that I will give for the life of the world is my flesh."**

Jesus now powerfully reasserts his central concern. The project is to eat the bread of life, to enter into the selfhood of Jesus and participate in his loving relationship with the Father. This sustenance is on another level from manna. Although it was given by God, manna was earthly food meant to sustain earthly life. Those who ate it died. Jesus is living bread, bread that sustains and transforms people through death. In fact, this bread is precisely Jesus' dying flesh given for the life of the alienated world, a world where death reigns. Jesus, the bread of life, will enter into and go beyond death. Those who eat this bread of life will die and rise with him.

Teaching

Why are some people attracted to Jesus? Why do the words of Jesus ring some people like a bell? Why do some people "leave all things and follow him"? (see Mark 10:28, for example). That is, why, do they see him as most important and reprioritize their lives so he is first?

This conversation with the so-called "Jews," people who are not attracted to him and who openly oppose him, provides a theological answer. This answer may or may not be persuasive. But in order to determine if it is applicable in any individual case, there is a need for inner work to detect the source of fascination with Jesus. The suggestion is: people are attracted to Jesus and enter into him because they already know the Father who sent him. In other words, the love of God is already in their hearts. So when they see that love blazing out of Jesus, they move toward it. Like is seeking like. It becomes a meeting of two fires, one may be only a brush fire but the other is a bush burning that is not burned up (see Exod 3:2).

Understanding this process might begin with the Johannine thunderclap that God first loved us (1 John 4:9). In the act of Creation, God has put his love into our hearts. In the language of the prologue, all things are created through the Word who is with God and who is God (John 1:1, 3). Creation is not a past event. After it was over, the Word did not recede back, so to speak, into its unity with God. Rather the Word is continuously present to Creation, sustaining and transforming it. This same Word that holds the Father and Creation in communion has become flesh, visible, audible, and tangible in Jesus (John 1:14). Therefore, those who have listened and been taught by the Word in Creation will recognize this Word in "the son of Joseph, whose father and mother we know" (v. 41) in the earthly Jesus.

How exactly will this recognition work?

In ancient spirituality, the love of God was considered a fire that pushed up the chest and moved out the eyes. This allowed a person to see whatever of God was on the outside because they were in touch with the inner love of God which was the source of their own being. This perspective is reflected in a piece of spiritual observation in both

Matthew (6:23) and Luke (11:34): if your eye is healthy, it is because your whole body is filled with light. In other words, the inner light of God floods out of the eye and allows you to see the divine in the outside world. But if your eye is bad, it is because your body is filled with darkness. One who is not in touch with the inner light of God cannot see it in the outside world. The problem with the religious authorities in St. John's Gospel is that they have "hardened hearts" (see, for example, John 5:42 or 12:37-43). The inner light has been extinguished, and therefore they are incapable of seeing the light of Christ. The remedy—one they will not accept—is to hang around with people whose hearts are not hardened, people who are coming to Jesus.

In his study of Meister Eckhart, Cyprian Smith develops this way of thinking: "God cannot be found or grasped in the external world, but only in the inner world. If we seek him outside, we shall find him nowhere; if we seek him within, we shall find him everywhere. This is not to say that only the inner world is real. Both are real; both have their own measure of importance. But it is the inner world which has the priority and the greater importance . . . Having discovered God within, we can discover him without; but never the other way round" (*The Way of Paradox: Spiritual Life as Taught by Meister Eckhart* [New York: Paulist Press, 1987] 51).

The flavor of this approach is captured in the popular saying attributed to God, "You would not be searching for me if I had not first found you" (see John 15:15). If we are attracted to Jesus, it is consoling to think it is because we already share the same Father. But the same Father can have quite different children. The lesser and greater must not be forgotten. Our intuitions may allow us to recognize Jesus' revelation; but Jesus' revelation goes well beyond our intuitions. In theological language, Creation and Incarnation are related, but Incarnation is intensified Creation, going well beyond what we could discover on our own. That is why when Jesus says, "No one can come to me unless drawn by the Father who sent me" (v. 44), I stumble on the word, "drawn." In my experience it is more like being pushed by a God who really wants us to experience what it is like to be God's child.

Twentieth Sunday in Ordinary Time

Proper 15

John 6:51-58

Receiving Communion

A Spiritual Commentary

[Jesus said to the crowd:] "I am the living bread that came down from heaven. Whoever eats of this bread will live forever; and the bread that I will give for the life of the world is my flesh."

The Jews then disputed among themselves, saying, "How can this man give us his flesh to eat?"

So Jesus said to them, "Very truly, I tell you, unless you eat the flesh of the Son of Man and drink his blood, you have no life in you. Those who eat my flesh and drink my blood have eternal life, and I will raise them up on the last day; for my flesh is true food and my blood is true drink. Those who eat my flesh and drink my blood abide in me, and I in them. Just as the living Father sent me, and I live because of the Father, so whoever eats me will live because of me. This is the bread that came down from heaven, not like that which your ancestors ate, and they died. But the one who eats this bread will live forever."

The central image in this conversational teaching is eating. Eating is an act of assimilation, an intimate act by which a part of the world becomes part of us. I often joke that when you look at me, you see at least sixty percent chicken. We are not separate from the world. In fact, we are physically constituted by the world. It is this eating dynamic that Jesus uses for his spiritual purposes. As we eat bread and it becomes part of us, so we must integrate the consciousness of Jesus and make it our own. The key concern is the transfer of consciousness from Jesus to us. As one spiritual teacher puts it, "When we eat material food, it becomes us. When we eat spiritual food, we become it."

"The Jews," picking up on the last word Jesus said, "flesh," ask: "How can this man give us his flesh to eat?" (v. 52). If they mean this

205

literally, some gruesome images are inhibiting their imagination. Although their question might be misguided, Jesus' evocative and symbolic answer extends the teaching. The image of eating "the living bread come down from heaven" (v. 51) is now transformed into imagery of eating his flesh and drinking his blood, the flesh and blood of the Son of Man. This division of flesh and blood symbolizes the death of Jesus and points to the way he is going to communicate his consciousness. Jesus' death is conceived as a movement from "a grain of wheat" into "much fruit" (John 12:24; see the Fifth Sunday of Lent, above). It is not a loss, but a transformative process through which he will be more. Part of that more is his increased accessibility. He will be available to more people as the risen Lord than he is as Jesus the historical individual.

The form of this accessibility will be participation in the ritual eucharistic meal. Eating the bread will be eating his flesh, drinking the wine will be drinking his blood. Through these symbolic acts the revelation of his dying will be communicated to those who eat and drink. What will they ingest? They will appropriate the embodied consciousness of Jesus, the abiding awareness of divine love transforming death into new life.

Although material food and drink can be assimilated without attending to the process, consciousness cannot be transferred in an unconscious way. The people will have to eat and drink in a certain way. The Greek word Jesus uses for "eating" emphasizes the "physical crunching" of food (see Francis J. Moloney, *The Gospel of John* [Collegeville, Minn.: Liturgical Press, 1998] 221.) Robert Nozick's description of "taking in food" suggests a path of development for the symbolic activity of rigorously chewing:

> [A]wareness is focused upon the activity of taking in the food, not simply on the food's qualities. We meet the food in the anteroom of the mouth and greet it there. We probe and explore it, surround it, permeate it with juices, press it with our tongues against the roof of the mouth along that hard ridge directly above the teeth, place it under suction and pressure, move it around. We know its texture fully; it holds no secrets or hidden parts . . . [(t)asting foods] is a mode of knowing them in their inner essence. (*The Examined Life* [New York: Simon & Schuster, 1989] 56–57)

This literal way of probing and knowing food is symbolic of what must occur if the mind of Christ is going to become our mind through eucharistic eating and drinking. We must assimilate the inner essence.

Teaching

When I was growing up, more than a few years ago, one of the liturgical practices was a meditation after communion. When people returned to their places after receiving communion, they usually knelt and, putting their head in their hands, focused on the presence of Christ who had just entered into them. It was a "mini-meditation" because the celebrant usually resumed the final prayer of Mass rather quickly. In those day priests were often clocked to see how fast they could say Mass. But many people stayed on after Mass to continue the interior activity they had begun.

I have no idea what other people did in that postcommunion quiet. In fact, I do not remember in any detail what I did. But I do know that for me it was the most meaningful part of Mass. It was guaranteed intimacy with Christ. For a short time during and after the host dissolved, God was immediately accessible to an inward glance. In my growing up years this was incredibly important. In my later years this importance has returned.

But there was also what I can only call a transcendent evanescence, a sense that this divine presence dissolved and went beyond. I could be there with it, but I could not hold onto it. And there was that moment when it was over, when somehow I knew it was time to move on. I was never sure if I left the presence of Christ in the church because I decided to leave, or if Christ, by the very nature of his vastness, decided to withdraw. But suddenly the everyday world was in my mind, modified by my time with Christ, but as insistent and demanding as always. I knew one eating would never do it. I would have to return again.

I enjoyed this post-communion activity, but I never fully understood it. Then I came upon three mystical prose poems of Pierre Teilhard de Chardin, collected under the heading "Christ in the World of Matter," (*Hymn of the Universe*, trans. Simon Bartholomew [New York: Harper & Row, 1965] 42–58). In all three stories a friend is telling Teilhard of his mystical experiences of Christ. The stories move Teilhard to new levels: "After listening to my friend, my heart began to burn within me and my mind awoke to a new and higher vision of things. I began to realize vaguely that the multiplicity of evolutions into which the world-process seems to us to be split up is in fact fundamentally the working out of one single mystery . . ."

The friend is a priest on a World War I battlefield in France. He carries the eucharistic species in a pyx (a small round container that is carried next to the heart.) "I suddenly realized just how extraordinary and how disappointing it was to be thus *holding so close to oneself* the wealth of the world, and the very source of life *without being able to possess it* inwardly, *without being able to either penetrate it* or to assimilate it." This is the emphasis of the Gospel text. There is a need to be incorporated into Christ by assimilating his consciousness, to eat his body and drink his blood.

So the priest "gave myself Holy Communion"—ate the flesh of the Son of Man. But what he expected to happen did not happen. Although the bread had become "flesh of my flesh, nevertheless *it remained outside of me*." He marshals his attention, humbles himself, purifies his heart—all in a "vain yet blessed attempt!" He envisions the host as always ahead of him, "further on in a greater permeability of my being to the divine influences." Although he continues to penetrate more deeply into the host, its center was *"receding from me as it drew me on."*

Since he could not reach the inner depths of the host, he decides to focus on the surface. "But there a new infinity awaited me." When he tries to hold onto the surface of the host, he found that what he was holding onto was "not the host at all but one or other of the thousand entities which make up our lives: a suffering, a joy, a task, a friend to love or to console . . ." The innermost depths of the host had eluded him and now the surface of the host was likewise eluding him, "leaving me at grips with the entire universe which had reconstituted itself and drawn itself forth from its sensible appearances." In eating the consciousness of Christ he discovered both God and the universe were beyond his capturing. He states simply, "I will not dwell on the feeling of rapture produced in me by this revelation of the universe placed between Christ and myself like a magnificent prey."

Christians eat the body and drink the blood of the Son of Man (the fully Human One) on a regular basis, some every Sunday, some every day. But anything done on a regular basis can become routine. For those of us prone to habituation, it is good to dip into the mystical consciousness of the Eucharist. Receiving communion can initiate entry into the consciousness of Christ, and the consciousness of Christ, no matter how it is presented, is always quite a trip.

Twenty-First Sunday in Ordinary Time

Proper 16

John 6:60-69 LM • **John 6:56-69** RCL

Coming to Believe and Know

A Spiritual Commentary

For users of the *Revised Common Lectionary:*

> [Jesus said to the crowd:] "Those who eat my flesh and drink my blood abide in me, and I in them. Just as the living Father sent me, and I live because of the Father, so whoever eats me will live because of me. This is the bread come down from heaven, not like that which your ancestors ate, and they died. But the one who eats this bread will live forever." He said these things while he was teaching in the synagogue at Capernaum.

The central message of John's Gospel is stated once again. Jesus lives by the life of the Father, a transcendent love. Although he participates in physical life, his identity flows from this life-giving relationship to God. He offers this same relationship to all who can enter into his consciousness and make it their own. This is a new consciousness. The past consciousness could not transcend death. This new consciousness opens people to eternal life. They share in Christ's identity, living by the Father.

This spiritual revelation is expressed and communicated in the physical and social images of flesh, blood, eating, bread, and heaven. This pairing of the spiritual with the physical and social sets the stage for the difficulty the disciples will experience. It is a difficulty associated with the synagogue teaching that stresses the complete transcendence of God and the complete finitude of people. What Jesus has to say does not fit easily into that theological mindset.

For users of the *Lectionary for Mass* and the *Revised Common Lectionary:*

> When many of his disciples heard [Jesus' words about eating his flesh and blood], they said, "This teaching is difficult; who can accept it?"

209

But Jesus, being aware that his disciples were complaining about it, said to them, "Does this offend you? Then what if you were to see the Son of Man ascending to where he was before? It is the spirit that gives life; the flesh is useless. The words I have spoken to you are spirit and life. But among you there are some who do not believe."

For Jesus knew from the first who were the ones that did not believe, and who was the one that would betray him. And he said, "For this reason I have told you that no one can come to me unless it is granted by the Father."

Jesus is the "bread come down from above" (see v. 58). His origins are in heaven; his manifestation is on earth. Moreover, Jesus is not saying this only about himself. He promises that all who believe in him will move from heaven to earth, from eternal life into temporal live, from the bosom of the Father into a community of friends.

This reverses the ordinary consciousness of religious people, in particular some of his disciples. They are set in their belief that God is completely other and people are completely earthbound. The origin of people is from the earth (Gen 2:7). They have glimmers of a higher world, but they do not belong to it. Jesus has it the "wrong way around." People are physical beings with spiritual intuitions, not spiritual beings seeking ever greater incarnations. Jesus' saying goes completely counter to normal expectations. It is difficult to both understand and accept.

Jesus knows their mental quandary. He understands the offense he is giving to their everyday consciousness. Perhaps the offense would be less if he, the Son of Man who is the full revelation of divine-human interaction, started with earth and ascended to heaven. At least then there would be the starting point with which they are familiar. But, of course, this would only be temporary appeasement. Heaven is "where he was before" (see John 1:1). It is always a matter of interaction between the physical and the spiritual, earth and heaven, ascending and descending angels (John 1:51), ascending and descending Son of Man. But in the consciousness of the Word Made Flesh (John 1:14; cf. KJV Bible), the initiative is always from above.

The flesh may run on its own biological life. But this life in itself is limited, and it perishes. However, this fleshy life is also enfolded in the life principle, in "the spirit that gives life" (v. 63). This spiritual life suffuses, transforms, and transcends the multiple forms it inhabits. When

Jesus speaks, he is talking about this transcendent spirit and life and how it is shared by all who can open to it. This consciousness change— not from flesh to spirit, but from spirit to flesh—is a difficult shift. Many will not be able to make the transition. They will walk away with their old mind in tact rather than stretch toward this new possibility. Even worse, one will betray the giver of this consciousness, and so threaten to destroy it. The ones who stay and develop will do so because they know they are children of the Father. They hear Jesus' words as drawing them back to their Source.

> **Because of this many of his disciples turned back and no longer went about with him.**
>
> **So Jesus asked the twelve, "Do you also wish to go away?"**
>
> **Simon Peter answered him, "Lord to whom can we go? You have the words of eternal life. We have come to believe and know that you are the Holy One of God."**

Staying with Jesus is always a decision. The disciples who left could not hack the consciousness shift. They were not ready to eat the food that the "bread" who "came down from heaven" had prepared. The twelve stayed because they were already eating. The words of Jesus had communicated to them eternal life. Therefore, they went through a process of coming to belief and knowledge. If Jesus could give them eternal life, his origins must be in God. He is of heaven, not of earth, the Holy One of God, the descending Son of Man. Although it is not finished, the consciousness shift of the Twelve is well under way.

Teaching

The last exchange between Jesus and the Twelve is very dramatic. Jesus confronts the inner group of the Twelve. Do they wish to leave as the others have done? Peter, a Gospel character not known to rise to every occasion, says there is no place to go. Jesus has everything they need. They will stay. Since we are cheering for Jesus' revelation to be received, we soar on the emotional high of Peter's fidelity.

The two options are leaving and staying. But the more intriguing possibility may have already happened. It is caught in Peter's reason for staying, "We have come to believe and know" (v. 69). Coming to believe and know is a process that begins with trusting enough—and ends with understanding enough.

Every so often I assign, as required reading in a course I teach, a text that is written from a very developed spiritual point of view. The author's point of view is not ordinary fare; and throughout the book she never lets up. The reaction of students is diverse but fairly consistent. Initially, there are a multitude of complaints. "Why can't she give more examples?" "Is this stuff orthodox?" "She can't be serious." "I can't tell you how much I disagree with this!" This is a book which, as teachers say, "You have to teach." I go over segments of the text in class and try to articulate in different language what she is trying to communicate. The students are not impressed or appeased. I tell them, "Hang in there." I use what little authority I have to encourage this perseverance.

About halfway through the book, some lights go on. Things are beginning to happen. There is more life in the group, even excitement. The comments change. "I think I have an example of that." "This is the real stuff, isn't it?" "I'm beginning to take this stuff seriously." "This book is really expanding how I see things." Soon many, but not all, are running with the material. They have come to believe and know. Somewhere along the way I tell them what a professor told me many years ago, "Never read a book you could write."

Spiritual teachers are more developed than those who follow them. So what they say and do is not going to be immediately understood by disciples. The consciousness of the followers is not a match for the consciousness of the teacher. Most often, the categories of the students are old wineskins (see Mark 2:22 and parallels). The new wine of the teacher bursts them. This means the followers must initially trust teachers, believe enough in what they say to explore it further. This trust is neither absolute nor forever. It does not mean anything goes, and it is not the goal of the relationship. Followers just have to "believe enough" because at this stage they do not "know enough."

Spiritual development within a faith tradition often walks this path from belief to understanding. When I was growing up, I struggled with the doctrine of the Trinity. What in the world was "one God in three persons" about? My teachers told me not to worry. "It is a mystery," they said, "a mystery we must believe in for our salvation." I stammered that in order to believe I had to know what it was about. They assured me that my ignorance was not an obstacle. I could believe on the authority of the Church who proclaimed this mystery under the inspiration of the Holy Spirit. In my own simple way of thinking, I could lean on the greater consciousness of the tradition until my own had developed. That's what I did. I said inside myself,

"This makes sense and it is important." This believing made me persevere until more understanding developed. Of course, part of that understanding was the idea of essential mystery. The more I understood the doctrine of the Trinity, the more mysterious it became.

Sometimes people think faith is the desired goal, and they think strong faith is an exercise of the will that fiercely holds on to what it cannot understand. However, in this way of thinking, faith is the first step. We have to find the larger consciousness to which we will apprentice ourselves. We have to trust and believe in that consciousness long enough to learn from it. Once understanding begins and grows, the external supports for belief are still appreciated, but they are no longer primary. If the consciousness is aligned with Love, if the Bread is true, if the "flesh" and Blood is nourishment, then life flows in us. We have come not only to believe but to know (see v. 69), and we stay because eternal life is flowing.

> And if the earthly no longer knows your name,
>   whisper to the silent earth: I am flowing.
>   To the flashing water: say I am.

> (Rainer Maria Rilke, *The Sonnets to Orpheus*, 2.29,
> trans. Stephen Mitchell [New York: Simon & Schuster, 1985])

Twenty-Second Sunday in Ordinary Time

Proper 17

Mark 7:1-8, 14-15, 21-23

Finding the Drivers

A Spiritual Commentary

[W]hen the Pharisees and some of the scribes who had come from Jerusalem gather around [Jesus], they noticed that some of his disciples were eating with defiled hands, that is, without washing them. (For the Pharisees, and all the Jews, do not eat unless they thoroughly wash their hands, thus observing the tradition of the elders; and they do not eat anything from the market unless they wash it; and there are also many other traditions that they observe, the washing of cups, pots, and bronze kettles.)

So the Pharisees and the scribes asked him, "Why do your disciples not live according to the tradition of the elders, but eat with defiled hands?"

He said to them, "Isaiah prophesied rightly about you hypocrites, as it is written, 'this people honors me with their lips, / but their hearts are far from me; / in vain do they worship me, / teaching human precepts as doctrines.' You abandon the commandment of God and hold to human tradition."

At the core of the Jewish tradition is the double commandment to love God and neighbor (Mark 12:29-30 and parallels). As generation succeeds generation, many ancillary traditions are created to adapt this love of God and neighbor to new situations. In theory, these traditions are always secondary to the center, to the loving heart of the tradition itself. They are evaluated by how they correspond to this center and heart. However, in practice, these traditions become functionally autonomous. They take on a life of their own. The distinction between the center and the periphery, the heart and the lips is obscured. The valid question of embodying the center and heart in particular traditions is reduced to an obsession with externals.

Also, the center and the heart are inside. They cannot be observed and measured directly. The traditions are external behaviors and often deal with objects (certain foods, cups, pots, bronze kettles, etc.). These are able to be seen and scrutinized. The heart may be hidden; but hands are available for inspection. Therefore, those who see themselves as guardians of the tradition (the center and heart) are prone to police traditions. They ask trivial questions because they have forgotten the important question. They no longer know the difference between God's commandment and human customs. But Jesus, the Son of God, lives out of the heart and center. He prophetically confronts their hypocrisy, their inability to adequately hold together the inner love of God and neighbor and the outer ways that love should be embodied.

> **Then he called the crowd again and said to them, "Listen to me, all of you, and understand: there is nothing outside a person that by going in can defile, but the things that come out are what defile.**
>
> **For it is from within, from the human heart, that evil intentions come: fornication, theft, murder, adultery, avarice, wickedness, deceit, licentiousness, envy, slander, pride, folly. All these evil things come from within, and they defile a person."**

The Pharisees and scribes are concerned with ritual defilement, eating with unclean hands, cooking with unclean pots, and, therefore, ultimately putting unclean food in you. The movement is from something outside designated as unclean going inside the person and contaminating them in the process. With this understanding all attention and energy is in the external world, fearing and avoiding an outer uncleanness that could inadvertently produce personal impurity.

Jesus, as all spiritual teachers, is concerned about moral defilement, how evil comes into the world. This happens in the exact opposite way of ritual impurity. Defilement begins and develops in the human heart, in the cultivation of evil thoughts, intentions, and imaginings. People work from the inside out; and if their minds are full of fornication, theft, murder, adultery, avarice, wickedness, deceit, licentiousness, envy, slander, pride, and folly, these become the drivers of actions. The Pharisees and scribes are obsessed with the ritual defilement and the external world. Jesus' attention is on the internal world and moral havoc it unleashes. He is intent on finding the drivers of immoral behavior.

Teaching

Although Jesus authoritatively points to the human heart and lists its evil imaginings, the actual drivers of destructive behavior are often not easy to discover. This is especially true if you are trying to find your own. When people cultivate their evil intentions and pursue them rigorously, they are knowingly wicked. But often the drivers are unconscious. Also, they are not classically evil like the list of Jesus. They are more pitiful, benighted, and stupid. Still they unfold into dangerous actions.

Therefore, an ally in righteous living is self knowledge. As we become aware of what drives us, we become free to cooperate or resist. To make sure I do not forget this condition of hidden drivers, I often retell the first time I learned this truth:

> Every night, when my father came home from work, he would do the same thing. I was six and every night I watched him.
>
> We lived on the second floor of a two flat. I could hear him coming up the stairs before I could see him. When he came through the door, I was there. He would pat me on my crew cut and take off his hat and plop it on my head. It would slide forward over my eyes and sideways over my ears. All this was done while he was walking, while he was making his way toward the bedroom, while I was following, pushing the hat back to see.
>
> My father was a policeman. He carried a gun in a holster at his hip. It was not slung low like the cowboy gunslingers in the serials I saw at the West End Theater on Saturday mornings. It rode waist high. Once, as we were walking toward the bedroom, I asked him if he could draw fast enough with the gun that high.
>
> "It's not like that," he said.
>
> On the top shelf of the closet in my mother and father's bedroom was a wooden safe. My father had it made to size and it was a snug fit, perfect height and perfect depth. On the shelf next to the safe was a key. With his back to me, my father would open the closet door, take the key off the shelf and open the safe. Then he would take off his belt and holster and take the gun out of the holster. The holster and belt would be rolled up and stuffed way back in the safe. Then he would open the cylinder of the gun. The bullets would slide out into his free hand. He would put the bullets in a dish that was inside the safe. I could hear them clinking as they rolled and settled into place. Then he would put the gun into the safe, lock it and put the key on the shelf. This is what he would do every night when he came home—as I watched.
>
> One night, after he had put the bullets in the dish, he turned and walked over to me. He was holding the gun by the barrel. Without say-

ing anything, he offered me the handle. I took it. Its heaviness surprised me. My arm fell to my side. I quickly heaved my arm up. It was all I could do to hold it upright. My father took it out of my hand, opened the cylinder and rolled it.

"This is where the bullets go," he said. "When you pull the trigger, the chambers move."

He paused.

"Do you want to play with it?" he finally said.

I nodded.

He gave me the gun. "Don't pull the trigger."

I went to the window and pointed the gun at the two-flat next door.

I looked at my father. He was watching me, but he said nothing.

I went over to the bed, hid behind it, then popped up and aimed.

My father said nothing.

I put the gun in my pocket and jerked it out. Fast draw.

My father said nothing.

I put the gun in my belt and pulled it out. Faster draw.

My Father said nothing.

I laid on the floor and took aim. Gunshot sounds came out of my mouth.

My father said, "Are you done?"

I nodded and handed him the gun. He turned and went to the safe. As he was locking the gun away, with his back to me, he said, "There—now you don't have to be figuring out how to get it all the time."

His words stunned me. It was not because they were critical or unkind. They were not. In fact, they were said in a completely matter-of-fact voice. There was no judgment in what he said. There was something far more shocking than judgment. There was truth. He was right. I *was* figuring out how to get it. But until he said it, I didn't know that was what I was doing. I did not know my watching was really a spying. I was "casing" the closet for a future raid, but I didn't know it. He knew me before I knew myself, and he gently showed me to myself.

As far as I can remember that was the first time I realized there was more going on in me than I knew. Of course, it was not the last time. Over the years I have been invited by certain events and strong armed by others into "going inside." I was often reluctant to undertake this inner scrutiny. The entertainments in the outer world always seemed more attractive. However, when I have managed to sustain an inner journey, there has always been a payoff. Most often the payoff has been painful. Knowing the hidden holdings of the mind is usually a blow to any scrubbed-up persona, any idealized self-image. But the pain is not as debilitating as the revelation is intriguing. Tearing the veil and seeing what has been cloaked is a temptation few can resist. I suppose this is part of what Jung meant when he said the development takes places not by "entertaining figures of light, but by making the darkness visible."

Twenty-Third Sunday in Ordinary Time

Proper 18

Mark 7:31-37 LM • **Mark 7:24-37** RCL

Resonating with Strength

A Spiritual Commentary

For users of the *Revised Common Lectionary:*

> **Jesus set out and went away to the region of Tyre. He entered a house and did not want anyone to know he was there. Yet he could not escape notice, but a woman whose little daughter had an unclean spirit immediately heard about him, and she came and bowed down at his feet. Now the woman was a Gentile, of Syrophoenician origin. She begged him to cast the demon out of her daughter.**

Jesus the Jew is among the Gentiles. The last time he was in Gentile territory he drove a legion of demons from a tormented man into 2000 pigs who rushed headlong into the sea (Mark 5:1-20). In response to this manifestation of the kingdom, the people asked him to leave. They were not ready. As far as he knows, nothing has changed. His preaching, teaching, healings, and exorcisms will not be welcomed. So instead of the countryside, marketplaces, and villages he withdraws into a house. He wants to escape notice.

But someone who is ready finds him. She is a Gentile woman coming on behalf of her daughter who is troubled by a demon. By Jewish standards, she is doubly unclean: Gentile woman and demon daughter. But even so, she has heard of Jesus and acted on what she heard, finding him in the house of his hiding. She has bowed at his feet, demonstrating her faith in the power of God that flows through him. She has begged him for an exorcism, not for herself but for the good of another. She has what Jesus is always looking for: perseverance, faith, and service. It must be disconcerting that these qualities are coming from uncleanness.

> **He said to her, "Let the children be fed first, for it is not fair to take the children's food and throw it to the dogs."**

But she answered him, "Sir, even the dogs under the table eat the children's crumbs."

Then he said to her, "For saying that, you may go—the demon has left your daughter."

So she went home, found the child lying on the bed, and the demon gone.

To her request for an exorcism, Jesus says no. There is a proper order to be followed. The Jews are offered the food of the kingdom first. It would not be right to pass over the children of the promise and carelessly give God's life and love to dogs, those who are unclean. Despite her qualities of perseverance, faith, and service, she is still an unclean Gentile. That trumps everything else.

The woman does not argue with Jesus' refusal. She does not retaliate or attack. Rather she resituates her request within the framework of his initial rejection. Even now, at this moment and not at some future time, the dogs (she and her daughter) could receive a single gift of God (crumbs) from among the many gifts that are given to the children (the Jews). She does not seek to be great or to be first. She seeks to serve her daughter's well-being, and she is willing to become least in order to make that happen. The spiritual secret of becoming least is so that God can become most. This is the attitude of the kingdom, the new humanity that Jesus is bringing about.

This is also the attitude that releases God's saving power in Jesus. Her "saying that" (literally, "because of this word") reveals how completely she is in sync with the divine will to heal. Jesus, whose will to heal is always waiting for cooperation, is so empowered that the healing takes place at a distance. He does not physically travel to the little girl. Her mother's faith, cooperating with the divine love animating Jesus' being, has so released the Spirit that the normal ways of mediation have been surpassed. Spirit is not confined to space and time. Geography means nothing when there is complete openness to the healing Spirit of God. Those who are least allow God to be most.

For users of the *Lectionary for Mass* and the *Revised Common Lectionary*:

Then [Jesus] returned from the region of Tyre, and went by way of Sidon towards the Sea of Galilee, in the region of the Decapolis.

Jesus is now a man on the move. He is back in Gentile territory. His conversation with the Syrophoenician woman has inspired him. It was not an isolated incident but a sign of where God might be active and so where Jesus must go. If one Gentile is ready, maybe more are.

They brought to him a deaf man who had an impediment in his speech; and they begged him to lay hands on him.

He took him aside in private, away from the crowd, and put his fingers into his ears, and he spat and touched his tongue.

Then, looking up to heaven, he sighed, and said to him, "Ephphatha," that is, "Be opened." And immediately his ears were opened, and his tongue was released, and he spoke plainly.

Then Jesus ordered them to tell no one; and the more he ordered them, the more zealously they proclaimed it.

They were astounded beyond measure, saying, "He has done everything well; he even makes the deaf to hear and the mute to speak."

More Gentiles are ready—somewhat. The tales of Jesus' wonder working has preceded him. They bring him a deaf man who also has a speech impediment. They expect the miraculous touch of Jesus' hands will cure the man. This expectation, miracle mongering, pollutes the atmosphere, divides and misdirects consciousness. It is as debilitating as the wailers and mourners who had to be put out of the house of Jairus and his wife (Mark 5:40). Jesus must take the man away from those who brought him. Their intention was good, but their understanding is weak. What Jesus has to do can only be done in private.

In Mark's Gospel Jesus distinguishes between the crowd and his disciples. The crowd hears the teaching in parables, but Jesus does not take them deeper. His disciples hear the teaching in parables, but he also interprets the teaching in private. In this way they come to know "the secret of the kingdom of God" (Mark 4:11, 34), The crowds are not ready for this private teaching, this secret of how God heals in Jesus.

Although the ears detect sounds and the tongue produces sounds, it is not the ears that hear or the tongue that speaks. The heart, the spiritual center of the person, is the source of hearing and speaking. If the heart is open to its divine source, then the person can hear and speak. If a person cannot hear or speak, it is because the heart is hard. Consciousness is closed off from the divine Source.

When Jesus puts his fingers into the man's ears, he reverses the flow of attention. The man no longer struggles to decipher sounds coming in from the outside. He listens inward, pulling his consciousness into his heart. Jesus is directing his attention into his spiritual center. Then Jesus spits on his hand and touches the man's tongue with his spit. Spit comes from the inside and symbolizes the Spirit. Jesus is connecting his Spirit, the Holy Spirit he received at his baptism, to the man's spirit. Now he and the man are interiorly in communion with one another.

Then Jesus looks to heaven. As Jesus' baptism revealed, the heavens are permanently opened. God is available; the Holy Spirit is always descending with love. But people must look upward. They must open their consciousness to the divine loving presence. This is a mighty effort. It must be done without distraction or wavering. Jesus accomplishes it with a sigh. Now the inward center of the man is united to the inward center of the beloved Son of God who is filled with the Holy Spirit. Jesus is opening the man to God through his own openness to God.

It is time to speak. "Be opened" is not addressed to the ears. It is a command to the heart to open to the love of God that it is experiencing by being united to Jesus, the Beloved Son (see Mark 1:10). When the heart opens, immediately the ears are unplugged and the tongue is loosed.

We now know what interiorly happened to free the Syrophoenician woman's daughter. Through the playful riddle Jesus and she meet in their hearts, in their inner connections with the loving and healing Holy Spirit. This meeting immediately released the Spirit into the world.

These are the spiritual dynamics hidden in Jesus' actions and words. Jesus did not just physically touch the man's ears and tongue, and immediately and magically the man could hear and speak—but this shallow and seriously incomplete rendition is what the people think. This is the story they are zealously spreading. Jesus is doing everything well. This is the crowd's story at the crowd's level. What happened in private has remained in private. The story of two people, one united to God and one not united to God, in intimate cooperation with the Holy Spirit to effect new human possibilities will have to be told at another time.

Teaching

Many years ago I was doing a workshop on storytelling in San Bernardino. There were many Native Americans there, some in traditional dress. At one of the breaks, I was gabbing with one of the participants. Then I turned and was face-to-face with a Native American woman, in traditional dress, about my height and size. She said, "You talk a lot about power, but you don't mean power."

"I don't?" I said.

"No," she said. "Power is like a fire. It flares up and burns out."

Then she stepped back, put her arm straight out, and steadily drew it across my eyes. "You mean strength," she said.

I knew I was being instructed by a spiritual teacher. And she was right. I did mean strength. The stories I told were celebrating a steady strength, an inner rootedness and certainty that could defy the vagaries of circumstances. They were tales of people moving from the inside to the outside. The women and men were proactive shapers of events, having the perseverance to turn negative situations positive.

But there was another implication in my temporary spiritual teacher moving me from power to strength. Power is explosive and tries to dominate by force. Strength simply holds fast to the truth, knowing the truth will outlast the lie. In the Gospel of St. Matthew, Isaiah is quoted as revealing Jesus as one who would not "quench a smoldering wick" or "break a bruised reed" (Matt 12:20). If a wick was almost extinguished, he would not put it out. If a reed was so bruised it was almost broken, he would not snap it apart. There was nothing in him that contributed to death. He was life; and he refused the ways of death. He was the meekness that will inherit the earth (see Matt 5:5).

I think steady, gentle strength is a key characteristic in the Gospel portrait of Jesus, especially the Gospel of St. Mark. His strength comes from his consciousness of being loved by God and being the bearer of the Holy Spirit into a world of suffering and alienation. This consciousness is constant. It permeates all he says and does. So many situations and so many voices try to pull him away from this inner truth. They try to turn him into both a sinner who he is not and into a Messiah who he is not. But he holds fast to his baptismal voice and vision.

But what really intrigues me is his endless quest to give this steady strength to others. He thinks nothing of crossing the boundaries of Jew and Gentile, and man and woman to find the resonating response he so desires. Wherever he is positively received, he stays. When he is rejected, he moves on—other towns, other people, other possibilities (see Mark 6:6-11). And he follows clues. If one Gentile can open completely to God, he will travel a great way to find others. He is driven by what gives him life, namely giving love and life to others.

I understand there is a theory about steady strength in family therapy literature. In seriously dysfunctional families there is often one person who is healthier than the others. If that person can hold onto her or his own health, the sparks of health in the other family members will slowly be revived. But if the healthy person gets sucked into the sickness, the family unit will enter more deeply into its destructiveness. This is a great testament to the power of one. But really it is the strength of one, the steady and gentle manifestation of health that refuses to participate in sickness.

This is one way we may be healed. Jesus, the healthy one, holds onto wholeness in a fractured world. He will not allow us to suck him into our sickness. Rather he brings us into himself. He sticks his fingers in our ears so we cannot hear the outside and are guided to the spiritual center of our heart. Then he places his spirit into us. He unites our center with his center which is open to God, Divine Love. Through this union with the Open One, our hearts open. We can now hear and speak the Word of God.

Twenty-Fourth Sunday in Ordinary Time

Proper 19

Mark 8:27-35 *LM* • **Mark 8:27-38** *RCL*

Disappointing Our Fantasy

A Spiritual Commentary

For users of the *Lectionary for Mass* and the *Revised Common Lectionary:*

> **Jesus went on with his disciples to the villages of Caesarea Philippi; and on the way he asked his disciples, "Who do people say that I am?"**
>
> **And they answered him, "John the Baptist; and others, Elijah; and still others one of the prophets."**
>
> **He asked them, "But who do you say that I am?"**
>
> **Peter answered, "You are the Messiah."**
>
> **And he sternly ordered them not to tell anyone about him.**

In following Jesus on the way, the question of his identity is inevitable. His activities of proclaiming, teaching, healing, and exorcising have forced speculation. In fact, the disciples have asked this question among themselves (Mark 4:41). Now Jesus turns the tables and, in a two-step progression, probes the understanding of both people and his disciples.

Everybody is right, but not right enough. The people have situated Jesus within the prophetic tradition. His ultimate identity is that the spirit of John the Baptist or Elijah inhabits him. This connotes he is ushering in the messianic age. Others would not go that far. He is one of the prophets, denouncing the failures of the covenant relationship with God and urging a return to the ways of God. Jesus fits this picture, but it is only a partial picture.

Peter takes it a step farther. Jesus is the Messiah, the awaited one. This is true but it is not for public consumption. Peter has the right word, but Peter does not have the right meaning.

> **Then he began to teach them that the Son of Man must undergo great suffering, and be rejected by the elders, the chief priests,**

225

and the scribes, and be killed, and after three days rise again. He said all this quite openly.

The inner meaning of "Messiah" is "Son of Man." The Son of Man is the one who lives in solidarity with God and others. This is certainly Jesus himself, but it is also the true name of all who follow him. It is the new humanity that the teaching of Jesus is bringing about. This new humanity will not be welcomed by the religious elite who live according to different values. They will reject the new humanity, make it suffer, and kill it. But their efforts will be in vain. God's energy ("three days") will resurrect it.

This picture of suffering, death, and resurrection puts everything in perspective. The healings and exorcisms of suffering people were revelations of God's love, a love that people had to understand and out of which they had to live. But they could easily be construed as random miracles that were not part of a deeper revelation and did not require a consistent and committed response. That is why Jesus silenced people, for fear they would spread misunderstanding and not the Good News.

That is also why he silenced his disciples after Peter's confession. "Messiah" is a concept with many meanings. Most of them have to do with glory and triumph for the Messiah himself and for all those who follow him. None of these meanings have to do with rejection, suffering, death, and resurrection. But this is what Messiah means, and this is how it is going to unfold. This is the straight truth, without sugar and without spin: "He said all this quite openly" (v. 32).

And Peter took him aside and began to rebuke him.

But turning and looking at his disciples, he rebuked Peter and said, "Get behind me, Satan! For you are setting your mind not on divine things but on human things."

Peter is not happy with Jesus' open speech. He obviously had something different in mind when he said, "Messiah." Although Peter is a disciple, he rebukes the Master, reversing the roles. Jesus' turning is not just a physical twisting. It symbolizes he is moving into a different and deeper level of consciousness. He trains this deeper level of consciousness on Peter and the disciples. One rebuke deserves another. Jesus reasserts his role, demanding Peter return to following him: "Get behind me" (v. 33). In rejecting the Son of Man interpretation of the Messiah, Peter has joined the ranks of Satan, the one who subverts

God's design. The reason is the way Peter's mind is working. It is set on human things, not on divine things.

David Rhoads contrasts "The Things of God" and "The Things of Humans." The Things of God are faith (Mark 2:5), courage (Mark 7:28), losing one's life for the Good News (Mark 8:35), being least and being servant (Mark 9:35; 10:43; Matt 18:1-5), and doing good (Mark 3:1-5; Matt 25:31-40). The Things of Humans are lack of faith (Mark 4:40), fear (Mark 5:36), saving one's life (Mark 8:35), being great, lording it over people (Mark 9:35; 10:42; Matt 18:1-5), and doing harm (*Reading Mark: Engaging the Gospel* [Minneapolis: Fortress Press, 2004] 88). If we had to honestly assess where our mind dwells, on the things of God or the things of humans, we probably would be shoulder to shoulder with Peter.

> **He called the crowd with his disciples, and said to them, "If any want to become my followers, let them deny themselves and take up their cross and follow me. For those who want to save their life will lose it. And those who lose their life for my sake, and the sake of the gospel, will save it.**

For users of the *Revised Common Lectionary:*

> **For what will it profit them to gain the whole world and forfeit their life? Indeed, what can they give in return for their life? Those who are ashamed of me and of my words in this adulterous and sinful generation, of them the Son of Man will also be ashamed when he comes in the glory of his Father with the holy angels."**

It is time to clear up what discipleship is and is not about, both for the disciples and the crowds. It is not about the chronic concern to save and enhance your life on the terms of "this adulterous and sinful generation." When we constantly strive to save our status and position in this world, we lose a larger life. There may be many reasons for this "saving-losing" effect, but it may be a simple feature of consciousness. When we give all our attention to one thing, other things are inevitably excluded. So it is crucial to bestow awareness on what is most valuable. This larger life is what is most valuable. So putting all our energy into gaining the whole world is not a profitable enterprise. It only means we will lose what is most valuable. It is a misplaced focus. Therefore, we must deny this tendency to center everything on this small sense of ourselves.

The larger, more valuable life is God's love. When we center ourselves in God's love, we will follow the impulses of that love. This love supports us as a servant of its basic energy to serve the well-being of others. Instead of wanting to become great, we become small. Instead of wanting to lord it over others, we grow in service. This way of thinking is deeply offensive to the rulers of this world, and they will not merely look the other way. They will make us suffer, but we must not shirk from our following. We must take up this cross as the inevitable price of loving in a loveless world. When we follow in this way, many will be ashamed of us. But it is the way of heaven, "the glory of his Father and the holy angels" (v. 38). It is valuing the things of God.

Teaching

I often have the opportunity to talk about the Gospels at retreats and workshops. Whenever I mention the "disciples' lack of comprehension" themes, I ready myself for a predictable question. Most often it arrives quickly. "If they (the disciples) were with Jesus on a daily basis and they did not 'get' what he was all about, how do you expect us (me) to get it?"

I usually stammer something about how the Gospels are written and what reading the Gospels can do for contemporary Christians. In the story of St Mark's Gospel, the disciples stumble consistently. Even at the end the women flee the tomb in fear and do not obey the young-man-in-white's command (Mark 16:1-8). But, as readers, we are in a different position. We can learn from their mistakes. We can watch the disciples not get it, and that allows us to get it. As Quakers might say, "As 'way' does not open for them, 'way' does open for us." Their failure provides the possibility of our faithfulness.

But lately I have become less sanguine about faithfulness. The disciples' lack of comprehension may be a prediction of our own inevitable failure. Their misunderstanding and our own comes from an entrenched way of thinking, a "thinking human things." This fundamental way of thinking is universally held. Even Jesus' straight speech cannot dislodge it. The problem with the Son of Man is that he disappoints one of our foremost fantasies.

We are little people. Even if we have rank, it is not high enough. Even if we have money, we are not wealthy enough. Even if we command respect, there is always one who ridicules us. We need an increase of importance. As eagerly as we want to promote ourselves, just as eagerly do we want to protect ourselves. We sense the fragility of our lives. A fall from the little grace we have haunts us. We fear becoming sick, and old, and dying. We never have enough or are enough. In a word, we "lack."

But we can fantasize. We can join Tyve's reveries from *Fiddler on the Roof* and sing, "If I were a rich man." We can spin scenarios of revenge, making our enemies the footstools under our feet (see Ps 18:38). We can close our eyes and see ourselves in charge, making decisions that help thousands and who respond with adulation. Of course, we will be healthy far into old age and die like Zorba the Greek, standing and howling out the window at winter. We may be little in reality, but we are large in dream.

The Messiah can feed this fantasy. When the Messiah comes, he will wipe away every tear (Rev 7:17; 21:4), seat people at table and feed them (Luke 12:37), heal every sickness (Matt 9:35), love and reward each person (Matt 25:34). He will save our lives and make us great. He will fulfill "the Things of Humans" that they cannot fulfill for themselves.

And in the early part of the Gospel of Mark, it certainly looked like that. Everything that attacked and oppressed the human was taken away. Satan was routed. Jesus, the fulfiller of fantasy, had arrived. Everyone flocked to him, although he always tried to move on. Everyone proclaimed his greatness, although he told them not to. He wasn't what they thought he was. But they couldn't hear that, because what they always fantasized had finally come to pass.

Jesus profoundly disappointed the fantasy of human fulfillment. The Son of Man goes a different way and offers a different way to all who follow him. He lives a life of trust in God and service of others. He does not harm others to secure his own life. In fact, saving himself is the last thing that is on his mind. Therefore, he does not mitigate our fear by making us great and assure us of our importance by allowing us to lord it over others. He will not sanction our own chronic concern with our status and position or look the other way while others suffer so we can save our life in this world. In short, he does not give us what we want. And when we know what we want with such certainty and pray for a Messiah to come and get it for us, who needs this Son of Man?

Twenty-Fifth Sunday in Ordinary Time

Proper 20

Mark 9:30-37

Welcoming the Least

A Spiritual Commentary

[After leaving the mountain] Jesus and the disciples went on from there and passed through Galilee. He did not want anyone to know it; for he was teaching his disciples, saying to them, "The Son of Man is to be betrayed into human hands, and they will kill him, and three days after being killed, he will rise again."

But they did not understand what he was saying and were afraid to ask him.

Jesus does not pursue fame or court recognition. He does not seek to be the center of attention. So as he travels through Galilee, he wants to avoid notice. This is especially true for he is teaching his disciples about the fate of the new humanity. This teaching is difficult to fathom; many would be puzzled. The teaching is blunt: although the Son of Man is guided by the hand of God, he will be killed by human hands. Those who set their minds by human things will do away with the one who sets his mind by the things of God. But this death will be transformed into resurrection.

Although they hear the words, the disciples cannot comprehend what he is saying. Their thinking is set on human things. Their thoughts are on avoiding suffering and pursuing status. Nothing can move these concerns from the center of their consciousness. Since their focus is completely on themselves, they naturally are afraid for themselves. So they fear to ask Jesus about anything that might sniff of danger, that might take them away from their dreams of glory.

Then they came to Capernaum; and when he was in the house he asked them, "What were you arguing about on the way?"

But they were silent, for on the way they had argued with one another who was the greatest.

"In the house" complements "on the way." The way is the following of Jesus, the action of trying to live the values of the kingdom. This way is more deeply probed "in the house," the place where Jesus teaches and reflects with his disciples in private.

"[O]n the way" they were arguing with one another. The argument was about what always causes arguments: who is the greatest. It seems they have no trouble quarreling among themselves. However, with Jesus it is different. "[O]n the way" they were afraid to ask questions about the teaching of suffering, death, and resurrection. Now in the house they become completely silent. There can be no progress when disciples wrangle with one another and avoid the teachings and questions of the Son of Man. Their silence and fear reveal the distance between how they think and how Jesus thinks.

> **He sat down, called the twelve, and said to them, "Whoever wants to be first must be last of all and servant of all."**
>
> **Then he took a little child and put it among them; and taking it in his arms, he said to them, "Whoever welcomes one such child in my name welcomes me, and whoever welcomes me, welcomes not me but the one who sent me."**

Jesus, the Teacher, sits down, gathers the Twelve who will guide the new humanity (notice that others must also be there, since a child is at hand), and instructs them in the ways of greatness. For Jesus the great are those who engage and cooperate with the loving energy of God. This loving energy is not concerned with its own honor and prestige, as the Pharisees suppose (Mark 2:7). Rather it goes out to encounter all and lift up their basic humanity. So if people would be first and align themselves with this energy, they would not seek their own glory but serve the real needs of others. "How it is" with God who is the first and greatest should be "how it is" with all who seek to be first and greatest.

When a spiritual teaching is given to an entrenched mindset, more often than not the mindset transforms the teaching rather than the teaching transforming the mindset. When the disciples hear this teaching of Jesus, they can quickly adapt it to their purposes. They have to endure a period of doing lowly stuff in order to get the higher stuff. If being a servant is the way to being first, they will be servants. All the time they will be thinking, "I'm better than these people I'm serving and one day everybody will know that. I'll have treasure in heaven" (cf. Mark 10:21). The disciples never let go of their own rendition of "first."

They just renegotiate their strategies about how to get to be the greatest. This way of thinking is reflected in Luke's ironic suggestion, "[W]hen you give a banquet, invite the poor, the crippled, the lame, and the blind. And you will be blessed, because they cannot repay you, for you will be repaid at the resurrection of the righteous" (Luke 14:13-14).

Jesus suggests another way to proceed and models it for them. He places a child in their midst, and he embraces the child. In this context a child symbolizes the least, one who does not have social status and importance. But the great of this world do not associate with the least of this world. So if this is the path to greatness, it must be explained. Jesus explains it in terms of his own consciousness, and how this consciousness would unfold in his followers. His explanation maps a process of mystical transformations. If they embrace a least one in Jesus' name, with his consciousness, that least one would become transparent to Jesus. But this transparency would unfold into a further transparency. Jesus will give way to the one who sent him. The disciples will begin with the last but arrive at the first, embrace the least but welcome the Source of All.

Teaching

When St. Francis kissed the leper, the leper became Christ. Before he kissed him, the leper was just a leper. It was in the act of kissing that he became Christ. It is in the way of welcoming that Christ appears. And Christ always brings his Father with him. So when we welcome Christ, we welcome the one who sent him. The dissolving lineup is "the leper into Christ" and "Christ into God."

Why does the process begin with the least?

When we begin with the least socially, we devalue the hierarchical ranking of society. Those at the top are surfeited with invitations. Those at the bottom are excluded. They have nothing to offer, no possibility of payback, so they are not welcomed. When we say that the path to Jesus Christ and God "the Father" is through welcoming those whom no one else will invite, we undercut class structures and turn everything, in that great word, topsy-turvy. To those with a maverick mind, this is always exhilarating activity.

But there is another meaning to the word "least." In this meaning it can be applied to the socially least and the socially most. This "leastness," that is in all people, is revealed by the type of welcome Jesus provides and encourages his disciples to imitate. Dag Hammarskjöld tried to point to it: "[People comment on] Jesus' 'lack of moral principles.' He sat at meal with publicans and sinners, he consorted with harlots. Did he do this to obtain their votes? Or did he think that, perhaps, he could convert them by such 'appeasement'? Or was his humanity rich and deep enough to make contact, even in them, with what in human nature which is common to all [people], indestructible, and upon which the future has to be built? (*Markings,* trans. Leif Sjöberg and W. H. Auden [New York: Knopf, 1964] 157).

The "least" means the bare, basic material that is common to all. It is beneath the accumulation of possessions and also beneath the lack of them. In Gospel language, it means to welcome the Son of Man in each person.

Rachel Naomi Remen, a doctor and spiritual teacher in the field of medicine, tells of a workshop with Carl Rogers, the proponent of client-centered therapy. Rogers began, "Before every session I take a moment to remember my humanity. There is no experience that this [person] has that I cannot share with him [or her], no fear that I cannot understand, no suffering that I cannot care about, because I too am human . . . I too am vulnerable. And because of this, *I am enough.*" Rogers then began a demonstration. He engages one of the doctors and they began to talk.

Remen gives her impression: "In the safe climate of Rogers' total acceptance, he began to shed his masks, hesitantly at first and then more and more easily. As each mask fell, Rogers welcomed the one behind it unconditionally, until finally we glimpsed the beauty of the doctor's naked face. I doubt that even he himself had ever seen it before . . . I remember wishing that I had volunteered, envying this doctor the opportunity to be received by someone in such a total way. Except for those few moments with my grandfather, I had never experienced that kind of welcome" (*Kitchen Table Wisdom: Stories that Heal* [New York: Riverhead Books, 1996] 218–19).

The doctor was usually welcomed in terms of his masks. When they all fell away, what was left was the "least," his basic humanity. It was Rogers' ability to welcome so thoroughly that allowed it to emerge.

Here, of course, is the breakthrough. The naked face of our shared humanity reveals the common Source of All. This is what is most beautiful and most valuable. This is the greatest and the first, and at the same time it is the least. Therefore, the teaching becomes clear; when we become the servant of this last, welcoming what is common to all, we paradoxically are first.

Twenty-Sixth Sunday in Ordinary Time

Proper 21

Mark 9:38-43, 45, 47-48

Being Salted with Fire

A Spiritual Commentary

[After Jesus had finished teaching the disciples,] John said to Jesus, "Teacher, we saw someone casting out demons in your name, and we tried to stop him, because he was not following us."

But Jesus said, "Do not stop him; for no one who does a deed of power in my name will be able soon afterward to speak evil of me. Whoever is not against us is for us.

The disciples have been warned that the desire to be great undercuts the work of the kingdom ("Welcoming the Least," above). But this warning has not been completely understood or integrated. In the disciples' defense, the drive to be great is deeply ingrained in the human condition. It works below the level of consciousness, coloring every situation, insidiously invading every perception. Jesus compared it to leaven (Mark 8:15). It infiltrates, inflates and puffs up, affecting everything.

It affects how the disciples react to the outside exorcist. They see someone casting out demons in Jesus' name, and they immediately perceive it as a threat. Is someone poaching on their territory? They guard their turf against anyone who might steal their importance. Their consciousness is so competitive that they do not even see the ones from whom the demons were cast out. The fact that the work of the kingdom has been done and humanity has been freed from bondage does not enter into the equation. They have become a tight-knit power group. When good is done and they do not benefit, they try to stop it. Following them, not following Jesus, has become the criterion of what should be permitted and what should be prevented.

The fact they "tried" to stop him may indicate that they failed. Then they are reporting this incident to Jesus to have him "stop" him. After all, he is exorcising in Jesus' name so Jesus could put an end to it. But Jesus has a different vision of what is happening.

His ultimate priority is the kingdom. If people are contributing to the kingdom and doing it in his name, then they will not denigrate what he is doing. They are part of Jesus' family because they belong to the divine will (Mark 3:34). The disciples are urged to have a more generous understanding of who is with them. All are for them, unless they prove otherwise. Until people exhibit hostility and hold values that go counter to the new humanity, it should be assumed they are actual or potential allies. It is not the disciples' role to exclude. People have to exclude themselves by their attitudes and behaviors. Therefore, the disciples should not try to guard their exorcist roles; they should welcome the expulsion of any demon by anyone. The work of the kingdom is wider than their group and so is the name of Jesus.

> **"For truly, I tell you, whoever gives you a cup of water to drink because you bear the name of Christ will by no means lose the reward. If any of you put a stumbling block before one of these little ones who believe in me, it would be better for you if a great millstone were hung around your neck and you were thrown into the sea.**

The kingdom is not only wider than the disciples; it is wider than exorcists. It includes those who offer hospitality and perform small tasks. However, those bent on greatness often fail to notice these people. Their desire for greatness not only leads to self-absorption in status and hoarding whatever is important, that is, the power of exorcism. It also shows itself in how the contributions of others are evaluated. In particular, it tends to overlook "little ones" who offer simple gestures of hospitality.

Those who "wish to be great" do not think of these support people in terms of participation and reward. In fact, instead of embracing them as Jesus modeled, they have a way of creating a disdainful distance (Mark 9:36). This comes close to lording it over people (Mark 9:35; 10:42; Matt 18:1-5), a counter-sign of the kingdom (see "Welcoming the Least," above). When people who are supposed to exemplify service act like lords, they cause the ones who are really providing service (cups of cold water) to second guess the kingdom. Is there really a new humanity in the making or is this the same old game masked by a mesmerizing rhetoric?

For Jesus the little ones will not lose their reward. Their hospitability creates the kingdom as much as proclamation, teaching, healing, and exorcism. This equal inclusion is prefaced by "truly I tell you" (v. 41), because it is startling to a consciousness obsessed by greatness. But the little ones have the proper consciousness. They do things because of Christ. They are believers and, as believers, they belong to Christ. So to embrace them is to embrace Christ, and to embrace Christ is to embrace the one who sent him (Mark 9:37). But if those "who wish to be great" do not embrace the least but cause them to stumble, to lose their faith in Christ and the kingdom, then these great ones had better redo their behavior. The rhetoric of disaster is meant to get their attention. Sinking to the bottom of the sea with a millstone tied around the neck is a terrifying fate. Well, those irretrievably sunken people will have it better than those disciples who are countersigns to the kingdom and cause "little ones" to lose their commitment (v. 42).

> **If your hand causes you to stumble, cut it off; it is better for you to enter life maimed than to have two hands and to go to hell, to the unquenchable fire. And if your foot causes you to stumble, cut it off; it is better for you to enter life lame than to have two feet and to be thrown into hell. And if your eye causes you to stumble, tear it out; it is better for you to enter the kingdom of God with one eye than to have two eyes and to be thrown into hell, where the worm never dies, and the fire is never quenched.**
>
> **For every one will be salted with fire. Salt is good; but if salt has lost its saltiness, how can you season it? Have salt in yourself, and be at peace with one another."**

The best way for the disciples to avoid causing scandal to others is to eliminate the cause of scandal in themselves. But this is not easy. The change of consciousness and action that Jesus is seeking is incredibly difficult. The drives to be egocentric, to save one's own life, to be great, to lord it over others, and to harm others in order to save yourself are the way of the world. As the way of the world, these ways of thinking and acting have become internalized into a "second nature." They are like a hand, a foot, and an eye (see 1 Cor 12). If these drives are to give way to other-centeredness, losing one's life for the Good News, being the least and servant of all, and not harming others, there must be clarity about what is at stake and a commitment to whatever surgery is needed. This is self-surgery, a voluntary sacrifice. So if the disciples are going to perform it, they must be convinced of its necessity.

What is at stake is the relationship to God. This is what is most important. Everything else is secondary. Staying related to God means life; breaking that relationship means hell. The way to stay related to God is to eliminate what breaks that relationship. When the disciples cut away what keeps them from entering life, the feared fire of damnation that never ends becomes a purifying fire. The emphasis is not on what was lost but on what was preserved. The fire becomes salt; purification becomes the preservation of what is essential. What is preserved through the purification is what is most valuable. Salt is a symbol of highest value. It is a treasure of incalculable worth, so excellent that if its flavor is lost, there is nothing higher that can restore it. Salt, then, is the relationship to God that brings peace among people. The excising of individual alienating traits makes possible the wholeness of people together. Jesus' final suggestion for those who desire to be great is: "Have salt in yourself, and be at peace with one another" (v. 50).

Teaching

The desire to be great comes with the territory of being alive. Thomas Aquinas called it *"desiderium naturale."* Everything living wants to persist and expand in being. In plants and animals this drive stays on the biological level. But in humans it becomes more complex and wide ranging. Not only do we want to biologically survive, we want to be important and esteemed, the center of attention and adulation.

This inner urge determines how we evaluate our lives. We weigh everything in terms of whether it promotes or diminishes us. Then we attach our happiness to promoting experiences and our sadness to diminishing experiences. The desire to be great takes the form of pursuing promotion and avoiding diminishment. These twin cravings, often unconscious, steer the course of our lives on a day-in, day-out basis.

There are many variations to this "greatness" project. The hierarchical structure of society becomes a natural benchmark for how we are doing. If we are aligned with the powerful, or if we are wealthy and famous, or if we are respected and admired, the inner drive is satisfied. But if we are poor and unknown, the inner drive is frustrated. Of course, it always helps to have someone worse off than we are. If upward comparison frustrates the drive to be great, downward comparison gives it a boost. This comparative mind puts us on the teeter-totter of depression and elation.

If this drive to be great is "natural" and the psychological structures that express and support it are so ingrained, how can Jesus encourage a movement to be least? People are heavily invested in the drive to be great. It gives them a rush, gets them up on Monday, and gets them through to Friday. When they hear the injunction to be a "child" and a "servant," they think of a life-denying impulse, appropriate for those with small appetites. They see those who embrace the "little ones" (v. 42) as not having the energy and zest to run with the big boys and girls. If the followers of Jesus deliberately espouse a lifestyle of least, they will be tempted to be resentful of those who strive to be great. If the way of service is to be undertaken, there must be an accompanying consciousness of why service is true greatness. Otherwise, it will certainly suffer severe complications.

There is no one way that consciousness of service as true greatness is awakened. But I came across a paragraph from a man interviewing a spiritual teacher who was trying to explain to him how people become aware of "essence" and how it makes possible changes in their behavior. What he describes might be helpful:

> "As an example, Ali pointed to the common feeling of anger —an aspect of personality. Begin looking into why this emotion recurs, Ali told me, and one might discover that at the surface level it is simply a way of asserting strength—of feeling separate and independent from other people. Explore a little more deeply, he elaborated, and it will turn out that the anger covers up an underlying experience of fear and weakness. "If you stay with that sense of weakness," he explained, "you'll begin to experience a hole in the belly, an emptiness, the feeling that you can't stand your ground, that something is missing. And if you feel that emptiness and you don't fight it or react to it but just stay with it, then the hole will begin to fill with a certain quality of essence. It feels literally like *liquid fire* [emphasis mine]. And then what you will feel is a real strength. Just by truly being yourself, you are strong. And that essential strength gives you the capacity to be truly independent without feeling angry." (Tony Schwartz, *What Really Matters: Searching for Wisdom in America* [New York: Bantam Books/Random House, Inc., 1995] 414–15)

Could this process show a pattern of how we might move from our psychological addiction to strategies of greatness to the consciousness of true greatness? We strive to be great because we feel we are not great. The sense that we lack significance drives us to lord it over people and chronically promote ourselves at the cost of others. The real drive is not to be great but to fill the hole in the middle of us that is empty. This hole cannot be filled by the frantic strategies for greatness. But we keep trying. Although we may sense this is the wrong way, we are not sure what is the right way.

The right way is to go "into the hole." Do not try to cover it over with deeds of greatness. The hole is really the entranceway into the kingdom. If we can dwell there, purified by its liquid fire, it will become salt. Our natural innate greatness will emerge as a gift. This is the truth that drives us but which we never quite grasp. We desire greatness because we are already great. It is not a quest for what we do not have; it is a quest to become conscious of what we already are. Then we can sense our greatness without the oppressive strategies of greatness, know our strength without having to be angry to feel it.

Sam Keen knows this quest and both the wrong way and the right way to pursue it. He was racked by the question "What can I do to give my life meaning, dignity, density?" In response he writes:

> My answer came suddenly jumping up and down in my mind with the force of an obvious fact long denied. I woke one night in Manhattan with the words, 'Nothing, nothing,' on my lips. As I started to laugh at the comedy of my seriousness, my vertigo began to subside. I saw that I had been obsessed with the wrong question. In the face of the uncertainty of life and the certainty of death no human act or project could render existence meaningful or secure . . . Either dignity and meaningfulness come with the territory or they must forever be absent. Sanctity is given with being. It is not earned. (*To A Dancing God* [New York: Harper & Row, 1970] 17)

This consciousness of greatness as gift means we do not have to exclude and overlook others to maintain our sense of importance. The project is not to be great but to find the way to express our natural greatness. This is what it means to be "salted with fire" (Mark 9:49). It is the simple consciousness of innate worth that we arrive at once we have been purified of all our grandiose projects and cut away all that keeps us from life.

Twenty-Seventh Sunday in Ordinary Time

Proper 22

Mark 10:2-16

Restoring Original Consciousness

A Spiritual Commentary

Some Pharisees came, and to test Jesus they asked," Is it lawful for a man to divorce his wife?"

He answered them, "What did Moses command you?"

They said, "Moses allowed a man to write a certificate of dismissal and to divorce her."

But Jesus said to them, "Because of your hardness of heart he wrote this commandment for you. But from the beginning of creation, 'God made them male and female.' For this reason a man shall leave his father and mother and be joined to his wife, and the two shall become one flesh. So they are no longer two, but one flesh. Therefore, what God has joined together, let no one separate."

Then in the house the disciples asked him again about this matter.

He said to them, "Whoever divorces his wife and marries another commits adultery against her; and if she divorces her husband and marries another, she commits adultery."

Jesus does not engage in the questions around divorce. When is it permissible? What are sufficient causes? What financial arrangements are appropriate? For him, the symbolism of divorce tells the whole story. It is what it is often called, a breakup. Things are loose, no longer in communion. It embodies separation consciousness. The original, unitive consciousness of creation is lost; and the one who came to restore creation wants it otherwise.

Separation consciousness focuses on surfaces where everything is unconnected and detached. Unitive consciousness focuses on depths where everything is mutual and in communion. Spiritually developed people live in unitive consciousness and work to allow that consciousness to have maximal impact on the world of separation. These two consciousnesses overlap. As Martin Buber said, "The seat of the soul,is where the inner world and the outer world meet. Where they overlap, it is in every point of the overlap" ("The Sphere of the In-between").

Marriage symbolizes unitive consciousness. The two are not two, but one. The ultimate source of this oneness is the "joining" energy that is the essence of God. God is love and, as Paul Tillich asserted, love is the power that drives everything there is toward every thing else there is. When a man and a woman live in unitive consciousness, the individual and discrete part of themselves—their bodies—come together in union. This physical intercourse is a sacramental revelation of the deeper spiritual truth of communion. The separate surface reflects the unitive depths.

Divorce symbolizes separation consciousness, a restricted awareness of individuals unconnected to one another. It is a breaking way of individuals from one another, but it is also a breaking away of the surface from the depths. Individuals scatter; they walk away from each other. This happens because their hearts have hardened. They have turned in on themselves; they cannot melt, flow, and merge. This is sin, a failure to sustain the original consciousness of creation. Jesus is the second Adam (see 1 Cor 15), the one who lives in unitive consciousness, and he wants all of life to be permeated by the truth of communion, the truth of "the Garden."

> **People were bringing little children to him in order that he might touch them; and the disciples spoke sternly to them.**
>
> **But when Jesus saw this, he was indignant and said to them, "Let the little children come to me; do not stop them; for it is to such as these that the kingdom of God belongs. Truly, I tell you whoever does not receive the kingdom of God as a little child will never enter it."**
>
> **And he took them up in his arms, laid his hands on them, and blessed them.**

Marriage symbolizes unitive consciousness on the horizontal level: people in communion with each other. A child symbolizes unitive consciousness on the vertical level: the person in communion with God.

The disciples, of course, are not aware of this symbolic potential of children. They are working out of conventional social awareness. Children are not important and so should not bother Jesus, who is important. Jesus has previously told them that embracing the child, then a symbol of the least, will bring them into the consciousness of Christ and through that consciousness to the consciousness of God (Mark 9:37). They do not seem to be ready for this. Jesus had to tell his disciples not to stop the outside exorcist (Mark 9:39); now he tells them not to stop the children. They are not practicing the welcoming attitude that will bring them into kingdom consciousness.

The clue about why the kingdom belongs to children is in the word "receive" (v. 15). Children, by definition, know they are not the cause of their own being. They have not forgotten their source, and they do not delude themselves by fantasizing that they are completely independent. Instead, they are aware of being in relationship. This is not an equal relationship. It is a relationship with their origin, their beginning. This relationship is not "over and done with," an event in the past. They are permanently present to God, and God is permanently present to them. There is no separation. "[S]uch as these" (v. 14) are those who live in communion with their Source.

Jesus embraces these children as their sibling. They share the consciousness of the same parent. In the center of his being, Jesus knows himself as the Beloved Son who is always receiving the Holy Spirit from the Father (see the accounts of Jesus' baptism). Then he lays his hands on them. The people brought the children so Jesus would touch them. But he does so only after he has named them as the path into the kingdom. In the Gospel, Jesus often touches the sick and possessed and heals them. It is his hands and their bodies that come into contact. But on a spiritual level, it is an awakened child of God stirring a sleeping child of God. The secret of the healings and exorcisms is the hidden finger of God (Luke 11:20). Finally, he blesses them with mission. If they receive the kingdom, they have to live it. "Such as these" can live in communion with God and at peace with one another.

Teaching

Contemporary spirituality often espouses a dimensional model. We are a mysterious unity of social, physical, psychological, and spiritual dimensions. Although consciousness focuses on one or another of these dimensions, all four are always present. Also, these dimensions mutually influence one another, but the nature and degree of this influence is difficult to gauge. Finally, these dimensions have their own laws and operations. As classic spirituality has always contended, the physical does not work like the spiritual: "What is born of the flesh is flesh, and what is born of the Spirit is spirit" (John 3:6).

When the distinct dynamics of the spiritual dimension are discussed, some wild ideas emerge. As spiritual, we transcend form. We are more than our physical, social, and mental natures. Ken Wilber traces this intuition back to a childhood experience:

> Almost every child wonders, at some time or another, "What would I be like if I had different parents?" In other words, the child realizes, in a very innocent and inarticulate fashion, that consciousness itself (the inner Witness or I-ness) is not solely limited by the particular outer forms of mind and body that it animates. Every child seems to sense that he [or she] would still be "I" even if he [or she] had different parents and a different body. The child knows he [or she] would look different and act differently, but *he [or she] would still be an "I."* The child asks the question, Would I still be *me* if I had different parents?—because he [or she] wants the parents to explain his [or her] transcendence, the fact that he [or she] would still seem to be and feel the same "inner I-ness" even though he [or she] had different parents. The parents have probably long ago forgotten their own transpersonal self, and so cannot give an answer acceptable to the child. But for a moment, most parents are taken aback, and sense that there is something of immense importance here that somehow they just can't quite remember. (*No Boundary: Eastern and Western Approaches to Personal Growth* [Boston: Shambhala, 1985] 134)

But not all adults forget. When Picasso was asked about his development, he baldly stated, "I don't develop. I am." Alice Munro, the Canadian short-story writer, said she was the same person at nineteen, thirty-nine, and sixty. "I think there is some root in your nature that doesn't change . . . I'm not absolutely sure of this, it's just something that I like to look at" (*Toronto Globe and Mail,* September 29, 2001).

Christians call this transcendent self the child of God. They stress our full reality transcends the physical, social, and mental dimension, but this transcendent self is itself grounded in the transcendence of God. When we are in this child of God consciousness, we know we are more than the circumstances that afflict us. We also know we can trust our ultimate relationship with the Source. When Jesus urges the disciples not to push away the children, he is pushing them toward this consciousness. The code phrase is: embrace the child and enter the kingdom.

Another distinctive feature of the spiritual dimension is its ability to be in another without displacing any of that other in which it is in. This is a particularly powerful potential of interpersonal living. Most of us know and acknowledge the distinction between an "I-It" relationship and an "I-Thou" relationship. When we have an "I-It" relationship with another person, we treat them as an object. We are the only consciousness and interiority present, and we deal with them strictly in terms of what is predictable and mechanistic. The person of the other does not enter our consciousness. We correct this reductionistic relating by moving to an "I-Thou" mode. Now we approach the other in a listening and receiving posture that allows for the revelation of the other as person. We know and love the other and the other knows and loves us (see the work of Martin Buber, *I and Thou*, several editions available).

Beatrice Bruteau takes this relating a step farther. She posits an "I-I" relationship. In this mode of relating, "the activities of the two subjectivities are confluent and simultaneous, instead of being responsive, alternating, as in dialogue. Each of them knows the other from the inside, from the subject side, in terms of the experience of actually doing what that subject does. And each totally loves the other by uniting with the other in this complete way" (*The Grand Option: Personal Transformation and a New Creation* [Notre Dame, Ind.: University of Notre Dame Press, 2001] 75).

When we are in our child-of-God consciousness, we have the potential of becoming a giver of our personal spirit into the spiritual identity of one we love. We can also be the receiver of the spirit of another into our spiritual identity. We are not self-enclosed individuals; we are reciprocal love-giving spirits. In the physical and social realms this is symbolized by marriage where "two . . . become one flesh" (v. 8) by the joining power of God.

Childhood and marriage can be understood from social, physical, and mental perspectives. But spiritual wisdom interprets them as symbols of distinctive aspects of spiritual consciousness. We are transcendent beings capable of freely entering into each other's interiority in knowledge and love. Once we grasp these spiritual dynamics, we return with vitality and zest to the physical, social, and mental dimensions of childhood and marriage. Jesus, the bridegroom and the child, left us instructions.

Twenty-Eighth Sunday in Ordinary Time

Proper 23

Mark 10:17-30 *LM* • Mark 10:17-31 *RCL*

Disowning Possessions

A Spiritual Commentary

For users of the *Lectionary for Mass* and the *Revised Common Lectionary:*

As [Jesus] was setting out on a journey, a man ran up and knelt before him, and asked him, "Good Teacher, what must I do to inherit eternal life?"

Jesus said to him, "Why do you call me good? No one is good but God alone. You know the commandments: 'You shall not murder; You shall not commit adultery; You shall not steal; You shall not bear false witness; You shall not defraud; Honor your father and mother.'"

He said to him, "Teacher, I have kept all these since my youth."

Jesus, looking at him, loved him and said, "You lack one thing; go, sell what you own, and give the money to the poor, and you will have treasure in heaven; then come, follow me."

When he heard this, he was shocked and went away grieving, for he had many possessions.

Then Jesus looked around and said to his disciples, "How hard it will be for those who have wealth to enter the kingdom of God!"

And the disciples were perplexed at these words.

But Jesus said to them again, "Children, how hard it is to enter the kingdom of God! It is easier for a camel to go through the eye of a needle than for someone who is rich to enter the kingdom of God."

They were greatly astounded and said to one another, "Then who can be saved?"

Jesus looked at them and said, "For mortals it is impossible, but not for God; for God all thing are possible."

The running man is eager, and the kneeling man is respectful. He is a true seeker, not like others who have approached Jesus with questions in order to test him. He calls Jesus, "Good Teacher" (v. 17). If he means that Jesus is ethical, he is certainly correct. If he means that Jesus is excellent in the art of teaching, he is also correct. But Jesus challenges that designation in the light of what he is seeking. If he is seeking to inherit eternal life, he will have to focus on the goodness of God. Eternal life is a gift of God. It flows from God's essential goodness. In fact, this entire teaching—both with the seeker and with the disciples—will focus on how to understand and relate to the goodness of God.

But the seeker's mind is elsewhere. He is centered on people doing the good in order to get the best. He is tied into the consciousness of action and reward. The teacher acknowledges this: "You know the commandments" (v. 19), and the teacher decides to affirm what he knows by listing the foundational good works. The seeker does indeed know these commandments. In fact, he has kept them from his youth. "Youth" is the operative word. This is a young man's spirituality, all eagerness, energy, and most of all, in contemporary terms, ego.

This seeker's path is not denigrated. Before Jesus takes him to another level, he looks at him and loves him. What the seeker has done so far has brought him to Jesus, and that is what Jesus sees. He has completed a phase and another phase awaits him. Love is the driving force of what Jesus will offer him. Although what Jesus is about to say will be challenging and difficult to grasp, he is not critiquing the seeker. When Jesus no longer focuses on the seeker's achievements but on what he lacks, it will not be from displeasure. Jesus' intention is to help him receive eternal life by answering his question about what he must do. But the type of doing Jesus will indicate is not the type of doing he has excelled at in keeping the commandments. A different attitude and energy will be needed to inherit eternal life. How does one receive life from a good God?

Suddenly Jesus suggests that he lacks one thing: "treasure in heaven" (v. 21). This observation goes back to Jesus' initial attempt to restructure his consciousness by having him connect goodness and God. Treasure in heaven means that what he must value above all else is his relationship with God. The path to this God-centeredness is to relinquish his possessions and give them to the poor. This will start the process of inheriting eternal life; following Jesus will develop and deepen it.

The seeker grasps this injunction ("When he heard this . . ." [v. 22]). But it shocks him so profoundly that he goes away in grief. When Jesus' penetrating gaze shifts to his disciples, he first widens his concerns to all those who have wealth and focuses on their difficulty in entering the kingdom. The disciples are perplexed by this comment. Then Jesus escalates the issue from difficulty to impossibility (even double-jointed camels can't get through the eye of a needle) and, in the minds of the disciples, from the wealthy to everyone ("Then who can be saved?" [v. 26]). This escalation moves the disciples from perplexity to astonishment. The way Jesus thinks is shocking, perplexing, and astonishing to the conventional consciousness of the seeker and of the disciples.

In their state of bewilderment, Jesus looks again at the disciples. This time he does not want to confound them with thoughts they cannot fit into their present mental structures. This time he wants to deliver the "thrust home;" he wants to calm the confusion he has created by bringing their conventional consciousness in line with his illumined consciousness. It is Jesus' consciousness that will open them to eternal life. This consciousness is enshrined in symbolic code: what is impossible for human beings is possible for God, "for God all things are possible" (v. 27). This saying is meant to be a "karate chop," dismantling the obstructing consciousness and opening the disciples to another way.

The Teacher insists that the center has to shift from the human to the divine. The good God wants to give eternal life, but humans must "look to heaven" as Jesus does so often (Mark 6:41; 7:34). However, humans are addicted to looking elsewhere, treasuring earthly things. Even if they pile up all the earthly things ("he had many possessions" [v. 22]), they will not inherit eternal life. It is not material possessions in themselves that are the problem. It is the inner allegiance to the consciousness of owning and accumulating. This consciousness and style of life has been developed in the social sphere, and it is a limited approach even in that sphere. But when owning and accumulating is transferred to the spiritual sphere, it is wrongheaded in the extreme. If the heart desires eternal life and pursues it by accumulating even good deeds (keeping the commandments), it will only come to grief. If the strategies of Jesus the Teacher work and consciousness stays focused on the goodness of God, it will become clear that dispossession on all levels is the way into the fullness of life. It is how we become receptive to the self-giving Spirit.

Peter began to say to him, "Look, we have left everything and followed you."

Jesus said, "Truly I tell you, there is no one who has left house or brothers or sisters or mother or father or children or fields, for my sake and for the sake of the good news, who will not receive a hundredfold now in this age—houses, brothers and sisters, mothers and children, and fields [—but] with persecutions— and in the age to come eternal life.

For users of the *Revised Common Lectionary:*

But many who are first will be last, and the last will be first."

Peter's "question that is not a question" could be paraphrased: "Look, let's not talk about the guy who walked away or rich people in general. We have not walked away. We have left everything to follow you. What's in it for us? What then will we have?" (see Matt 19:27). The disciples' consciousness has not moved beyond *quid pro quo*. Is the sacrifice worth it? They are looking for reward.

Jesus' prediction of excess might be a serious response to Peter's concern. If they have left their families of origin and choice and their native homesteads, they will gain the extended families and homesteads of all who follow Jesus (Mark 3:31-35). For those who left a few, a hundredfold awaits. There will be more of everything except fathers. Since they left their fathers to follow Jesus and his Father in heaven, earthly fathers have been symbolically displaced. Of course, there will be eternal life in the age to come because they have fulfilled the path that Jesus laid out for the seeker, leaving everything and following him.

But what if this is Jesus the Teacher tweaking Peter's recalcitrant mind? Peter is fearful of being cheated. He may have left everything, but his mind has not. He is still looking for things, and he is a little worried by what he has just witnessed. The rich seeker has just walked away, and then Jesus has said that the rich in general cannot get into the kingdom. Where is this leading? Is the underlying fear that the good God might not come across?

Jesus addresses this fear with the comic exaggeration worthy of the abundance at the ending of the book of Job (Job 42:10-17). Everything will be returned with interest, but of course there will be a few persecutions. The good God is not stingy. But the spiritual law of consciousness is always applicable. If you want to be first (as the disciples do), you will be last. But if you are last, thereby opening yourself to the goodness of God, you will be first. All blessings of God, whether in this age or the age to come, have to be received; and the owning and accumulating mindset cannot manage that openness. Although Peter and the disciples will be offered everything, their grasping minds might not allow them to receive it.

Teaching

If you bought this book, you own it. It might even be on a shelf with other books that you own. Perhaps the shelves are in a house that you own. Perhaps, there is a car that you own, but right now your teenage daughter is driving it. Even if you say the bank owns the house and car, you are paying them off in order to own them. People in religious orders may not own anything individually, but the order has possessions. Even people who don't "have a pot to piss in," are scrambling for pot money. We are all owners and have an owning spirit.

What is it that spiritual traditions in general—and Gospel spirituality in particular—have against owning material possessions?

Material possessions are the tip of the iceberg. The iceberg is the inner drive to own and accumulate. This drive, in turn, arises from a profound sense of insecurity. The earth may remain forever, but there is quite a turnover in individuals (Eccl 1:4). When we accumulate wealth and possessions, we relieve the basic anxiety that, in our present form, we are under constant attack. When the barn is full, the wolf is not at the door. A sense of safety replaces fear. Storing up things in the present make us feel that the future is protected. Of course, the larger the accumulation is, the greater the sense of safety.

When spiritual traditions scrutinize this consciousness of insecurity and the corresponding strategy of accumulation, they point out its serious moral defects. When people accumulate wealth, they have to protect it. Therefore, most of their time and energy is spent in hanging on to what they have accrued, for it is ownership that brings the sense of safety. This separates them from their neighbors whom they see as a threat to this wealth, and the need for feeling safe makes the idea of sharing with others ludicrous.

The drive to assuage insecurity can be ruthless. It pushes people into such self-centered behaviors that they commit injustices. Even more, they tolerate any injustice as long as it benefits them. The Letter to Timothy speaks a truth many people know from their own experience: "[T]he love of money is the root of all kinds of evil, and in their eagerness to be rich some have wandered away from the faith and pierced themselves with many pains" (1 Tim 6:10).

These moral defects are matched by the spiritual ignorance that suffuses the whole project. Accumulation is futile in the face of death. In Jesus' parable the man with the bumper crop decides to build extra barns. But God reminds him that he is a fool (ignorant), and asks the question, "the things you have prepared, whose will they be?" (Luke 12:16-21). Temporal life, as temporal life, is radically insecure. No strategy within time can change that. Although there is more to spiritual wisdom than the acceptance of death, it often begins and is sustained by that consciousness:

> In the [nineteenth] century a tourist from the States visited the famous Polish rabbi Hafez Hayyim. He was astonished to see that the rabbi's home was only a simple room filled with books. The only furniture was a table and a bench.
>
> "Rabbi, where is your furniture"? asked the tourist.
>
> "Where is yours?" replied Hafez.
>
> "Mine? But I'm only a visitor here."
>
> "So am I," said the rabbi.
>
> (in Anthony De Mello, *The Song of the Bird* [Garden City, N.Y.: Image Books, 1984])

Accumulation for security denies death.

Therefore, the way to deal with temporal insecurity is to accept it as the way of things. But at the same time we realize it is not our entire identity. Each person is a child both of time and eternity. We live in the rhythms of transcendence and finitude. The project is to live in time and be centered in eternity, to be in the world but not of it (see John 15). This will turn our lives around. We no longer will be racked by anxiety and driven to domination. If we can cultivate this combined consciousness of time and eternity, we will have an inner life of peace and an outer life of service.

But we will still have to own things, accumulate some wealth, and plan for the future. This is the way of social responsibility, but we do not want it to be the way of spiritual and moral folly. The spiritual wisdom about the blending of time and eternity will help us engage these projects without domination or delusion. In other words, even while we have possessions, we have to disown them. We cannot allow them to own us, to enter so deeply into our identity that we can open neither to God nor to neighbor.

Twenty-Ninth Sunday in Ordinary Time

Proper 24

Mark 10:35-45

Putting Others First

A Spiritual Commentary

James and John, the sons of Zebedee, came forward to Jesus and said to him, "Teacher, we want you to do for us whatever we ask of you"

And he said to them, "What is it you want me to do for you?"

Along with Peter, James and John belong to the inner circle. Perhaps it was that distinction that emboldened them to request a cart blanche. They want to reverse the order Jesus had previously insisted on (Mark 8:33). They want Jesus to do their will rather than they doing Jesus' will. But they prefaced this request calling Jesus a teacher. And the teacher is always intent on uncovering the hearts of the disciples. Nothing uncovers the heart like voicing desire. The first desire made it clear that they are fixated on themselves and in hot pursuit of something else. So without answering their question, Jesus inquires about what they want. Their question has been answered with a question. The teacher has turned the tables.

And they said to him, "Grant us to sit, one at your right hand and one at your left, in your glory."

But Jesus said to them, "You do not know what you are asking. Are you able to drink the cup that I drink, or be baptized with the baptism that I am baptized with?"

They replied, "We are able."

Then Jesus said to them, "The cup that I drink you will drink; and with the baptism with which I am baptized, you will be baptized; but to sit at my right hand or at my left is not mine to grant, but it is for those for whom it has been prepared."

251

They want to flank Jesus in glory. Was the image of the transfiguration with Elijah and Moses on either side of Jesus their model? (Mark 9:4). What is in their hearts are power and prestige, and Jesus is the star to which they have hitched this aspiration. As soon as Jesus hears what they want, he knows they do not know. He is the wrong star for glory hounds.

What Jesus knows is a process: a cup of sorrow that becomes a cup of salvation, a baptism that is both death and resurrection. This definitely refers to Jesus' upcoming passion and resurrection. But it also means the whole way of life he advocates: denying yourself, taking up the cross, and losing your life for the sake of the Gospel and in service of others (Mark 8:34-35). Death and resurrection come as a package. Also, the attitude should not be bearing with bad times in order to get to good times. Dying and rising are two sides of the one experience of freedom and life.

James and John do not hesitate. But have they grasped the significant way Jesus has changed their desire? Since they have agreed to the cup and the baptism, Jesus can grant this request. But anyone who follows Jesus can be sure the pattern of his life will be the pattern of theirs. It may not be the exact same conflict that Jesus precipitated, yet the path will be death and resurrection and not an endless upward escalator to glory. Thus their original request cannot be granted. Jesus does not control everything. He follows the will of God and trusts that God's plan will be fulfilled in the way God desires it.

What a frustrated ending for their grab for glory! They get the Cross and Resurrection, with greater emphasis on the Cross. But the right and left hand places are not in Jesus' gift. So the goal that drives them can no longer be this form of aggrandizement.

> **When the ten heard this, they began to be angry with James and John.**
>
> **So Jesus called them and said to them, "You know that among the Gentiles those whom they recognize as their rulers lord it over them, and their great one are tyrants over them. But it is not so among you; but whoever wishes to become great among you must be your servant, and whoever wishes to be first among you must be slave of all. For the Son of Man came not to be served but to serve, and to give his life as a ransom for many.**

Spiritual and social climbers always upset other spiritual and social climbers. The drive to be first makes others feel last and conflict erupts.

We become angry when our self-will is compromised by the self-will of others. The grab for glory by two ignites the grab for glory in the other ten.

This gives Jesus an opportunity to show another way. In competitive rankings, someone always is higher than someone else. This higher translates into oppression. Those on top push around those beneath them. Importance and power take on a sinister cast. The greater ones experience their superiority when they constrain others against their will. Their estimation of themselves rises to the extent that they can keep someone else lower. This is the way of the larger world, but it is not the way of the new humanity that Jesus is bringing to birth.

Disciples experience greatness when they heal, exorcise, and teach—and through these activities free others from what imprisons and debases them (see Luke 10:17-20). This service unites them with the Holy Spirit and they bring others into the kingdom. This is the way of the Son of Man, the new humanity. This other-centered way of life buys back people from captivity.

Teaching

The Gospel of St. Mark stresses that putting others first entails denying ourselves and taking up our cross (8:34). "Denying yourself" points to what we will have to give up in order to serve others. Often these are the things that make us feel secure in the social world: status and wealth. Although "denying yourself" certainly involves an interior attitude of detachment, it also means some degree of actual relinquishment. "Taking up your cross" points to all the persecution we will receive as we engage a life of putting others first. The Gospel stresses the ordeals we will have to endure in pursuing this counter-cultural life. Overall, the putting of others first seems to entail exactly what the Gospel asserts: suffering.

But a favorite saying of Gandhi, who lived life for others, was, "Renounce and enjoy." He was more aware of the suffering of a self-centered life than the sufferings of an other-centered life. "For those whom ego overcomes, sufferings spread like wild grass" is a saying attributed to the Buddha. To renounce our own self-will—to relinquish our demand to have everything the way we want it all the time—is to be free to entertain what we previously would have pushed away. Our ego is a very small piece of the world. When we strenuously attach ourselves to it, we reduce our enjoyment. Detachment is the door into a larger world.

But it is a difficult door to open:

> I catch myself in self-importance ten times a day—check that, five—well,
> maybe once. It's appalling anyway. A little flashbulb goes off and I'm
> exposed . . . like Jimmy Olsen caught Superman changing clothes in the
> phone booth.
>
> Of course, whoever I'm with has probably been seeing all this self-
> importance in me for hours before I ever notice. And my colleagues . . .
> they've been shrugging or giving up for years. So there's no sanctuary.
> And I've stopped trying to hide it. No, that's a lie! Don't trust this man!
> Don't print this interview!
>
> What I've done really is I've *begun*. I've just started to watch myself as
> I go through these little prances. I actually have this exercise I sometimes
> perform. What I do when I catch myself being Mr. Administrator of So-
> cial Services is I get up out of my chair, walk away a few steps, stand for
> a moment, and then turn around and walk back and sit down again. The
> one who is now seated is usually not the same one who was there before.
> I'm no longer that guy, Mr. Administrator. For a while, anyway.
>
> I should add that this exercise frequently appears quite mad to other
> people in the room, particularly if they're people who have come to me
> for some kind of assistance. ("This is the guy I've come to for help?")
> Funny. So I perform these exercises at considerable cost to my aura of
> authority, you understand. But it is definitely worth it. Freedom is price-
> less . . . worth whatever the cost. (in Ram Dass and Paul Gorman, *How
> Can I Help?: Stories and Reflections on Service* [New York: Knopf/Random
> House, Inc., 1985] 33–34)

This is a man struggling to change his work role from an ego asset into
service of others. But "Mr. Administrator" hangs on. What keeps him
going is he glimpses the greater freedom and joy on the other side of
self-centeredness.

Part of the joy of "denying yourself" and "putting others first" is the
reduction in inner and outer conflict. Jesus indicates this is a possibility
when he recommends this approach to the angry and splintered
apostles. Chuang Tzu has a brief parable about a person who is crossing a river in a skiff: If an empty boat collides with the person's own
boat, the person does not get angry. But if one sees a "someone" in the
boat, the first person will curse and shout. If the boat were empty, there
would be no anger (in Thomas Merton, *The Way of Chuang Tzu* [New
York: New Directions, 1965] 114–15). The teaching is that someone
who has let go of his ego does not cause resistance. "His [or her] steps
leave no trace," as Chuang Tzu (Zhuangzi) says. This means that one

does not trigger the reactive ego in others. "Denying yourself" brings the joy of peaceful coexistence with others.

When our attachment to our ego and its supports has been modified to such an extent that we sense a new freedom for action and new peacefulness with others, we can focus on others. However, our service to others is not a subservient "whatever you want." James and John might have got this impression from Jesus, and so they bluntly asked him to fulfill their fantasies. Jesus makes it clear that he is not available for that project. Neither are we. Service means discerning the lure of God in the life of others and committing ourselves to their response. This commitment may bring us into conflict with people who are invested in maintaining oppressive structures. So in order to be faithful to service, we will have to "take up our cross." But there is joy in being part of the divine-human energy that is fashioning a new humanity. It is not the joy of the ego that wants to claim and proclaim its influence. It is the joy of the soul that soars, cooperating with the invitation of the Spirit.

Thirtieth Sunday in Ordinary Time

Proper 25

Mark 10:46-52

Begging for Sight

A Spiritual Commentary

As [Jesus] and his disciples and a large crowd were leaving Jericho, Bartimaeus son of Timaeus, a blind beggar, was sitting by the roadside.

In spiritual traditions blindness is the inability to notice, understand, and integrate the spiritual dimension of life. Without this ability, we have no true wealth:

> When you know yourselves, then you will be known, and you will understand that you are children of the living Father. But if you do not know yourselves, then you live in poverty, and you are the poverty.
>
> (Gospel of Thomas, 3)

In this condition of not knowing we are sons and daughters of the Living One, we become beggars. But it is not a scrounging for money to sustain physical life. We beseech others who have this ability to see the spiritual to share it with us.

As Christians, our begging blindness is not for spiritual sensitivity in general. It is for the spiritual revelation of the death and resurrection of Jesus of Nazareth. It is because we are blind to this revelation that we sit by the roadside. This is the road out of Jericho that leads to Jerusalem, the place where the revelation of death and resurrection will take place. We need to go along in order to see, but only Jesus can move us from our stationary position off the road to a following behind him on the road.

When he heard it was Jesus of Nazareth, he began to shout out and say, "Jesus, Son of David, have mercy on me!"

Many sternly ordered him to be quiet, but he cried out even loudly, "Son of David, have mercy on me!"

We cry out to Jesus as the Son of David because Jerusalem is the City of David, where God's covenant of unconditional love will be carried out (1 Chr 17:10-15). This is the light that will cure our blindness. We become a bold beggar, shouting out. There are always obstacles to overcome. Often it is other people who are disturbed by our begging, by our naked desire. Our blatant and insistent plea for mercy offends their more moderate ways. They try to quiet us. If our desire is not strong enough, we will be left behind. Our blindness will be permanent.

Jesus stood still and said, "Call him here."

And they called the blind man, saying, "Take heart; get up, he is calling you."

So throwing off his cloak, he sprang up and came to Jesus.

If our cry is loud enough and refuses to be silent, the one who hears all cries for liberation will stand still. He will stop on his journey toward the destiny of his revelation in order to call us to join him. Everyone who begs from their heart for sight is heard by the clear-sighted one. The other people who previously blocked access now facilitate it. In our blind and begging condition we were unimportant. Only the one who embraces little children could hear us (Mark 9:36; 10:16). But once we are called by Jesus, we become important and worthy of their support. Our blind and begging condition makes us ready, but it is the call by Jesus that raises us off the ground. We already know our old life of blindness is over, so we courageously throw it off. It lightens us enough to spring toward Jesus. But our new life of sight has yet to begin.

Then Jesus said to him, "What do you want me to do for you?"

The blind man said to him, "My teacher, let me see again."

Jesus said to him, "Go; your faith has made you well."

Immediately he regained his sight and followed him on the way.

Jesus tests our desire. He cannot grant any wish. He is not a fairy godmother and we are not James and John, desiring glory (Mark 10:37). We recognize that he is our Teacher and, as our Teacher, he can bring us into greater understanding of divine-human ways. We have always desired this, and in the past we have seen. But Jesus on his relentless way to Jerusalem transcends this earlier way of seeing. His death and resurrection is a new revelation; old eyes are blind to it (see Mark 2:22).

Jesus calls no attention to himself. He does not focus on the power that flows through him. He just tells us to go because our faith, the single, unquenchable desire of our heart, has opened our eyes. We see again, and we know where we will go. We cannot go back home. With our new eyes we must follow him into the new revelation. We join the other, behind him on the road, afraid but wide-eyed: "They were on the road, going up to Jerusalem, and Jesus was walking ahead of them; they were amazed, and those who followed were afraid" (Mark 10:32).

Teaching

Reb Mendl studied at the House of Learning. "He gathered knowledge with burning eagerness, but after a while a yearning for something more began to glow in him." Reb Mendl was not satisfied with mere intellectual knowledge. He thought that when he studied past masters, he should be able to enter into their presence. In particular, when he poured over Rabbi Isaac Alfasi, he wanted to be able to experience him. He wept in anguish when he was not able to do this.

One night Alfasi appeared to him in a dream, saying only, "You are to go to Elimelekh." Reb Mendl had never heard of this man, but he left immediately to search for him. After much wandering, "weary and in tatters, hungry and freezing," he managed to reach Reb Elimelekh's house. "The secretary refused to admit this person who looked like one of the beggars that had lately pestered the Rebbe." But Reb Mendl forced his way in and found the Rebbe.

"Who sent you?" asked Reb Elimelekh.

"Alfasi did," said Reb. Mendl.

Reb Elimelekh stared at the stranger for a long moment, then said, "You can stay with me." (Abraham Joshua Heschel, *A Passion for Truth* [Woodstock, Vt.: Jewish Lights/New York: Farrar, Straus and Giroux, LLC, 1995] 64–65)

The desire to understand spiritual revelations can consume people. This desire is not intellectual curiosity. It is a sense that salvation lies in greater and greater penetration of the mystery of God and humanity (and thus the mystery of Jesus Christ, God and human)—a mystery to which someone else has the key.

Reb Mendl is not content with the traditional ways of the House of Learning. He will not be content with Alfasi's ideas; he will drink his spirit. The dream figure of Alfasi sends him to Reb Elimelekh. The journey is not known beforehand. By the time he arrives at Reb Elimelekh's house, his desire has transformed him into a beggar. He will not be denied, and Reb Elimelekh sees this passion and welcomes it. Alfasi might have sent him, but it was Reb Mendl who walked the way.

The son of Timeaus is driven to see and understand the revelation of the Son of David. When the Son of David hears his begging for mercy, he perceives the fury of his desire. The crowd cannot crush it. Jesus matches this passion with a call that brings him to his feet. Seeker and sought meet. But the one with the revelation has met many who have not been able to comprehend it. Jesus knows he has not changed; he will do what he will do. So if someone can see and understand, it is not because Jesus has done something different. It is because their faith has allowed them to follow his way. Faith cures blindness by creating in consciousness a passionate quest for deeper revelation.

Any great desire eventually turns us into beggars. In Nikos Kazantzakis' *Zorba the Greek,* Zorba tells the boss that the first time he heard the *santuri* (a musical instrument), it took his breath away and he could not eat for three days. He knew he had to learn the instrument. His father berated him. "D'you mean to say you'd turn into a strummer?" But Zorba took all his money, money he had saved for marriage, and bought a *santuri.* He went to Salonica and threw himself at the feet of a Turk, Retsep Effendi. He begged him to teach him, even though he had no money. "And you're really crazy about the *santuri?*" The twenty-one year old Zorba answered, "Yes." "Well, you can stay, my boy" ([New York: Scribner Paperback Fiction, 1981; Simon & Schuster, 1953] 11–12).

No one has the money to purchase a great desire. We must beg the merciful to teach us, and more often than not, their perception of our passion will bring us to what we desire.

For Christians, followers of Jesus, our great desire is to understand and enter into the revelation of the Cross and Resurrection. Every day I beg the Father of Jesus to have mercy on my blindness. It is a tribute to the thoroughness of my blindness, that it is only recently that I stopped waiting for mercy and have come to understand that it is begging that clears the cataracts.

Thirty-First Sunday in Ordinary Time

Proper 26

Mark 12:28-34

Writing on the Heart

A Spiritual Commentary

One of the scribes came near and heard [Jesus and the Saddu-cees] disputing with one another; and seeing that Jesus answered them well, he asked him, "Which commandment is the first of all?"

Not all religious leadership rejects Jesus. One of the scribes respected Jesus' positions. Now he wants to hear more. Although he does not address Jesus with a title, this is not a hostile inquiry.

There were over six hundred prescriptions in the Law. Naturally, questions about priority arose. Which was most important? How should they be ordered and interrelated? Is there one that contains all the others? If there are many, the human mind asks about one. If there is one, the human mind asks about many. Balancing the one and the many is essential human activity.

Jesus answered, "The first is, 'Hear O Israel: the Lord our God, the Lord is one; you shall love the Lord your God with all your heart, and with all your soul, and with all your mind, and with all your strength.' The second is this, 'You shall love your neighbor as yourself.' There is no other commandment greater than these."

The first commandment, the one from which all others flow, concerns the one God. Divine oneness is absolute, the Creator of All. Therefore, creatures should imitate this oneness by bringing themselves into complete coordination with the One. Heart, soul, mind, and strength should be united in loving communion with God. When this happens, a second commandment arises. The one God makes all people one; the neighbor must be loved as yourself. Although these are two, they are inseparable. Therefore, they form one commandment, "the first."

This twofold first commandment is engaged by an interior act of love. This establishes the proper flow, from the inside to the outside, from unitive consciousness to unitive acts. This is precisely what is threatened when believers are faced with many laws. They ask what is the law, and what does it entail, and how can they keep it. Their consciousness is outside and the emphasis is on obedient behavior. The inner world that accompanies the behavior is overlooked. The law can be kept with a hard heart, a dark mind, a sick soul, and only a minimum of strength. This causes a split between the inside and outside and fuels the conflict between the spirit and letter of the law. It also grounds one of God's deepest laments:

> [T]hese people draw near with their mouths,
> and honor me with their lips,
> while their hearts are far from me."
> (Isa 29:13)

Then the scribe said to him, "You are right, Teacher; you have truly said that 'he is one, and besides him there is no other'; and to love him with all the heart, and with all the understanding, and will all the strength,' and 'to love one's neighbor as oneself,'—this is much more important than all whole burnt offerings and sacrifices."

When Jesus saw that he answered wisely, he said to him, "You are not far from the kingdom of God."

After that no one dared to ask him any question.

The scribe approves of Jesus' answer and repeats it for emphasis. He stresses that God is absolute and beyond comparison. Therefore, there is no competition for the complete devotion of the creature. It is not a matter of this god or that god; it is a matter of *God.* The scribe also sees an implication. The liturgical practices that relate people to God are less important than the inner attitude of loving God and neighbor. Jesus and the scribe are on the same page. Indeed, the scribe is slowing integrating the double commandment into his way of thinking and seeing ramifications.

If the scribe approves of Jesus, now Jesus approves of the scribe. But he also points to a further development. The scribe answered wisely because wisdom is always a hearing of the Word that leads to doing. The scribe heard Jesus' word and realized the priority of love of God and neighbor over cultic obligations. If this realization is pursued, it will change how he worships. This realization also moves him beyond questions of Law and toward the experience of the kingdom of God. But it does not get him there.

In the Kingdom of God detailed legislation and Temple sacrifice are over. It is not a matter of theological debate about which commandment is first or of just recognizing that love of God and love of neighbor takes precedent over burnt offerings. It is a more radical recognition that a community that includes Jews but goes beyond the boundaries of Judaism is emerging. Jewish cultic practices are being replaced by universal practices of prayer: "My house shall be called a house of prayer for all nations." (Mark 11:7; NAB references to Isa 56:7; Jer 7:11). Jesus sees a development in the scribe, but he also sees that more is needed.

By evaluating the scribe not in terms of his legal knowledge but in terms of the kingdom of God, Jesus has shown that he is at a depth that legal wrangling cannot reach. In fact, Jesus has consistently undercut the theological positions of the religious elite by taking them into water over their head. Even in this friendly encounter, he does not settle for agreement. He dramatically takes the conversation to the next level. Who wants to dare a dialogue with this Son of Man?

Teaching

In the Book of Jeremiah, God says, "I will put my law within them, and I will write it on their hearts; and I will be their God, and they shall be my people. No longer shall they teach one another, or say to each other, 'Know the LORD,' for they shall all know me, from the least of them to the greatest" (Jer 31:33-34). The Law had previously been written on stone tablets. People had to look outside themselves to see what to do. They were quick to say, "I don't know that law." Now since the Law and the Lawgiver will be in their hearts, all will know God. The proper flow will be established, from inner realization to outer action.

This inner consciousness of love of God and neighbor has priority because there are not enough laws to cover the territory of the human. Six hundred is just a start. There are an endless variety of human situations, and within that endless variety there is endless nuance. Laws are unable to foresee everything and predict proper behavior. But people who are equipped with a steady, loving interior will find a way to embody that love in the unforeseeable situations of life.

In my old neighborhood there was a steady stream of mentally ill and handicapped people who would beg. One man who had no legs below the knees would sit outside Walgreens. He would arrive in his wheelchair and, with powerful upper body strength, lift himself out of the chair and onto the ground. He did this in winter as well as summer. A large plastic cup was positioned between the stubs of his knees.

I always gave him some money, usually on my way out of Walgreens. Then one day as I was approaching the store, I saw a woman squatting down next to him and talking with great animation. As I turned to go into the store, I heard her say, "So you haven't always lived in Chicago . . . ?" She was inquiring about his life, caring for him in a personal way. My dollar or two tossed in his cup seemed impersonal, even demeaning.

But more to the point, how did she come upon this generous form of presence? There were no laws to guide her. But I think there was an inner consciousness of love that bumped into a situation and found a way to express itself. Love of the transcendent God makes us one with our neighbor, but it does not tell us what to do in every situation. But if we can hold onto the consciousness, a way will open, a way impossible to forecast, a way beyond prescription.

Dr. Frederic Craigie makes the same point when he tells the story of an oncology nurse who was working with a cancer patient. The patient was experiencing many painful losses and was on the verge of despair. The nurse was not able to get the man to talk at any length. Not knowing what to do, she invited him to go for a walk in the garden outside the facility. On the ground was a dead butterfly. Without comment she picked up the butterfly and gave it to him. This opened the man up and he began to talk about his life. Craigie comments:

> Taking a walk and picking up the butterfly are creative processes that are not deduced from a model. Certainly there is no psychotherapy algorithm which says, "go outside, find a dead animal, and give it to the patient." To the extent that what we as would-be healers do is inductive and creative, it places a premium on our ability to be open to inspiration, or in-spiriting. It places a premium on our spiritual well-being, and on our ability to be receptive to the movement of the Spirit in using us in sometimes unforeseen ways as agents of change and healing. (Frederic C. Craigie, Jr., "The Spirit and Work: Observations about Spirituality and Organizational Life," *Journal of Psychology and Christianity* 18 [1999] 43–53)

A consciousness in tune with God and neighbor is alert to possibilities that no law could ever foresee.

But this inner consciousness of love of God and neighbor also has priority because there are many laws that do cover a lot of territory. In particular, they are prescribed behaviors that we are asked to follow. For example, consider a retirement community that has "respect" as one of its guiding values. In order to implement respect, the leadership has created a list of tips:

1. Use Mr., Mrs., or Miss with last names unless they invite you to call them by their first name.
2. Try to be the same height as the older person (for example, if they are in a wheelchair, pull up a chair; if they are in bed, sit down beside them).
3. Address questions directly to them, not indirectly through caregivers.

The list goes on. Yet, as helpful as these tips are, they are not enough. It is always a person who acts. Therefore, where they are "at" internally when they engage in these behaviors is important. Even the most objectively respectful action can be undercut by an inner, unmindful or disrespectful attitude. All the tips begin with words such as "Use," "Try," "Start," "Speak," "Touch," "Accept" for the person who is initiating an action. But with what consciousness is the action being performed?

Both where there are no laws and where there are many laws, the question of the proper flow from inside to outside is important. If God writes the double commandment to love in our hearts and we learn how to read it daily, we move within the Law and beyond the Law.

Thirty-Second Sunday in Ordinary Time

Proper 27

Mark 12:38-44

Spotting Discrepancy

A Spiritual Commentary

As [Jesus] taught, he said, "Beware of the scribes, who like to walk around in long robes, and to be greeted with respect in the marketplaces, and to have the best seats in the synagogues and places of honor at banquets! They devour widows' houses and for the sake of appearance say long prayers. They will receive the greater condemnation."

As the Son of Man, Jesus is a fully realized and integrated human being. He embodies the double commandment to love God and neighbor (see the previous Sunday). Any thought, feeling, or behavior that is discrepant with these twin, foundational loves has been purified. If someone asked him what his message was, he could respond, "My message is my life." The thoughts of his heart and the words of his mouth are in perfect harmony (see Ps 19:14).

As fully realized and integrated, Jesus quickly spots any lack of realization and integration. So his teaching includes unmasking the discordant messages and behavior of the religious elite. These men can recite the *Shema:* Hear, O Israel: "The LORD our God is one" (Deut 6:4; KJV), and they do so often. Also, they are informed about the love of neighbor (Lev 19:18). But these teachings at the heart of Israel have not been taken to their hearts. The result is hypocrisy, pretense, and duplicity. They say one thing and do another. Jesus is watching.

Basically, self-love has replaced love of God. What the scribes like about being a scribe is not the Law and the righteousness that comes from deep understanding and obedience. They love all the superficial externals: long robes, salutations in the marketplace, and the best seats at synagogues and banquets. What they gravitate toward is anything that makes them the center. Even when they pray, it is for the sake of appearance. They do not genuinely open themselves to God. Their complete dedication is to how they are being perceived. The ego, always unsure of itself, needs constant adulation. The scribes are owned by their egos.

Also, self-love has replaced love of neighbor. In this passage the neighbor is a widow whose meager resources are plundered by scheming scribes. The widow is a symbol of the most vulnerable in Israel. Therefore, God cares for her in a special way for God is "Father of orphans and protector of widows" (Ps 68:5). God also makes justice toward the widow a condition for residing with the people of Israel (Jer 7:6). But the most vulnerable is also a prey for the most rapacious. Could the scenario be that the widow in her desperate circumstances prays to God for help? And who is there to help her with those prayers but scribes who allegedly know the ins and outs of divine favor. Of course, there is a fee, and the longer the prayers the more the fee. Their concern for the widow is a pretense for enriching the self.

> **He sat down opposite the treasury, and watched the crowd putting money into the treasury. Many rich people put in large sums. A poor widow came and put in two small copper coins, which are worth a penny.**
>
> **Then he called his disciples and said to them, "Truly I tell you, this poor widow has put in more than all those who are contributing to the treasury. For all of them have contributed out of their abundance; but she out of her poverty has put in everything she had, all she had to live on."**

Somewhere in the writings of Nelson Algren, a populist Chicago novelist, there is an anecdote about an orphan and a widow. The orphaned boy goes to a Catholic school. The priest tells him he needs five dollars to say a Mass for his deceased father. If Masses are not said for him, his father "will never see God in the face." The boy is very distraught. He goes home and with tears in his eyes tells his mother, "Dad will never see God in the face if we don't have a Mass said." The widow gives her son the five dollars, and he gives it to the priest who says the Mass. A little later, the priest corners the boy again with the same message. His deceased father will never see God in the face unless there are more Masses said. The distressed boy begs his mother for another five dollars. "If we don't do it, Dad will never see God in the face." The widow holds her ground. "Then let him look at God's ass," she says.

The long-ago widow of this Gospel story does not have the chutzpas of this contemporary widow who can distinguish the parts of God's anatomy. Throughout the Gospel Jesus has consistently championed human needs over the hardened practices of the synagogue. Now he targets the Temple treasury. When he sits opposite the treasury, it symbolizes that he is opposed to the whole temple atmosphere around money. It is a public affair with the rich parading their large sums. But Jesus is not concerned with the rich. They are never exploited. They give to the temple out of their surplus. Piety will never carry them away. Like the scribes, the rich take care of themselves.

But the widow divests herself of all support. Her generosity plays into the devouring greed of the Temple. Those who are supposed to protect her leave her, literally, penniless. What is most frightening is that she cooperates with her exploitation. This is a condition that is often mentioned in the literature on oppression. The exploited are so thoroughly co-opted that they do not see what is really happening. They even unconsciously contribute to it. This mistake is common. In St. Luke's Gospel, Jesus says, "The kings of the Gentiles lord it over them; and those in authority over them are called benefactors" (Luke 22:25). The oppressed think their oppressors are actually benefiting them. Is the house of God to which the widow goes really benefiting her when contributing to it despoils her own house? Jesus named the Temple "a den of robbers" (Mark 11:17; NAB reference to Jer 7:11). Has the woman freely donated the last of her livelihood or has a subtle theft occurred? The widow may not grasp all that is going on, but the Integrated One who is sensitive to all duplicity has not missed it.

Teaching

The Gospels have a keen sense of hypocrisy. In Isaiah God criticizes people who

> . . . draw near with their mouths
> and honor me with their lips,
> while their hearts are far from me."
> (Isa 29:13)

This split between the inside (heart) and outside (lips = words) is the condition of the majority of religious elite. Also, it is assumed that they are aware of their condition and consciously embrace it. Of course, if this is the case, they are active agents of evil.

However, there is a cousin to conscious hypocrisy. It is "value discrepancy." Hypocrisy is a conscious deception for the purposes of promoting and protecting yourself. Value discrepancy is an unconscious lack of integration. For example, a husband says he loves his wife, but he talks only about himself and never inquires about her feelings. The value of love should unfold into a less self-centered way of life with an active concern for his wife's feelings. But the value is not integrated. Hypocrisy would be: he tells her he loves her but in his heart he does not and his maintaining this pretense in some way benefits him. Value discrepancy is: he really loves her, but he has not broken old self-serving tapes and learned how to attentively listen to another. The response to hypocrisy is prophetic denunciation; the response to value discrepancy is awareness and improvement.

Value discrepancy often shows up in organizational life. I do a fair amount of work in faith-based health care. The hospitals and the larger systems of which they are a part are values driven. There are mission statements where values such as "compassion," "respect," "stewardship," "equality," etc. are spelled out. These values are supposed to permeate the organization and penetrate all its operations.

However, if you talk to an individual or a particular group, they may point to a policy or a behavior that directly contradicts the values. If they are angry about this discrepancy, they may even suggest hypocrisy. They may say that the people on top do not really believe in respect, but this rhetoric "keeps the troops happy"—while management does contradictory things for their own promotion.

But more often than not the value discrepancy is not an evil strategy. It is simply a failure of integration, and there are many reasons for it— some of them quite justifiable: Things grew too fast. Policies were created out of expediency rather than values. Leaders caved in to different pressure groups. The cultural values of business and organizational life that most executives have unconsciously internalized trumped the stated values. It happened by not being mindful. "Now that we see it, we recognize we are not who we say we are."

Although sometimes value discrepancies are blatant, often they are difficult to spot. This is especially true if the discrepancies are long-standing ways of acting and obligations that are taken for granted. Only thoughtful and highly integrated people notice the gap between what is preached and what is practiced—which brings us to Jesus, the widow, and the temple treasury.

It is difficult to see the exploitation of the widow because Temple theology and policy is well established. The Law obliges all to support the Temple. Personal piety builds on that law and goes beyond it. Donating is a sign of one's sincerity and commitment. To give to God's House is to give to God. In fact, all you have comes from God, and to give it back is an act of vibrant faith. Do the priests and scribes profit from this? They do, but that is incidental. This is about the total claim faith makes on true believers. The manifest objective of this way of thinking is to support the House of the God of Israel.

However, the latent functioning of this theology and practice is another matter. God's chronic concern has been for the poor and the vulnerable. This revelation preceded the Temple and was one of the driving forces of the Exodus from Egypt. No Temple policy should generate the expectation that the vulnerable should make themselves more vulnerable, and no widow should be allowed to impoverish herself. The house of the "Father of orphans and protector of widows" (Ps 68:5) does not devour the houses of widows. The teaching of Jesus reveals this value discrepancy.

Thirty-Third Sunday in Ordinary Time

Proper 28

Mark 13:24-32 *LM* • Mark 13:1-8 *RCL*

The Gospel text for users of the *Lectionary for Mass* for the Thirty-Third Sunday in Ordinary Time is Mark 13:24-32. A spiritual commentary and teaching for that text is given for the First Sunday of Advent.

Living In-between

A Spiritual Commentary

As [Jesus] came out of the temple, one of his disciples said to him, "Look, Teacher, what large stones and what large buildings!"

Then Jesus asked him, "Do you see these great buildings? Not one stone will be left upon another; all will be thrown down."

The disciple is impressed by the power and grandeur of the Temple. It is a magnificent edifice. But also it is a symbol for a way of life. The Temple is the religious and economic center of Israel. Its theology and practices permeate the life of the people. The disciple's gawking amazement suggests he thinks it will last forever. It is just too large to fall.

Jesus does not see the same building as the disciple. Jesus sees the foundation cracking and the facade crumbling. Minor repair is impossible. Everything will come down; every stone will be dismantled. It is a fig tree that has not borne fruit (Mark 11:13-14, 20). It is not God's dwelling place; it is a den of thieves (Mark 11:17).

When he was sitting on the Mount of Olives opposite the temple, Peter, James, John, and Andrew asked him privately, "Tell us, when will this be, and what will be the sign that all these things are about to be accomplished?"

Then Jesus began to say to them, "Beware that no one leads you astray. Many will come in my name and say, "I am he!" and they will lead many astray. When you hear of wars and rumors of wars, do not be alarmed; this must take place, but the end is still to come. For nation will rise against nation, and kingdom against

kingdom; there will be earthquakes in various places; there will be famines. This is but the beginning of the birth pangs."

Jesus, the Teacher, is seated opposite the Temple, symbolically opposing all it stands for. He has predicted its fall. His inner circle of disciples is looking for privileged information. They are concerned not only about when all this will come down but also what will be the signs that this destruction is about to happen. This is more than a neutral interest in a timetable. They are looking for an edge, a way of preparing for what was predicted.

Jesus' rendition of the collapse and its aftermath is horrifying. Things will get worse before they get better. In fact, the dismantling of the Temple and its way of life will have social and cosmic repercussions. Nations will clash; people will starve; the earth itself will be in upheaval. False people will come, mimicking Jesus, and saying they know a way forward. But they do not; they will only lead the disciples astray. But as confusing and catastrophic as this will be, the proper perspective is that it is the beginning. The death of this way of life is the birth of a new way.

Teaching

Many people have undergone the type of major collapse that Jesus predicted. Their theological, social, and political worlds have suddenly disappeared. Others have suffered less (but still) harrowing forms of dismantling: the sudden death of a loved one, a Friday afternoon layoff, a stock market crash. But unscheduled and traumatic change is a fact of everyone's life. And we do not skate through it.

Change may happen quickly. But transition is a slower process. It is how we psychologically adjust to the change. It entails grieving over what has been lost, feeling we are without our bearings, and looking forward to something new. The problem is when we are in the midst of transition, we cannot envision the new. We have to take T. S. Eliot's difficult advice:

> I said to my soul, be still, and wait without hope
> For hope would be hope for the wrong thing.

> "East Coker," [2.3] in *Four Quartets* [New York:
> Harcourt, Brace and Co. 1943)

The time of transition itself has been characterized as that moment when the trapeze artist has let go of one bar and has not yet grabbed the next bar. It is midair living. The identity we had is gone and the identity we will have has not arrived. So, depending on the intensity and duration of the transition, we gain a reputation as not being ourselves. We eat too little or too much. We slough off work or become addicted. We are silent when we should talk and talk when we should be silent. We decide to tell the truth and then are forced to cover it with a lie. We start things we don't finish and we try to finish things we didn't start. We are tired of our friends asking how we are and hurt when they don't ask how we are. As I overheard someone say about me in the middle of a transition, "Oh, don't mind him and his long hair. He's numb." In the in-between time of transitions we have joined that legion of our fellow human beings who, in a past moment of arrogant stability, we labeled as "not knowing their [derriere] from their elbow." Welcome to confusion so profound it is anatomical.

Transitions are so discombobulating it is difficult to see any value in the in-between state. It is easy to look to the future and bet on our innate resiliency. "Hang in there. You'll get through." However devastating the loss may be, we will find a way to deal with it, to adapt and continue. It may take time, but a stable future awaits us. Even if we do not get completely over it, we will get beyond it. As our unhelpful friends say, "Life goes on, and so will you."

Spiritual teachers, an unconventional lot, take a different tack. They say, "Don't hurry to a new security." They think there is potential in the present process of floundering. It is not in the hope of reaching the next bar but in the interval of being between bars. The potential is in midair living.

Without tongue in cheek, spiritual teachers suggest that the in-between time is an opportunity to remember that we are always more than what is happening to us. We are not only immersed in transition, we transcend it. Our soul is not only related to the changing temporal order but to the unchanging eternal order.

When we lead a stable life on the physical, psychological, and social levels, this spiritual truth often eludes us. When disruption occurs— and we either choose or are forced to change—an invitation emerges in the middle of the transition. Since we are between earthly stabilities, we may just shift awareness to our heavenly connection. In doing this, we begin to develop our spiritual potential.

In mystical, biblical terms the in-between time is the third day of creation. On that day God drew up out of the waters dry land and separated "the waters under the sky" from the dry land (Gen 1:9, 13).

The waters symbolize the formlessness and turmoil of transition. The appearance of dry land gives humans a place to stand in the midst of the swift and dangerous currents. What God did on the third day of creation, God does every day. Divine reality is always supplying a place to stand. However, we most need this divine grounding when we have lost our human grounding, when we are in the midair between the bars.

Beatrice Bruteau has some helpful advice:

> Don't we superficially answer the question, "Who are you?" by citing our occupation, our relation to spouse or parent or child, our nationality, our religion, our race, our wealth, our fame, our achievement, or perhaps some special feature that looms large in our social life such as sexual orientation, or some physical or mental handicap, or a drug dependency, or a prison record? This is often how we think of ourselves and other people . . . However, all those descriptions are mere combinations of appearances in our experiences. They change constantly. That's not what we mean by a real self. The real self is what is back of all those descriptions, quite independent of them. ("Global Spirituality and the Integration of East and West" *Cross Currents* 35 [1985] 194–95)

The underlying idea is to understand ourselves as a hierarchy of different aspects and to disidentify with the real but lower aspects. In doing this, we will coincide with the higher reality of our transcendent self, a self that allows us to relate to our transitions rather than be swallowed up in them.

For those of us addicted to our descriptive selves, moving to the transcendent self seems like a fallback position. When we cannot have what we really want, we reluctantly stand on the ground God provides in the turmoil of sea change. But once we have negotiated a new set of earthly stabilities, we quickly forget the sense of transcendence that sustained us in the midst of change.

This seems to be "the way of things spiritual." We remember the spiritual when we need it and we forget it when we don't. The Sufi poet, Rumi, wrote that when we realize a spiritual truth, we should "enjoy this being washed / with a secret we sometimes know, / and then not" ("Story Water" in *The Essential Rumi,* trans. Coleman Barks and others [San Francisco: HarperSanFrancisco, 1995]). The "being cleansed" means that the dirt that covers our eyes is washed away. Without clouded vision we know a secret, the transcendent grounding of our lives in God, that we will not know at another time. Rumi does not lament this fleeting state of affairs or berate us for our forgetfulness. He offers a more pleasurable option: enjoy it, as the unexpected gift of midair living.

Christic the King

Proper 29

John 18:33-37

Foregoing Force

A Spiritual Commentary

[Pilate asked Jesus:] "Are you the King of the Jews?"

Jesus answered, "Do you say this on your own, or did others tell you about me?"

Pilate replied, "I am not a Jew, am I? Your own nation and the chief priests have handed you over to me. What have you done?"

A political man asks political questions. Herod is king of the Jews. If Jesus says he is the king of the Jews, he is fomenting rebellion. Then the procurator has a charge.

But a spiritual person answers political questions in a spiritual way. Jesus' basic self-understanding is that people are drawn to him in order to receive divine love. If Pilate is asking this on his own, then he could be one of those drawn. Attraction to Jesus is not confined to Jews, and the title "King of the Jews" could be code for the unsurpassed importance of the divine love Jesus reveals. But then again, it might not be Pilate's question. He might have heard it from others, and he is checking it out.

Political persons stay political. Jewish kings are a question for Jews, so naturally he has heard it from Jews. It is Jesus' own people who have told him. They did it in order to provide grounds to execute him. If Jews turn against a Jew and hand him over to a Roman, Pilate wants to know why.

> **Jesus answered, "My kingdom is not from this world. If my kingdom were from this world, my followers would be fighting to keep me from being handed over to the Jews. But as it is, my kingdom is not from here."**
>
> **Pilate asked him, "So you are a king?"**

Jesus answered, "You say that I am a king. For this was I born and for this I came into the world, to testify to the truth. Everyone who belongs to the truth listens to my voice."

Jesus tells Pilate he is not a pretender to the throne. The social-political kingdoms of this world are built on violence and maintained by force. Jesus' disciples are not fighting to keep him out of the clutches of the religious authorities who have brought him to Pilate. The reason is the realm of which Jesus is the highest member is not this alienated world of fighting.

Pilate catches none of this distinction between an earthly realm and another reality. He is back to what he knows best. He heard the word kingdom, so it should be clarified. Is Jesus saying he is a king or not? This is what the political guardian wants to know.

Political men reduce everything to political terms. "King" is Pilate's word; he is the one who is using it. Jesus, the spiritual man, has another self-designation. He is a witness to the truth. He lives within and reveals the ultimate relationship to God and creation. Those who are fixated on political power cannot open to this spiritual depth. But those who are aware of the spiritual will hear Jesus' voice. The truth they know will draw them to the truth he is.

Teaching

Foregoing force is such an awesome decision.

In the Gethsemane scene in Luke, Peter, in a preemptive strike, cuts off the ear of the servant of the High Priest (Luke 22:50-51). Jesus says simply, "No more of this," and heals the man, restoring his ear. Jesus has spent his entire ministry giving people ears to hear, he is not about to start taking them off now. The symbolic import is that the beginning of violence is the end of dialogue. That is why Peter's sword severs the ear. Combatants can no longer hear one another. Ears have to be restored for dialogue to happen and for violence to end.

Jesus refuses the sword of Peter. He is committed to the Word as the only form of interpersonal influence. If he belonged to this world, he would advocate fighting to secure his safety. But the world that he comes from relies on love as its sole strategy and protection. Jesus witnesses to God's unconditional love. The wager is that when people hear about this love, they will recognize it as what they have always wanted. Perhaps, it will be an after-the-fact recognition. Once divine love has been revealed, people will realize it is what they have been looking for all along. But before the revelation, they would not have been able to explore their inner drives with enough depth or clarity to discover their communion with love.

So Jesus is not only a revelation of divine love; he is a mirror to the unknown territory of the human heart. People know themselves when they see him, and so they cannot help but be attracted. "I have other sheep that do not belong to this fold. I must bring them also, and they will listen to my voice. So there will be one flock, one shepherd" (John 10:16). "Listening to the voice of Jesus" is certainly an irenic rendition of leadership and influence. But it is the approach that Jesus takes before the power of Rome. No muscle, no force—only the magnetism of the revelation.

Foregoing force includes not making threats (see Matt 5:39; Luke 6:29). If you do not get the revelation of divine love and are not attracted to it, Jesus will not terrorize you with prospects of worldly disasters and/or afterlife punishments. The conventional religious persuaders of reward and punishment will not make an appearance. Also, betting it all on attraction means forsaking snobbery. If you do not get the revelation of divine love and are not attracted to it, Jesus will not intimate that you are a little slow on the uptake. His only strategy is to reveal the truth again. Also, it definitely excludes torture and death as a way to win over adherents. In other words, many of the strategies of influence that Christians have espoused might be rejected by the One who only knows how to witness and wait.

Perhaps dialogue takes the place of force. David Bohm makes a distinction between discussion and dialogue: "Discussion" has the same root as "percussion" and "concussion." It connotes a hitting against, where sounds do not blend but where one wins out over another. Discussion can follow this form. Ideas are batted around; one or more are accepted by people and many more are rejected. However, dialogue suggests a free flow of meaning that becomes shared by all involved (see Peter Senge, *The Fifth Discipline: The Art and Practice of the Learning Organization* [New York: Doubleday/Currency, 1990] 241–44).

Most people have experienced rough and tumble discussions resulting in winners and losers, and there is certainly a place for that in debating situations. But Jesus' preferred form of influence would seem to be more like a flow of shared meaning, where people come to a revelation of the truth together.

This theory seems very difficult in practice. It certainly did not work with Pilate who could not hear Jesus' voice and dismissed it briskly, "What is truth?" (John 18:38). When things seem difficult in practice, it is time to return to theory and regain desire. Jesus is the revelation of divine love, and divine love addresses human freedom as an invitation. When human freedom is not capable of responding affirmatively, divine love continues the conversation. Christ is not king because he can bend human will with his might. He is king because out of love he foregoes force and continues to talk. Peter may cut off ears, but Jesus restores them.

Scripture Index